# DIVERSE TRANSNATIONAL CARE

## Ageing and Migration in Bolivia

Tanja Bastia and Claudia Calsina

First published in Great Britain in 2025 by

Policy Press, an imprint of
Bristol University Press
University of Bristol
1–9 Old Park Hill
Bristol
BS2 8BB
UK
t: +44 (0)117 374 6645
e: bup-info@bristol.ac.uk

Details of international sales and distribution partners are available at policy.bristoluniversitypress.co.uk



British Library Cataloguing in Publication Data
A catalogue record for this book is available from the British Library

ISBN 978-1-4473-6520-4 paperback
ISBN 978-1-4473-6521-1 ePub
ISBN 978-1-4473-6522-8 OA ePdf



Cover design: Dave Worth
Front cover image: Tanja Bastia
Bristol University Press and Policy Press uses environmentally responsible print partners.
Printed and bound in Great Britain by CPI Group (UK) Ltd, Croydon, CR0 4YY

Bristol University Press' authorised representative in the European Union is:
Easy Access System Europe, Mustamäe tee 50, 10621 Tallinn, Estonia,
Email: gpsr.requests@easproject.com

Some of the testimonies we have included in this book refer to experiences of physical and sexual violence.

# Contents

# Series editors' preface

*AGEING IN A GLOBAL CONTEXT*
*Series editors: Chris Phillipson (University of Manchester, UK),*
*Toni Calasanti (Virginia, Tech, USA) and Anna Wanka*
*(Goethe-Universität, Frankfurt am Main, Germany).*

As the older population continues to expand across the Global North and South, new issues and concerns arise for consideration by academics, policy makers and practitioners worldwide. *Ageing in a Global Context* is a series of books, published by Policy Press in association with the British Society of Gerontology, which aims to influence and transform debates in what has become a fast-moving field in research and policy. The series seeks to achieve this in three main ways: first, through publishing books which re-think key questions shaping debates in the study of ageing. This has become especially important given the pressures on health and social care systems, alongside the complex nature of population change, both of these elements opening up the need to explore themes which go beyond traditional perspectives in social gerontology. Second, the series represents a response to the impact of globalisation and related processes, these contributing to the erosion of the national boundaries which originally framed the study of ageing. From this has come the emergence of new concerns explored in various contributions to the series, for example: the impact of cultural diversity, changing patterns of working life, patterns of inequality through the life course, the role of ethnicity in later life, and building age-friendly communities. Third, a key theme of the series is to explore interdisciplinary connections in gerontology. The various books provide a critical assessment of the disciplinary boundaries and territories influencing later life, creating, in the process, new perspectives and approaches relevant to the development of gerontology in the 21st century.

*Diverse Transnational Care* represents an important addition to the Ageing in a Global Context series. The issue of transnational care has developed as a significant strand of work in the field of ageing, reflecting the importance of migration streams both within countries and those which cross international boundaries. But the complexity of such care remains under-researched, notably so in the context of the different types of experiences and pressures faced by societies in the Global South. The research by Tanja Bastia and Claudia Calsina, drawing on intensive fieldwork in Bolivia, provides a detailed study of the effects of international migration, and its implications for older people managing their lives in the absence of their children.

The study demonstrates the highly differentiated nature of the impact of migration on older people, reflecting variations in social class, gender and regional difference in migration practices. Through the 100 interviews with men and women carried out for the research, a detailed picture is built up by analysing the three main pillars of transnational care: financial and material resources; health and care; and emotional wellbeing. The resulting study represents a unique picture of the lives of older people in Bolivia together with their relationships with their adult children. The research explores both the vulnerabilities experienced by older people but also the contributions which they make in supporting their children as they move in search of greater economic opportunities. The book represents an important contribution to the literature on transnational care, as well as broadening our understanding of the lives of older people in an important country in the Latin American continent.

# List of figures, tables and boxes

# Glossary

| | |
|---|---|
| **a medias** | modality by which somebody who needs land asks those with surplus land whether they can use it and in return they pay the rent with half the harvest |
| **acullicar** | chew coca |
| **adulto mayor** | older citizen |
| **aguinaldo** | extra payment received for Christmas, equivalent to a monthly wage |
| **anticrético** | a modality of accessing housing where the tenant pays a large deposit that is then returned in full by the owner at the end of the contract. This modality allows property owners to access capital that they can use to finalise or expand their property, invest elsewhere or just earn interest in the bank, while the tenants effectively live in the house 'rent free', save for the loss of interest they would have earned elsewhere on their lump sum. The practice is inscribed in Bolivian property law. The contract usually specifies that if the owner does not return the lump sum, the house will be sold so that the person renting can have their lump sum returned. |
| **bachillerato** | high school diploma |
| **barbechar** | prepare the land for sowing |
| **Caja de salud** | national health service |
| **cañahua** | Chenopodium pallidicaule, a grain similar to quinoa |
| **cargos de autoridad** | communal responsibilities |
| **cariño** | love |
| **catequista** | teacher of Catholic doctrine |
| **centro de salud** | health centre |

| | |
|---|---|
| **Chaco** | area in the south of Bolivia |
| **chuño** | sun- and cold-dried potatoes |
| **costumbre** | custom, routine |
| **cuidado** | care |
| **derrame cerebral** | brain haemorrhage |
| **embolia** | stroke |
| **Encuesta de Hogar** | household survey |
| **fiesta** | party, also used for community fête |
| **grupos originarios** | indigenous population/group |
| **huerto, huertito** | vegetable plot. *Huertito* is the diminutive version |
| **mamita** | mum, diminutive, used in the way that 'love' is used in northern England, as in, for example, 'thank you, love' |
| **mita-mita** | literally, half-half. Refers to a system of renting land by which the person renting the land gives half of their produce to the landowner |
| **morenada** | folkloric dance of the Bolivian highlands |
| **Nación o Pueblo Indígena Originario Campesino o Afro boliviano (NPIOC)** | Indigenous or Afro-Bolivian communities |
| **parentesco** | fictive kin relations |
| **patrimonio** | estate |
| **patrón** | landowner. Until the agrarian reform of 1953, people living on the land were not free to leave it as they owed labour to the landowner |

| | |
|---|---|
| **peón** | labourer |
| **poliglobulia** | polycythaemia |
| **Prosol** | a Community Solidarity Programme with the aim of redistributing income from the natural gas sector for the benefit of indigenous and peasant communities in the Tarija region |
| **quinche** | a structure made of cane or wood filled in with mud |
| **Renta Dignidad** | monthly cash transfer given to people over the age of 60 years in Bolivia. Literal translation = dignity payment |
| **rentista** | pensioner, who receives a contributory pension |
| **reproducción social** | social reproduction |
| **salud** | health |
| **sembrar partido** | sow the land |
| **territorios indígena originario campesino** | land recognised as belonging to indigenous communities |
| **Tigo** | national telecommunications company |
| **wawa** | baby, child |
| **Yacimientos/ Yacimientos Petrolíferos** | state oil company |
| **yunta** | pair of oxen |

# About the authors

Tanja Bastia is Professor at the Global Development Institute at the University of Manchester. She draws on feminist geography and development studies for her research on transnational migration, intersectionality, gender and age. She has been conducted multi-sited ethnographic research with Bolivian migrants in Bolivia, Argentina and Spain since the year 2000 and recently held a Leverhulme research fellowship to develop her research into ageing and migration. She has edited *Migration and Inequality* (Routledge, 2013), co-edited (with Ronald Skeldon) the *Routledge Handbook of Migration and Development* (Routledge, 2020) and is the sole author of *Gender, Migration and Social Transformation: Intersectionality in Bolivian Itinerant Migrations* (Routledge, 2019). https://orcid.org/0000-0002-2025-7706

Claudia Calsina is currently pursuing a PhD in Social Sciences and Humanities at the Universidad Mayor de San Simón (UMSS) and the School of Global Studies of the University of Gothenburg. She has a master's degree in Gender, Identity and Citizenship (Cádiz, Spain, funded by the Carolina Foundation) and is a social pedagogue. She is a researcher at the Centre for Planning and Management of the UMSS and has worked as a consultant for different public institutions and non-governmental organisations. She specialises in gender issues and has publications on issues of migration and transnational care, gender violence and femicide. https://orcid.org/0000-0003-0890-0006

# Acknowledgements

We would like to acknowledge our gratitude to the multiple funders who have made this book possible. The Manchester Institute for Collaborative Research on Ageing (MICRA) funded the pilot project in 2013, which allowed us to do the data collection in Cochabamba. The British Academy and Leverhulme funded the second part of the data collection in Santa Cruz and Tarija, through their small grants projects. The Leverhulme also funded the final part of the data collection in La Paz and Oruro, as well as supported Tanja through their Research Fellowship (RF-2016–450). We are also extremely grateful to both the Leverhulme and the University of Manchester's Library Research Services for funding the Open Access publication, making sure that this book is available to the wider public.

Tanja would like to thank her co-writers on other projects that informed some of the writing in this monograph, particularly Russell King and Aija Lulle for collaborating on an article on migration, ageing and development, on which we have drawn on for parts of Chapter 2; Penny Vera-Sanso and Julie Vullnetari, for collaborating on a *Progress in Development Studies* special issue on ageing and development; and Erika Busse and Maria Calderón, for their friendship and multiple academic collaboration.

Tanja would also like to thank colleagues at the Global Development Institute, particularly those in the Social Development teaching cluster for covering teaching and other responsibilities during the sabbatical, which allowed time for revisions and final submission of the manuscript; and the Research Group on Migration, Refugees and Asylum, including Tanja Müller for convening the group, Uma Kothari and Oliver Bakewell for providing a supportive environment, and Matt Walsham and Luis Eduardo Perez Murcia for covering teaching while I was on the research fellowship. I am also very grateful to members of MICRA, particularly Christopher Phillipson, for their support and encouragement in both the projects and in writing this book. Susie Miles and Nicholas Merton provided me with the tools and clarity for the final push, through their 'Being a Leader' training. Anna Richardson and Emily Ross at Policy Press and Bristol University Press have smoothed over the whole writing process and ensured that we felt supported throughout, for which we are very grateful. Two reviewers provided generous comments and very useful feedback on the first version of this monograph.

In Bolivia, Tanja would like to thank Maria Esther Pozo, for the initial collaboration during the pilot project, Sahara Roque Rocabado and her family, for their friendship and for always welcoming her to their home, and Pablo Regalsky, for incisive comments and reading the first full draft of the manuscript. Claudia would also like to thank María Esther Pozo for her support and guidance throughout the years, the CEPLAG and its director, Carmen Ledo and the whole team for offering a collaborative environment for learning and academic development.

The findings that we report on here have been enriched by presenting preliminary findings at a number of events. Particular thanks go to Michelle Gamburd and Cati Coe for very meaningful exchanges related to their own research on ageing and migration.

A number of people helped during the data collection process, carrying out interviews, providing contacts and support during fieldwork, including Sahara Roque Rocabado and Silvia Jaldín in Cochabamba, Pilar Lizárraga and Carlos Vacaflores of Comunidad de Estudios JAINA in Tarija, Felina Albornoz, Nataly Zuñiga and Abad Arana in La Paz, Carmen Soraya Paiva Fernandez and señora Ángela Sánchez Arambiza in Santa Cruz.

In Bolivia, we arranged dissemination events at key points in the research project, particularly after the pilot in Cochabamba and following the completion of the data collection in Tarija. In both instances we invited municipal and regional authorities, local researchers and grassroots organisations representing older people. Help-Age International Bolivia also participated at these events. Besides presenting preliminary findings, we also wanted to create a space in which grassroots organisations representing older people were able to put forward their concerns to the local municipal and regional authorities. In many of our interviews as well as informal conversations with older people and the organisations that represent them it became clear that they felt that they were not listened to nor heard by the people who make the policies that affect their everyday lives. We felt that creating this space was the minimum we could do given the time and information that many of these people have provided us with. Unfortunately, the completion of the data collection in Oruro and La Paz coincided with the beginning of the COVID-19 pandemic so the events we had planned to organise in these two regions never happened.

In the UK, Tanja organised an online event in December 2020 to mark the completion of the data collection and present some of the preliminary findings. These findings were also presented at various academic conferences and seminars, including at the Universities of Southampton, Keele, Kings College and the LSE. Claudia presented a paper at the 5th Latin American and Caribbean Congress of Social Sciences, 'Democracy, Justice and Equality', organised by the Latin American Faculty of Social Sciences, held in Montevideo, Uruguay in November 2022.

Tanja would like to also thank her family: her partner Juan for his support and understanding and always being there; her two children, Islay and Adair, for their sense of humour and for bringing so much joy; her mother, for early encouragement and support; and both her grandmothers, who passed during the writing of this book, for their unconditional love.

We would like to dedicate the book to our collaborator and Tanja's friend, Sahara Roque Rocabado. Without her help, the research on which this book is based would not have been possible. We would also like to dedicate the book to all our respondents, who took time out of their daily lives to share their experiences with us.

We will donate royalties from the sale of this book to HelpAge International, who work to support older people worldwide.

We take full responsibility for any errors.

1

# Introduction

## Ageing and migration in the global context

Despite common perceptions that ageing is mostly affecting higher-income countries, by 2050 80 per cent of the people over the age of 60 will be living in developing countries (HelpAge International and UNFPA, 2012). Rapid ageing is therefore a global challenge, but one that will be particularly affecting countries in the Global South, including Latin America (Shetty, 2012; Baars et al, 2014). Yet, we still know relatively little about ageing outside of richer countries in the Global North (Skinner et al, 2015). Even in disciplines such as development studies, ageing as a process and older people have been relatively sidelined from both research and policy interventions (Lloyd-Sherlock, 2004; Vera-Sanso, 2023; Vera-Sanso et al, 2023). This book focuses on ageing in the context of high and diverse Latin American migration streams. Its aim is to analyse what kinds of consequences migration has for the migrants' parents who have remained in Bolivia, the migrants' country of origin.

In the Global South, poverty is over-represented among older people (Lloyd-Sherlock, 2010; Farah Henrich et al, 2012). Existing literature suggests that migration can exacerbate the vulnerability of older people and can contribute to new forms of poverty in later life (Vullnetari and King, 2008; Barrientos, 2009; Bastia et al, 2021a). However, the literature on the consequences that migration has for migrants' parents is quite thin and skewed towards distress migration and the migration for lower-income work (Toyota et al, 2007; Stefoni et al, 2022; Miyawaki and Hooyman, 2023). This book explores the consequences of migration for older people through the use of intersectionality, a framework which emerged from feminist and anti-racist theory to analyse the intersections of gender with other axes of inequality, such as class and ethnicity (Crenshaw, 1989; 1991; Bastia, 2014). It asks: *How do transnational care practices differ across socio-economic status?*

We purposefully selected interviewees from a range of socio-economic and livelihood backgrounds, from rural, urban and peri-urban areas and in five different and quite diverse regions, with the aim of exploring the diversity that exists in transnational care practices.

## Diverse transnational care practices

Our starting point is Baldassar et al's (2007) pathbreaking work on transnational caregiving, which shows that it is possible to care at a distance and across national borders (Baldassar et al, 2007). Baldassar et al's (2007) work on transnational caregiving has shown that physical proximity is not an essential requirement for the giving and receiving of care in later life. Instead, caregiving is possible in transnational social fields, spanning physical distance and crossing national borders. This literature argues that transnational care often takes different forms. For example, personal care, which requires physical proximity, is often substituted for other forms of care, such as financial assistance to a local relative or a paid assistant, who can provide hands-on care (Baldassar et al, 2007). Visits by migrant children allow for quality time spent with the ageing parent in the 'home country'. Regular communication makes up for the loss of proximity. However, Baldassar et al's research was carried out in Australia, mainly with migrants whose parents live in resource-rich countries, such as Italy. Taking a 'Southern perspective', it is clear that the degree to which these transnational care practices are available or accessible will differ between lower- and higher-income countries, and different groups of people within these countries.

Research carried out in countries of origin, such as that of Vullnetari and King (2008), already found some differences with this general model of transnational caregiving. In their research in Albania, Vullnetari and King (2008) found that migrants' parents were often in a more vulnerable situation than the one described by Baldassar et al (2007), especially those who were living in remote areas with limited contact with their children abroad. Age also played a significant part in their study. They distinguished between 'young old', who were in their 50s and 60s, and 'old old', who were in their 70s and older (Vullnetari and King, 2008). People in these different age groups were likely to have significantly different needs in relation to healthcare and support, for example. While those in their 50s and 60s are still likely to lead active and healthy lives, those in their 80s and above are more likely to be frail and needing support. They also found that while capacity and ability to care may exist, supportive families are not always the norm.

Other studies, albeit carried out within context of internal migration, found that the stayers' vulnerability was linked to their social networks (Kreager, 2006). Better-off families were better able to use migration to reinforce their position, in contrast to poorer families whose social networks were too shallow and weak to overcome their disadvantage. Kreager (2006) also found that cases where all children are away and not contributing were very rare and that they generally contributed, even if small amounts.

Migration, therefore, can provide the means for households to maintain their status but it can also be the source of vulnerability. Examples of the latter include when migrants do not send remittances; when grandchildren are left in the care of older people; when assets are sold to raise capital; and when illness creates the need for physical hands-on care in proximity (Schröder-Butterfill, 2004; Kreager, 2006; Kreager and Schröder-Butterfill, 2007). However, it is also important to recognise that transnational care norms are not static and that being involved in the process of migration also changes the normative assumptions on which the care of older people is built. Ho and Chiang (2017), for example, argue that notions of filial piety prevalent in Chinese culture are now changing because of the rise of transnational families in which co-residence, a prerequisite for caring for older and ageing parents, is no longer achievable (Ho and Chiang, 2017).

## Why Bolivia

Bolivia is a suitable country to begin addressing these questions. Bolivia is highly differentiated in terms of class and ethnicity. It is also one of the poorest countries in Latin America with a variety of migrations, including regional, South–South migrations to Argentina, Chile and Brazil and longer-distance, South–North migrations to the United States, Spain and Italy. Building on 100 interviews carried out in five different regions of Bolivia (Cochabamba, La Paz, Oruro, Santa Cruz, and Tarija) and across rural, urban and peri-urban areas, this monograph makes a significant contribution to the literature of ageing, migration and transnational care.

The findings from the data gathered indicate that the ability of older people to cope with the absence of their adult children varies significantly by residence, socio-economic status and the type of migration they engaged in. In rural areas, the older 'left behind' find it very difficult to cope with their children's absence. Remittances are irregular, communication unreliable and the migrants' parents need to continue working on the land to survive, although many also draw health benefits from working the land. Peri-urban areas are very entrepreneurial and the older left-behind, particularly mothers, take an active role in managing their children's remittances. Urban areas tend to have better-off, educated migrants, whose work abroad reaps benefits that are more lucrative for both migrants and their parents. However, there are also some exceptions to these broader trends, with some older people in rural areas investing in agricultural production; and some cases of extreme vulnerability in urban areas (Bastia et al, 2021a).

Underpinning this heterogeneity are:

- different migration streams – regional, less lucrative from rural areas, more diversified from peri-urban areas and South–North migrations from urban areas;
- different understandings of the family and the role that adult children play in their parents' later life; and

- a weak state infrastructure and very unequal access to social and physical support in later life.

Within this context, transnational caring therefore becomes highly differentiated and mediated by class, gender and ethnicity in relation to which migration opportunities are available, but also in terms of expectations of the adult child–older parent relationship.

This monograph presents rich and new empirical material from the Latin American region on the effects that migration has on the older left behind and on transnational care practices. The findings demonstrate how transnational caring is not available to everyone in equal measure.

Compared to other regions of the world, Latin America sits somewhere in the middle of the ageing spectrum. As a region, it is not as 'young' as Africa, for example, nor as 'old' as Asia (UNDESA, 2013; ADB, 2024; Oxford University, 2024). A recent document published by the Economic Commission for Latin America and the Caribbean (ECLAC) indicates that there are 88.6 million people aged 60 an over in Latin America and the Caribbean, representing 13.4 per cent of the total population (ECLAC, 2022). Estimates indicate that this will increase to 16.5 per cent by 2030 and 25.1 per cent by 2050, doubling the current proportion (ECLAC, 2022). However, there are also significant country-level variations. Bolivia (together with French Guiana and Haiti) is in the initial stages of the ageing process, where fertility is over 2.5 children per woman and the proportion of people over the age of 60 between 7 and 10 per cent of the population (ECLAC, 2022). For comparison, Chile and Argentina are classified as being in the advanced stages of ageing and many Caribbean countries, including Cuba, in the very advanced stages of the ageing process, where older persons account for over 21 per cent of the population (ECLAC, 2022). While not being at the extreme of the ageing spectrum, the challenge for countries such as Bolivia lies not in the proportion of its population that is over the age of 60 years old, but in the weakness of its institutional structure, particularly in relation to pensions and health services, as we will show.

To investigate the relationship between migration and ageing, we carried out one hundred interviews with men and women aged 60 years and over from the regions of Cochabamba, Tarija, Santa Cruz, Oruro and La Paz (see Appendix for the full list of interviewees and key details). The interviewees were selected on the basis of their age and residence, aiming to gather data that would represent the experiences of migrants' parents with differing socio-economic backgrounds living in rural, urban and peri-urban areas. As such, there was great variability in terms of education, livelihoods and migration experiences.

Broadly speaking, the experiences documented in the interviews represented the wider context of international migration, which differed in each region. In Cochabamba, interviewees had adult children in Argentina, Brazil, the United States, Spain and Italy. Many of the interviewees themselves also had previous personal experience of international migration, particularly to Argentina and Venezuela. In Tarija, most interviewees had adult children in Argentina. This represents the very strong connections from Tarija, particularly the rural areas, and migration for work in the neighbouring country. Many of the children had started migrating from a very young age, when they were still young teenagers. The interviewees had therefore aged while their children have been living and working abroad, which was different in Cochabamba, where migration was a more recent experience. Santa Cruz experienced a significant out-migration to Spain, particularly after the 2001 Argentinean crisis, with a very strong participation of women. Direct international migration from rural areas was hard to find in this region as most international migration took place from peri-urban and urban areas. Most experiences we collected from rural areas were of 'step migration', from rural areas to the city and then on to another country, generally Spain. In La Paz, interviewees' children had migrated regionally to Brazil, Argentina, Chile, Uruguay, Colombia, Mexico, the United States, and various destinations in Europe (Italy, Spain, France and Belgium). Of particular importance was regional migration, particularly for jobs deemed unskilled, like the garment sector (Argentina and Brazil) but some also migrated to pursue their studies and for professional jobs, within the region as well as to Europe. In the case of Oruro, there were cases of regional migration for agriculture and the garment sector, particularly to Argentina and Chile, migration to Europe (Spain, UK and Italy) for domestic work and care of older people, and to a smaller degree, professional jobs within the region and to Europe (see Bastia and Calsina Valenzuela [2022] for a summary).

Given the large number of interviews, it is impossible to do justice to all the interviewees. The chapters that follow therefore include the most representative experiences of each region and area, as well as those that contrasted with the general trends.

Based on this data, we show that transnational care differs across socio-economic status and that not everyone has access to transnational care. Transnational care practices rely on the ability of migrants and parents to communicate, visit, have a minimum of resources and institutional support available, besides the fact that family relations need to be amicable, if not supportive and loving.

## Layout of the book

The book is organised around three main pillars of transnational care: financial and material resources, including remittances; health and care; and emotional wellbeing.

Chapter 2 discusses the main literature that covers ageing, migration and transnational care practices. It shows that many disciplines, including geography, gerontology and development studies, have traditionally sidelined ageing in the Global South, and paid much greater attention to ageing in the Global North. This needs to change, not only because older people in low- and middle-income countries generally face much more precarious conditions, but also because most of the growth in ageing will come from countries in the Global South. This chapter also shows that the literature on ageing and migration has similarly tended to focus on countries of the Global North. We make the case for paying greater attention to older 'stayers' – the migrants' parents – particularly those who remain in countries of the Global South.

This chapter also lays out the main conceptual tools that we use in the main part of the book, including the concepts of transnational care and migration circuits. Finally, we make the argument that greater attention needs to be given to the diversity and heterogeneity of older 'stayers'.

Chapter 3 elaborates on the methodology, including details about data and funding, our sampling strategy, methodology and the main methods we have used in this book – the semi-structured interview. We provide details of fieldwork and data collection, discuss the ethical dimensions of our research, including working across different languages for both collecting data and writing. Here we also explain how we went about analysing our material and the process of co-writing.

In Chapter 4 we review the broader ageing and migration context in Bolivia. We begin with an overview of Bolivian migrations and then go on to focus on older people in Bolivia, including a review of the public policies that govern national and regional policies for older people in Bolivia. We then sketch out migration history and practices in the five regions where we conducted data collection, including any particularities that are relevant for later understanding the empirical chapters.

Chapters 5 and 6 represent our first analytical pillar. In Chapter 5 we discuss financial and material resources and the ways in which migrant children sometimes participate in influencing these. Chapter 6 covers remittances: whether parents receive remittances, how these are spent and also the many instances where they refuse to receive remittances from their adult children abroad.

Chapters 7 and 8 represent our second analytical pillar: health and care. In Chapter 7 we discuss the main health issues that affect our interviewees and how they address them. In Chapter 8 we discuss care, both the ways in which our interviewees arrange their everyday care needs and also how they often continue to care for others.

Chapters 9 and 10 cover our third analytical pillar: emotional care and wellbeing. In Chapter 9 we describe parents' responses to their children's migrations. In Chapter 10 we cover communication, and how older people maintain contact with their migrant children and whether they are able to visit children abroad – or their children visit them. In this chapter we also discuss the many strategies migrants' parents employ to maintain their emotional wellbeing, whether this manifests as continuing to work, being active in local associations or attending church.

In the last chapter, Chapter 11, we summarise our main findings and discuss the broader implications of our research.

2

# Ageing and migration in the Global South

## Introduction

The project on which this book is based began with our interest to try to understand the consequences that international migration has for the migrants' parents. Both migration studies as well as gerontology were at the time largely focused on higher-income, Western countries. They both largely maintain this focus ten years on. In this chapter we run through the literature on ageing and migration to show how some of its findings and assumptions are significantly different if approached from a non-Western perspective. By doing this, we also show how this literature could be enriched if researchers adopted a broader framing, one that includes non-Western, lower- and middle-income countries.

To do this, we draw on a number of literatures, including that developed by gerontologists who work in non-Western contexts; development studies, including migration and development debates; development geography; and the growing literature on South–South or regional migration.

## Ageing and migration

Broadly speaking, we situate our research within the 'ageing–migration nexus' (King et al, 2017; Sampaio, 2022). This literature emerged over the last couple of decades as a result of the realisation that much of the research on migration was very much skewed towards the younger generation (Lulle and King, 2016; King et al, 2017). While it is true that most migrants are in their 20s and 30s when they first migrate, this is not to say that people do not migrate when they are older (Bastia et al, 2022b). According to the United Nations Department of Economic and Social Affairs (UNDESA), the average age of migrants across the world was 39 in 2019 (UNDESA, 2019), with some striking differences between continents: 30.9 years for migrants living in Sub-Saharan Africa but 42.7 years in Europe and 43.5 years in North America. While one in seven international migrants was below the age of 20 in 2019, approximately 32 million migrants, or 11.8 per cent of the global migration stock, were aged 65 years or over (UNDESA, 2019).

In addition, even the migration of younger people has repercussions for those who are in their later stages of their lives. Younger people have older

8

relatives, who are affected by the migration of the younger generations (Toyota et al, 2007; Vullnetari and King, 2008; Bastia, 2009; Conkova et al, 2018; Bastia et al, 2021a). Migrants, particularly women, also seek work in care of older people and, as such, become part of the complex transnational relationships that are often relied upon to provide care for people as they age and in the last years of their lives, a process that raises ethical concerns for some (Berlinger and Kaebnick, 2013; England and Henry, 2013; Bastia, 2015; Amrith and Coe, 2022). This happens in countries of the Global North as well as those of the Global South (Parreñas, 2001; 2012; Amrith, 2010; Martínez Espínola and Delmonte Allasia, 2022). Moreover, even when migrants undertake their migration journeys when they are young, they might age 'in place' at their destination as they get older, or undertake new journeys to return to their places of origin once they have fulfilled their migration objectives or when additional needs arise for them to return (Hunter, 2011; 2018a; Buffel, 2017; Ciobanu et al, 2017; Sampaio and Walsh, 2023).

These different scenarios have all been examined in the ageing and migration literature (Sampaio, 2022). However, as with the migration literature more generally, this literature has also been largely focused on the Global North or the higher-income countries in Europe and North America, particularly the United States, which attract the majority of the migration flows and where most of the research funding is available. So, a global perspective has been missing in both the migration literature and in the ageing and migration sub-literature. Although these countries do receive the largest number of migrants in absolute terms, important regional centres of migration exist in every region and the currently expanding literature on South–South migration attests to the importance of taking into account these migration flows (Crawley and Teye, 2023).

The ageing and migration literature so far has dealt with three main themes: the migration of older people; the ageing of migrants in destination countries; and older people who have stayed in countries of origin.[1]

Warnes et al (2004) and Warnes and Williams (2006) were the first ones to propose a typology of older migrants, set forth in two review papers, in which they showed how diverse older migrants are. Lulle and King (2016), who build on this work, propose a typology that includes:

- older people who remain in the country of origin when their children and grandchildren migrate;
- international retirement migrants, who migrate to benefit from a better climate, scenery, leisure and lifestyle; and
- the ageing process of labour migrants, which includes: staying put in the country of destination, returning to the country of origin, or a combination of both, engaging in what they term 'back-and-forth transnational lifestyle' (Lulle and King, 2016: 7, following Bolzman et al, 2004).

Here we follow their typology and suggest that the transnational element crosses all the others and is always present, whether the person moves or not. We therefore discuss older people on the move, including the different reasons for the move; 'ageing in place', which tends to refer to ageing in place of destination to describe the process of ageing following a previous move; and older people who have stayed in their countries of origin following the migration of their children and, sometimes, grandchildren. What will become evident, as the review progresses, is that most of this literature has focused on the Global North and that only the 'retirement migration' literature has thus far shown any sign of starting to embrace a more global perspective.

## Older people on the move

As for migration in general, categorising and defining the reasons behind somebody's migration proves challenging. Migrants may state one reason as their main motivation for migration. However, their decision and desire to migrate is often made up of many different reasons. Economic motivations tend to prevail as the main motivation. This is as much a reflection of actual economic needs as of the researchers' main interest. Feminists writing about migration in the 1980s have explored in depth how the researchers' main interest in economic migration has tended to tinge all migrations with this quality (Anthias, 1983; Phizacklea, 1983). King and Lulle (2015; Lulle and King, 2016) have explored more recently in much depth how migration that is on the surface presented as a labour migration is in actual fact also a deep search for fulfilling one's own dreams and desires (King and Lulle, 2015; Lulle and King, 2016). However, while recognising this complexity, it can also be said that, as for any person, older migrants undertake their migration journeys for a variety of reasons. The main ones that have been explored in the literature are retirement migration, return migration, the migration of older people to join younger family members, and migrating for work. We discuss each in turn.

*Retirement migration* has by far outstripped all the other types of migration as a source of interest for researchers. As has been acknowledged elsewhere (Bastia et al, 2022b), this might not be a reflection of the numeric or political importance of this type of migration but might have more to do with the attractiveness for Northern researchers to carry out fieldwork in locations that are deemed desirable (see also Lulle and King, 2016).

This literature begun with a focus on Northern Europeans retiring to Spain and Italy (Williams et al, 1997; King et al, 2000), but more recently expanded to examining retirement to destinations in the Global South, including Mexico (Truly, 2002; Sunil et al, 2007; Balslev Clausen and Velazquez Garcia, 2011), Costa Rica (Janoschka, 2011; Janoschka and Haas,

2014), Ecuador (Hayes, 2014; 2015), Malaysia (Green, 2013; 2015; Ono, 2017) and Thailand. Some have termed this type of migration 'residential tourism', based on the fact that the type of migration resembled an extended holiday stay (Jurdao Arrones, 1970; Huete et al, 2008). Others, however, have highlighted how retirement migration is often a response to the precarity that older people experience in their own countries as they age (Repetti and Calasanti, 2024).

This strand of the literature has examined the reasons why some retirees seek retirement locations abroad, as well as the broader implications of their choices. It has shown that some who are able to afford these journeys, the costs of relocations and potentially also financing a double residency, choose to relocate to enjoy the better weather and different scenery, but also to be able to access cheaper housing and living costs. The fact that established communities of co-nationals already exist provides an additional attractive dimension (King et al, 2000; Casado-Díaz et al, 2004). Others, particularly US retirees, choose to move to Central and South American locations, because they are unable to afford the very high costs of privatised healthcare in their home countries (Hayes, 2014), which has also been found to be a factor for 'pension-poor' retirees in Thailand (Botterill, 2017). Savaş et al (2023), for example, in a recent review article on international migration for retirement show that some of the best-known examples of people who move to a country other than the country of their usual residence around the time of their retirement includes British people who move to the south of Spain, North Americans retiring to Mexico and, more recently, Japanese nationals moving to Malaysia.

Although these types of migrations have generally been linked to retirement, Janoschka and Haas (2014) prefer the term 'lifestyle migration' to indicate that similar migrations are undertaken by people of all ages, who seek out a lifestyle that is different to the one that they have access to in their home countries. Important to note, though, is that regardless of the terminology, choosing to spend one's retirement years, or indeed, a larger part of one's life elsewhere, is often linked to a personal history of travel and tourism to that particular destination (Botterill, 2017).

Besides motivations and the personal experiences of the retirees/lifestyle migrants, this literature also examines the social, environmental and developmental implications of the migration and settlement of significant numbers of foreign nationals, in their later stages of their lives, in these target destinations. Some argued that the retirees provide a positive economic stimulus to what were essentially quite impoverished areas in the south of Spain (Williams et al, 1997). They bought properties and their relocation stimulated the development of a local housing market, with additional service provisions, creating jobs that attracted younger Spanish internal migrants (Huete et al, 2008). Others, however, pointed out that the type of development created was unplanned, lacking both urban and tourism planning (Huete et al, 2008), that went hand in hand with irreversible local environmental damage and significant segregation between the local and the migrant communities (Membrado Tena, 2015). Similar arguments have also been made for Costa Rica (Janoschka, 2011) and Ecuador (Hayes, 2018).

Those focusing on the social consequences of this migration have likewise raised concerns and highlighted tensions in the cross-national marriages between older Western men and younger Thai women (Laliberte Rudman, 2006; Koch-Schulte, 2011; Scuzzarello, 2020).

We can see in this strand of the literature that while it began with a focus on Europe and the United States, it has more recently expanded to include retirement destinations in the Global South (Savaş et al, 2023).

Older people *returning to their countries of origin* has been studied for a longer time, at least since the 1970s, when the return of retirees to Italy attracted attention as to their developmental potential (Cerase, 1974). Going along with the more popular view that older people tend to be a 'cost' to the economies, wherever they reside, Cerase (1974) also argued that while younger people's return to their countries of origin, in this case Italy, can lead to economic innovation, the return of retirees and older people had little developmental potential. However, more recent studies have shown that older people who return to their countries of origin can bring benefits, both for themselves as well as for the places they left when they were younger. Hunter (2018b), for example, details the important role that returning retirees play in North and West Africa, contributing to their villages' development through financial investments and continued participation in Hometown Associations. Return, for these men, also means beginning a new life, rather than the 'social death' associated with older age in Western countries (see Chapter 6).

The transfer of pensions to countries of origin can benefit the local economy, as it provides an injection of foreign currency. However, the move to return to their countries of origin can also be an opportunity for the retirees to achieve personal and professional goals that they have not been able to either pursue or achieve while they were working and living abroad. Sun (2014; 2016) has researched Taiwanese retirees who have returned from the United States to access good quality healthcare but also to contribute to the development of their home country. While 'retired', they find new jobs in Taiwan, contributing to universities, hospitals or working as consultants. The degree to which such a movement will be beneficial, at least economically, will largely depend on whether the returning retirees have been able to accrue pension benefits and whether they are able to claim these benefits from their home countries, once they return there. As has been shown, these benefits are not always transferable (Sinatti, 2015).

Besides financial considerations, such as whether the pension is transferable or sufficient for the returning migrant and his/her family to live on, the permanence of a return decision will also depend on the extent to which the returning migrant and his/her family will be able to cohabit harmoniously. Long-term separations, which are sometimes only sporadically broken by visits 'back home' can lead to strains in family relationships and family members becoming 'strangers' over time (Hunter, 2018b). Unless migrants and their family members have been able to preserve some kind of familiarity and closeness during the separation, a return is unlikely to be permanent and may lead to a further emigration (see Hunter, 2018b for more details).

Because of these perceived and actual benefits that returning retirees can bring, many countries of origin have specific policies to encourage the return of their citizens once they retire. Examples include Cape Verde, Cote d'Ivoire, Ghana and Senegal (Amassari, 2009; Åkesson and Eriksson Baaz, 2015; Kleist, 2015).

The *migration of older people to join younger family members* has also been researched but to a much lesser degree. The work of King et al (2014) has illustrated well the hopes and perils of moving at a later age to join adult children, effectively to be able to exercise their grandparenting roles. Building on their long-term research on Albania, this research shows how the migration of younger people often robs their parents of the opportunity to be grandparents to their grandchildren. Some, therefore, then decide to follow their children and join them in their countries of destination or travel backwards and forwards between their places of origin and their children's destinations (Díaz Gómez and Marroni, 2017). While this move allows them to practice and be grandparents, the living arrangements and social context is often fraught with difficulties, which range from living in crowded spaces, not speaking the language of the country that they are staying in, and interpersonal tensions related to different views about child-rearing (King et al, 2014).

In a study of national and transnational family networks of older adults in Guanajuato, Mexico with children emigrating to the United States, Montes de Oca et al (2008) propose a classification of other situations of old age:

- older adults who remain in the communities of origin (although during their youth they made trips to other locations, they returned and did not leave their communities again for the rest of their lives);
- older adults who have never migrated, but have been affected by this phenomenon at the family level;
- the 'swallows': older adults who have migratory experience, and in old age alternate their residence between the community of origin and the place of residence of the children, thus strengthening the transnational bond; and

- old age identified as having absent older relatives, either due to abandonment, disappearance or death (Montes de Oca et al, 2008).

Other studies, such as that of Díaz Gómez and Marroni (2017), use the category 'grandmothers of migration' to refer to the mobility and agency capacity of older women from Michoacán, Mexico, who migrate to the United States to care for grandchildren. In turn, they are grandmothers who are caregivers and cared for in migratory contexts.

Research into *older people migrating for work* has received the least attention. As with migrants of younger ages, older people's personalities and personal characteristics predict their likelihood of undertaking a migration journey (see Van Dalen and Henkens, 2007; Jokela, 2009). Lulle and King's research (2016) in this sense is pioneering, not only because it puts older migrants, that is, older people who undertake their migration journeys for the first time, firmly on the map of migration studies, but also because of their conceptualisation of the reasons behind these migration. As explained earlier, while focusing on labour migration, they recognise that migration for work envelops many different dimensions of people's lives and so-called 'labour migration' journeys can also be undertaken for pleasure, curiosity, or to satisfy personal and intimate desires (Lulle and King, 2016).

## Ageing 'in place' in countries of destination

The ageing of migrants who migrated when they were younger has been covered in parts of the literature on labour migration as well as that on diasporas, with slightly different emphases. Research on labour migrants who are 'ageing in place' generally focuses on the choices they make when these labour migrants reach retirement age and the consequences that these choices have for them. Hunter (2011; 2018a) has found that older migrants in France are disadvantaged compared to the native population of the country of destination. While staying in their countries of destination might give them access to better healthcare and higher pensions, his research shows that older migrants live quite isolated lives, with weakened family-based networks (Hunter, 2011; 2018a; Ciobanu and Hunter, 2017). Research on Filipina migrants in the United States also testifies to the difficulties that ageing migrants face in retiring, in this case, from jobs that involve caring for older people who may actually be younger than the carers themselves (Nazareno et al, 2014).

Others, however, have found that migrants have a rich engagement in civic participation, which includes volunteering in co-ethnic and cross-ethnic communities (Torres and Serrat, 2019). Research into ageing diasporas has been more predisposed to acknowledging a heterogeneity of experiences among ageing migrant communities (Mehta and Singh, 2008), including how older people play an active role in changing ageing cultures themselves (Lamb, 2009). A transnational perspective and a recognition that ageing for migrant communities takes places within transnational social fields, wherever the ageing migrants may find themselves, forms a cornerstone of this literature (Buffel, 2017). This acknowledgement of transnational social fields also puts the spotlight on ambivalences that ageing migrants experience, both in terms of the choices they are able to make but also how they feel about their complex identities and sense of belonging as well as the difficulties they face in accessing care in older age (Gardner, 1999; 2002; Cylwik, 2002; Ciobanu and Ramos, 2015; Näre, 2017).

As can be seen from the examples mentioned in this section, much of the existing research on ageing in place and on ageing in contexts of migration continues to be focused on higher-income countries, mainly Europe and the United States (for an example, see the edited collection by Karl and Torres [2016] or Torres and Hunter [2023]). While this may be a fair reflection on the geographical locations that host most of the migrants globally as well as those locations that have experienced most of the demographic ageing to date, as already mentioned in the Introduction, this is rapidly changing. We therefore need to be able to expand our geographical horizons and our understanding of ageing in contexts of migration globally.

## Older 'stayers' in countries of origin

The only strand of the ageing and migration literature that has paid a fair amount of attention to places of origin and countries other than the main migration destination areas is the literature on older 'stayers', the older family members – usually the migrants' parents – who stay in their countries of origin while younger family members migrate (Haagsman and Mazzucato, 2020). Although initially most of the literature on the 'left behind' was generally concerned with the welfare of the migrants' children and in that sense had 'forgotten' about the older left behind, this has started to change during the last decade or so (Toyota et al, 2007).

Initially most of the studies were tinted with a focus on vulnerability. The research on the consequences that the mass migration out of Albania had for the welfare of the older generation that stayed in the depopulated villages and had to make do with living in relative abandonment from both the state and family support, led to the popularisation of the term 'orphan pensioners' (King and Vullnetari, 2006; Vullnetari and King, 2008). While some of this research continues to document the vulnerability that older 'stayers' experience as a result of migration by the younger generation internationally (Conkova et al, 2018; Iossifova, 2020) or internally (He and

Ye, 2014), approaches to the question of older stayers have over time become more complex and questioned the supposed vulnerability of this group of people (Biao, 2007; King et al, 2017).

This literature is not confined to countries of the Global South. A recent review of the literature on transnational caregiving has found that for half of the studies on transnational care, the migrants' countries of origin were in Europe (Miyawaki and Hooyman, 2023).

Authors researching ageing and migration in transnational contexts that include lower- and middle-income countries have proposed a more complex understanding of the care-work involved (see Dossa and Coe, 2017; Yarris, 2017; Gamburd, 2020). Yarris (2017) for example, has researched the care that grandmothers provide in Nicaraguan transnational families, analysing how care is reconfigured as a result of the migration of women from Nicaragua. Rather than conceptualising this as a 'care deficit' as in the traditional view based on the global care chains framework (Hochschild, 2000), Yarris argues that the care that grandmothers provide is a source of wellbeing for the children as well as other members of the transnational families (Yarris, 2017). Gamburd (2020) provides us with one of the most detailed ethnographies of transnational care as seen from the origin country point of view. Based on longitudinal ethnographic work in a Buddhist village in Sri Lanka, Gamburd's vivid descriptions bring to life not just the care that grandparents provide for their grandchildren when their parents migrate, but also the strategies that older people enact to secure their own care and wellbeing in older age (Gamburd, 2020). Coe (2022), similarly, focuses on the migrants' countries of origin to examine the changing landscape of care in West Africa, particularly in Ghana, where what she defines as 'market-based solutions' have become much more common as a source of care for older people in the last decades (Coe, 2022).

In this monograph we build on this more recent research on transnational ageing but with a focus on the countries of origin and the migrants' parents. While doing this, we also build on the tension that was already highlighted over a decade ago by Biao (2007), albeit for an internal migration context, in which he argued that it was not the migration of relatives that led to the abandonment of the migrants' parents in China's rural areas, but an abandonment of the state. We found a very similar situation in Bolivia, as will become clear throughout this monograph.

### Transnational ageing

Transnational ageing cuts across many of these categorisations, given that it is used to describe how processes of ageing take place transnationally, across places of origin and destination. Therefore, we would argue that transnationalism and transnational social fields, whether these are acknowledged or not, play a role in influencing all the various scenarios identified thus far: those of older people on the move, whether they then eventually age 'in place' (that is, at destination) as well as those who do not migrate but stay in countries of origin.

Clearly, we need to acknowledge that ageing in low-income countries has been investigated, but it has played a relatively minor role in the general literature on ageing and how it is theorised (Vera-Sanso, 2006). As with migration research in general, the existing literature on ageing and migration focuses primarily on South–North migration, thus overlooking South–South migration even though it constitutes almost half of all cross-border movements (Ratha and Shaw, 2007; Crawley and Teye, 2023).

There is an extensive literature dealing with the migration of domestic workers and carers, many of whom find work in the care service for older people, both in residential homes and as direct employees of the family of the person cared for. Different studies evidenced the feminisation of migratory flows, especially but not exclusively from the Global South to the Global North, coining concepts such as 'global chains of affection and assistance' (Hochschild, 2000), 'internationalization of care' (Parella, 2005), 'global care crisis' (Pérez Orozco, 2021) and 'transnational circuits of care' (Romero, 2018). This literature is not usually included in the 'ageing–migration nexus' but it does provide rich insights into how the process of ageing in destination countries is supported by migration and transnational networks of support. Studies focusing on places of origin have tended to categorise these migrations as a zero-sum game, where places of origin tend to miss out on the care of the women who have migrated (Hochschild, 2000). However, this approach has also been critiqued through a number of studies that have shown that systems of care at origin are always in flux and migration is merely one of the reasons that leads to a reconfiguration – rather than a loss – of care practices in places of origin (Bastia, 2019; Herrera, 2013; 2020).

However, rather than putting an emphasis on the 'here' or the 'there', we would argue that a comprehensive and original way of understanding transnational relations in contexts of ageing has been put forward by Walsh and Näre (2016) in the introduction to their edited collection on *Transnational Migration and Home in Older Age*. While much of the literature cited so far is influenced by a here/there or origin/destination framing, Walsh and Näre (2016) aim to move away from the methodological nationalism that informs much of the migration literature as well as transcend the here/there dichotomy. In this monograph we do focus on the country of origin, but only to balance out the overwhelming focus of both the migration and the ageing literatures on the countries of destination.

The literature on transnational care, to which this monograph aims to contribute, adopts this transnational perspective but also aims to contribute to a better and richer understanding of the experiences of stayers in countries of origin.

## Transnational care

Transnational care as a field of interest emerged after the turn of the current century among scholars working on migration and interested in understanding caring arrangements in contexts of international migration. Baldassar et al (2007)'s work is pathbreaking in this field. In their early work, Baldassar et al (2007) took issue with the gerontological literature, in which it was generally assumed that physical proximity is a requirement for care. Based on their research with migrants in Australia, who in various ways cared for their parents who had remained in their countries of origin, they argued that physical proximity is not an essential requirement for the giving and receiving of care in later life. Instead, they showed how caregiving is possible in transnational social fields, spanning physical distance and crossing national borders. They build on the work of Basch et al (1993), in which they developed the concept of transnational social fields to define social processes and relationships that take place across transnational fields (Basch et al, 1993).

The authors identify five main elements that make up transnational care. First, providing economic support, which for some migrants' parents is absolutely essential to make ends meet. Second, emotional and moral support, such as listening and talking, which, they argue, is 'the *bedrock* of transnational family relations' (Basch et al, 1993: 87, emphasis in original). They distinguish between routine support, crisis support and support provided at the time of emigration. Third, accommodation. Fourth, practical support, which they argue is particularly important for mother–daughter dyads/relationships. Fifth, personal care, which, as indicated earlier, can be substituted by financial assistance, or can be provided through visits. While care can take place across transnational social fields, it often takes different forms from proximal care. For example, personal care, which requires physical proximity, may be substituted for other forms of care, such as providing financial assistance to a local relative or a paid assistant, who can then provide hands-on care (Baldassar et al, 2007).

We use these different elements to build our own analytical framework around three main pillars of transnational care:

1. material elements, which we distinguish between financial and material resources, such as income, housing, land, and so on, and remittances, the financial resources that are sometimes sent by migrant children to their parents, but also the other way around;
2. personal care, which we organise around access to health services and the care that our interviewees receive, as well as give to other family members; and

3. emotional wellbeing, which we organise around the ways in which our interviewees responded to their children's migrations and other elements that help support their wellbeing, including communication with their children abroad, visits (both ways) and associational life.

These different types of support and care are not discrete and independent of one another. As the authors acknowledge, there is a certain 'degree of exchangeability ... between types of support and care', especially in relation to personal care, to which migrants often cannot contribute (Baldassar et al, 2007: 107). However, research carried out in migrants' countries of origin shows that there is not just an important interplay between different types of support, but also a significant tension between the decision to migrate or to return, and the provision of care for older people.

However, as we already know, much of care-work is gendered. Gamburd's research in Sri Lanka (2020), already mentioned earlier, shows the complex interplay between gender and intergenerational relations in contexts of high out-migration and the tension inherent between the need to provide care of older people vis-à-vis the need to provide financially for one's own family. In her research context, individuals can gain social prestige and karmic merit by offering to care for elders (Gamburd, 2020: 44). However, they also need to balance the need to fulfil their financial and caring obligations towards their own children and partners with the caring expectations towards their own or their in-laws' ageing parents. Gendered expectations assume that women are generally more likely to leave a job to take up caring responsibilities, while men's responsibility is to earn an income. However, if a man cannot fulfil his breadwinner role, his wife is then expected to do so and often does so through migration. In this case, a woman's obligation to support her family financially 'supersedes her duties as a caregiver to an elderly parent or in-law but may not supersede her obligation to her children, particularly her teenage daughters' (Gamburd, 2020: 55).

That women are more likely to leave their jobs to care for elders has also been observed in Britain, where women provide 75–85 per cent of relative care (Finch, 1989: 27). Men do provide care but generally only when they are looking after a disabled wife. Finch (1989) argues that there is a clear hierarchy of obligations for who offers personal care. First, marriage relationships take primacy, so the spouse takes on the caring responsibility. Second, the parent–child relationship, which is highly gendered, with daughters being much more likely than sons to take on care responsibilities. Third, members of the same household. Fourth, gender, where women are much more likely to provide care but also to not receive care in periods of illness, given that 'women are presumed to be able to cope domestically in circumstances where men are presumed to be unable to manage' (Finch, 1989: 29).

In context of high levels of out-migration, the second 'hierarchy of obligation', or the parent–child relationship, is most likely to get disrupted and this is particularly the case where the migration is highly feminised, so where women are more likely to migrate. This is because it is women – or daughters – who are most likely to take up caring responsibilities of their ageing parents. However, one could also see how the first 'hierarchy of obligation', or taking care of a spouse, becomes more difficult to fulfil when adult children have migrated, particularly for those whose livelihoods depend on some level of help from their adult children (for example, farming, as we will see in Chapter 5).

Moreover, it is also interesting to see how care for older people is in tension in people's decisions not just in relation to their financial obligations but also how some types of care may seem more or less important. For example, childcare is seen as more important, because if parents are not there to educate their children, children can 'go bad' and the reputation of the whole family will suffer. Care for older people, on the other hand, is seen as less important and more easily outsourced, despite the fact that there is a fairly clear order of preference for elder caregiving, in which immediate family comes first, extended family or fictive kin come second, and bought-in help come last (Gamburd, 2020).

These examples highlight the importance of context and the fact that it is difficult to generalise in relation to either gender or care. In fact, our intersectional approach, in particular, stresses the importance of taking into account the social and cultural specificity of the context within which we carried out our research. As others have argued, there is no generalisability in intersectionality, as there is no universal intersectionality (Magliano, 2015; Pinto Baleisan and Cisternas Collao, 2021). For us, this means that we have had to deal with *multiple contexts*, hence our emphasis not just on gendered and intergenerational power relations and socio-economic differentiation, but also the very different regional contexts where we have conducted our research.

In their conclusion, Baldassar et al (2007) list a number of requirements that enable transnational care: active kin work; the capacity and ability to engage in transnational caregiving; finance; access to technology; time and mobility; ability (relatively good mental health); being able to delegate caring responsibilities to others, if unable to take on care responsibilities oneself; a sense of moral requirement; negotiated family commitment; license to leave (parental support for the migrant's decision to migrate); supportive kin; and familiarity with mobility. Therefore, while adopting Baldassar et al's concept of care, as already discussed, we have also simplified it as a way of structuring our analysis around the three pillars that we adopt in this book: material and financial resources, including remittances; health and care; and emotional wellbeing.

The degree to which these will be available will differ in lower- and higher-income countries, between different groups of migrants in countries of destination, and between different groups of parents in countries of origin. The authors themselves found significant differences between migrant and refugee interviewees within their sample (Baldassar et al, 2007). These were related to both levels of income as well as migration status. However, we would argue that the degree to which these requirements are available and accessible is inherently framed by unequal access to both resources as well as different types of migration circuits. This is why in our research we have highlighted socio-economic differentiation and aimed to examine to what extent socio-economic positioning affects the ability to practice (both give and receive) transnational care.

Our approach of starting from the place of origin also addresses a methodological bias. Baldassar et al (2007) did not include in their study examples of left-behind parents who were abandoned or who had little contact with their migrant adult children, not because these do not exist, but because the starting point for their methodology were the migrant (adult) children at destination. Migrants provided contact details of their parents and the authors built their contacts with the migrants' parents from the destination area. Although they did find variation in the strength of the relationship between migrants and parents based on differential access to communication technologies, different ability to speak the grandparents' language and variations in parents giving migrants 'license to leave', all migrants had some kind of functional relationship with their parents, or they would not have provided the parents' contact details. The authors themselves acknowledge a bias towards well-functioning transnational families because they had to gain permission from the migrants to contact their parents.

In a more recent article, Kilkey and Merla (2014) expand on the notion that state policies and international regulations influence the maintenance of transnational family solidarity. However, their starting point is also two countries of destination: the UK and Belgium. They distinguish between four types of care provision: direct provision of physical co-presence; direct provision at a distance; coordination of support; delegation of support. However, they do not take into account lack of care or situations where no support is provided; nor do they explicitly focus on socio-economic differentiation.

Research carried out in countries of origin, on the other hand, while providing evidence of how transnational care is experienced by the receivers of this care, has highlighted instances where this care is deficient or non-existent. Vullnetari and King's research, for example, shows how following mass out-migration, it was not uncommon to find 'orphan pensioners' in Albanian villages and rural areas (King and Vullnetari, 2006; Vullnetari and King, 2008). Older people were struggling to cover their basic necessities being far away from urban centres and in the absence of their adult children. More recent research in Bulgaria paints a similar picture, where older people living in rural areas face multiple hardships as a result of the absence of the younger generation (Iossifova, 2020).

However, we should be careful in always linking migration to greater vulnerability for migrants' parents. Research in Indonesia shows that while between 29 per cent and 76 per cent of elders were vulnerable or prospectively vulnerable at the time the research was conducted, migration itself was not an automatic cause of vulnerability. Adult children who moved away continued to contribute, albeit in small amounts. Cases where all children were away and not contributing were very rare. This research concluded that vulnerability is linked to the intergenerational transmission of poverty, more than being a specific outcome of migration (Kreager, 2006).

In some of our previous writing on this, which was based on our interviews in Cochabamba only, we have already identified some examples of older parents who were not only struggling to meet their own needs, but who also had caring responsibilities towards grandchildren (Bastia et al, 2021a; 2021b).

Therefore, there are two points we would like to highlight here. First, that it would be wrong to assume that migration only leads to greater vulnerability. Migration can be the source of vulnerability, but it can also provide the means for households to maintain or improve their status. Examples of the former include when migrants do not send remittances; when grandchildren are left in the care of older people without proper support or when the needs of the grandchildren cannot be met by the grandparents or vice versa; when assets are sold to raise capital; and when illness creates the need for physical hands-on care in proximity (Schröder-Butterfill, 2004; Kreager, 2006; Kreager and Schröder-Butterfill, 2007). While all of these scenarios do happen, as others have already argued, there is a danger of falling into the 'vulnerability trope' (King et al, 2017) by *assuming* that migration will always lead to greater vulnerability. As we show in the chapters that follow, while it is true that a significant share of the older population in Bolivia does experience sometimes significant vulnerabilities, this is more often the case due to the lack of a solid infrastructure that would support older people well into their later lives; and not a result of migration itself.

Moreover, older people are heterogeneous, and they are positioned very differently in relation to livelihood opportunities, access to health services or to support networks. As we will show in the chapters that follow, there is no one experience of migration that unites them all. They all experience their children's migration in very different ways and, while for some, their children's migration may lead to an increase in their vulnerability, others might benefit from it.

Second, involvement in the process of migration also changes the normative assumptions on which care of older people is built on. As Ho and Chiang

(2017) find, notions of filial piety prevalent in Chinese culture are now changing because of the rise of transnational families in which co-residence, a prerequisite for caring for older parents, is no longer achievable. On this last point, Gamburd (2020) also talks about how moral expectations and practices of care change through increased access to mainstream education – children spending time away at university. The transnational care we refer to in this book is therefore not made up of fixed, inherited norms but constantly in flux as a result of societal changes, of which migration itself is a part.

## Care

Care has been widely discussed in feminist theory, from the early work of Tronto and Fisher (1990) to more recent calls for care to be given proper consideration as a foundation of democratic principles, including the drawing up of care manifestos (Tronto and Fisher, 1990; Tronto, 2015; The Care Collective et al, 2020). These writings argue that care is a foundation of everyday life, but one that has largely been ignored by mainstream politics and policies, as well as mainstream social theorists, largely because the majority of care-work is carried out by women. As such, while being essential for the reproduction of people, societies and economies, care is undervalued and continues to be largely invisibilised.

Many definitions of care exist. Tronto and Fisher (1990) defined care as follows:

> On the most general level, we suggest that caring be viewed as *a species activity that includes everything that we do to maintain, continue, and repair our 'world' so that we can live in it as well as possible.* That world includes our bodies, ourselves, and our environment, all of which we seek to interweave in a complex, life-sustaining web. (Cited in Tronto and Fisher, 1990: 34; emphasis in original)

Definitions often distinguish between care as an activity versus a broader understanding of care as an emotion, as in caring about somebody.

There are also contending concepts that have been used by feminist researchers. For example, many have highlighted the tensions that exist in focusing on care versus social reproduction, which arguably places greater emphasis on the structures within which care takes place, as well as on the ways in which it contributes to the reproduction of the working force (Kofman and Raghuram, 2015). Others have argued that care as a concept is Eurocentric (Green and Lawson, 2011).

While we do acknowledge the limitations of the term care, and overall have a preference for the wider term social reproduction, we have decided to use care as a key focus in our work. One of the reasons for this is that the term is easily translatable into Spanish and also can be easily understood colloquially, that is, there is a term – *cuidado* – that is easily understood by everyone. Social reproduction is also translatable into Spanish, that is, there is a Spanish equivalent – *reproducción social* – but this is not easily understood outside of specialised circles, either academic or those that engage with feminist social critiques. We wanted this book to be accessible to the wider population, not just researchers.

A second reason for using care is that we also wanted to keep this term because of its associated term, 'transnational care'. We could have switched to 'transnational social reproduction' but felt that we would have been weakening the link with the original term and associated discussions, if we had made this decision.

## Migration circuits

Different types of migrations lead to different outcomes. There is a clear hierarchy of desirability in terms of migration destinations, which is further made more complex by different modes of migration, which are, again, hierarchically ordered in terms of their desirability. South–North migrations are often preferred. They lead to higher-paying jobs and the potential to settle in a high-income country. However, they require higher levels of capital, including financial, social and human capital. Regional, South–South migrations, on the other hand, are more easily accessible, in terms of paperwork, financial investment and contacts, but usually lead to smaller returns, also because in some cases these migrations constitute patterns of circular migration. Wages in Bolivia's neighbouring countries, such as Argentina, Chile or Brazil, are lower than in some of the South–North destinations, such as the United States, Italy or Spain. Argentina and Brazil are also more likely to experience quite regular, periodic crises, although, as we have seen more recently, these are also common in higher-income countries. Anecdotal evidence, for example, suggests that Bolivians are currently returning from Argentina in significant numbers given 'life there is unsustainable'.[2]

This hierarchy of destinations is illustrated well by the recent work of Parreñas et al (2019), in which they examine the mobility patterns of domestic workers in the United Arab Emirates from the Philippines and Indonesia. While establishing the itinerancy and precarity that current migration policies engender, they join a number of other scholars who have also shown the existence of a marked, yet shifting, hierarchy of desirability in migration destinations (Pratt, 2012; McKay, 2016; Parreñas et al, 2019; Silvey and Parreñas, 2020).

Bolivians have historically shown a preference for regional migration to Argentina for garment and agricultural work and to the United States for more skilled work but migrants shifted their attention to Spain and Italy because of the inability of making a living in Argentina at the beginning of the new millennium. The shift in destination was a result of Argentina ceasing to be a desirable destination, rather than an explicit strategy to diversify destinations, increase income or seek more lucrative work (Bastia, 2019).

In addition to this hierarchy of destinations, there are also more and less desirable modes of migration. While the United States might be a desirable destination, for some migrants the only way to access this destination is through undocumented migration. Undertaking a journey through irregular means and not being able to secure legal status carries penalties that will have consequences not just for the migrant herself but also for her family members who have stayed in her country of origin. For example, visits may not be possible given that leaving the destination would imply not being able to return to it, unless another irregular journey was undertaken, with all the risks and costs that implies.

In this book we also depart from most studies of migration, which focus on migration from the point of view of destination. We focus instead on examining migration as it is seen from the Global South and through diverse migration circuits, including South–South regional migrations.

While most of the research and policy work on migration focuses on migration from the Global South to the Global North, almost half of all cross-border migration takes place between countries of the Global South (between 34 and 41 per cent of all cross-border movements, depending on which source is used [IOM, 2013]). So-called 'South–South' migration has been gathering more attention in recent years (Crawley and Teye, 2023), despite the challenges that have been raised in relation to the use of the term (Bakewell, 2009). This figure is likely to be significantly underestimated, given that movements between countries of the Global South are not as tightly controlled, monitored or counted as those taking place from the Global South to the Global North.

Intraregional migration in Latin America and the Caribbean is long-standing and rooted in the region's identity (Neira Orjuela, 2022). Even more so in recent decades, the increase in intraregional migratory flows from Colombia, Ecuador, Peru and Bolivia to some of the main Latin American countries whose economies are wealthier, such as Brazil, Chile and Argentina, is striking (Neira Orjuela, 2022). Much of the most recent research and policy attention has focused on the massive exodus of Venezuelan migrants to other countries within the region and systems of asylum to accommodate forced migrants (Acosta et al, 2019; Blouin, 2019; 2021; Gandini et al, 2020; Freier and Vera Espinoza, 2021; Gissi et al, 2021; Martínez Espínola and Delmonte Allasia, 2022; Cintra et al, 2023; Zapata et al, 2023). Smaller migration streams, but which are just as significant, particularly for the countries of origin, have also been researched (Cela et al, 2022a; 2022b; Marcelin and Cela, 2023).

Paying attention to the diversity of migration, including what we might call South–South or regional migration, means that we have a fuller picture of migration and its consequences. For example, we can find that shades of undocumentedness also exist in regional migration flows and address what these might mean for transnational care and the wellbeing of the migrants' parents. By taking this approach and not limiting our view on migration to specific destinations, we also come across instances of skilled migrations that take place along South–South migration routes.

As we will see in the chapters that follow, some migrants are also able to secure better paid, professional positions by migrating regionally to a neighbouring country. This is most likely to happen for those with middle-class backgrounds who have first migrated to finalise their further education or pursue more specialist trainings, such as master's degrees. We tease out class-based distinctions throughout our empirical chapters to highlight the types of possibilities that are open to different people to highlight the diversity – and also inequalities – inherent in migration possibilities and thereby also transnational care.

But, who counts as a migrant? The formal definition of a 'migrant' is somebody who has moved from one place or one country to another and stayed in their 'destination' for a certain period of time, for example a year (De Haas et al, 2020; Skeldon, 2021). However, migration is clearly a much more complex process. Migrants are located in 'networks, relationships and communities' (O'Reilly, 2012): 4). They are not isolated individuals making choices on their own. Clearly, migration takes many different forms. In our interviews we have come across seasonal and circular migration, return migration, internal migration that had preceded international migration, international migration that was undertaken to secure a position in the city, distress migration, for example, to flee a violent relationship, regular visits, or migration to secure health treatments, among others.

We also recognise that not everybody is able to move and while in our sample we have focused on those who have adult children abroad, their experiences are closely interwoven with those whose aspiration to migrate remains just that, an aspiration (see Carling, 2002; Carling and Schewel, 2018). In migration studies there is now increasing recognition of how remaining in place is part and parcel of a world that is on the move (Mata-Codesal, 2015). The increasingly strict and highly controlled barriers that higher-income countries erect to keep out those migrants they deem undesirable mount costs on those who try but are unable to secure their migration project (Jones, 2016). Some migrants try to reach their destination multiple times and, if they cannot reach their destination, are faced with an unpayable level of debt (Bastia, 2019).

Migration is therefore a process which profoundly changes the world, for both the migrants themselves as well the societies they move from, through and to.

By taking into account the different migration trajectories and routes, as well as the different position that the migrants' parents are situated in relation to the socio-economic hierarchy in the places of origin, we aim to challenge some of the assumptions that continue to prevail in the literature on transnational care. First and foremost, we show that there are multiple forms of migration. Second, and following on from this, we illustrate how these different forms of migration have different consequences for the migrants' parents. Third, we also show how migrants' parents are often actively involved in their children's migrations. They are seldom passive recipients of their children's decisions to migrate. They often contribute to their children's migration projects, sometimes actively encouraging their children to migrate. At times they also manage remittances and investments. While doing this, we also make a significant contribution to our knowledge of the ageing literature, given this is also overwhelmingly focused on the Global North, as we discuss in the next section.

## Ageing in the Global South

The world is rapidly ageing due to declining fertility rates (Phillips and Feng, 2018: 96–97). This has been known for a while. What is less known is that low- and medium-income regions of the world are ageing rapidly too. According to UNDESA, four-fifths of the world's population aged 60+ years will be concentrated in the Global South by 2050 (UNDESA, 2015). Globally, the total of older people will increase from 962 million in 2014 to 2.1 billion in 2050. Based on data from UNDESA (2017), there are 228 million people aged 60+ in China, 125 million in India and 68 million in Africa. Meanwhile, in Europe (including Russia) there are 182 million. As well as these absolute numbers, the share of older people in the total population, already a phenomenon well advanced in the Global North, will grow sharply in the Global South – for instance, from 9 to 19 per cent in India (2017–2050) and from 6 to 10 per cent in Africa, the world's 'youngest' continent (Phillips and Feng, 2018; Rishworth and Elliot, 2018). Latin America and the Caribbean is also experiencing a rapid ageing process. By 2060, the proportion of people aged 60 and over in this region is projected to surpass that of Asia and Oceania and be closer to the corresponding values in North America and Europe (ECLAC, 2022).

Ageing can be defined as a biological process of becoming older but the way in which biological ageing is understood and experienced is very much socially and culturally specific (Lulle, 2024). What ageing means in practice will depend on the context and on who is ageing. While in our research we have chosen a threshold to identify our interviewees (aged over 60 years old), we see ageing as a process that often starts when people become aware that they are getting older. This might happen when they start experiencing ill health that is more associated with older age. In the Global North ageing might also be associated with reaching particular stages in one's life, such as retiring or becoming grandparents. But in the Global South this is less likely to be relevant, because pensions are not widely available (Barrientos, 2009). In some contexts, it is also more common for women to bear children from a younger age, so their mothers become grandmothers when they are still deemed to be relatively 'young'.

However, it is important to distinguish between what some have called 'third' and 'fourth' age as this refers to a distinctive shift in the wellbeing of the person getting older (Williams et al, 2012; Ahmed and Hall, 2016). The former is usually the stage, frequently covered by lifestyle research and targeted by policies and individual choices, of 'active' and 'successful' ageing. The latter is the frail old age of bodily and/or mental decline when regular support is needed by family or healthcare providers (Higgs and Gilleard, 2017).

Moreover, active ageing and successful ageing models of individual responsibility and independence, which celebrate 'active' ageing, do not necessarily map on to all societies in the Global South where, in some contexts, 'successful ageing' is less about individual self-reliance and more about dignity, respect, family support, spiritual development and physical relaxation (Gardner, 2002; Gamburd, 2020).

Thus far, the focus of much of the literature on ageing has been on the Global North. Existing reviews show that we still know relatively little about ageing in the Global South (Harper and Laws, 1995; Skinner et al, 2015; 2018); although there is a growing literature by anthropologists and gerontologists that focus on lower-income countries (Lloyd-Sherlock, 1996; 2010; Schröder-Butterfill, 2004; Vera-Sanso, 2004; 2006; 2012; Kreager, 2006; Kreager and Schröder-Butterfill, 2007; Lloyd-Sherlock et al, 2012; Coe, 2016; 2017; 2022; Yarris, 2017). Given the figures indicated earlier, it is imperative that we bring greater balance in our understanding of ageing across the world, including because the rapid ageing trends in lower-income countries give rise to concern.

First, health infrastructure is much more precarious in the Global South than in higher-income countries (Kowal et al, 2010; Tan, 2022). Moreover, even in lower-income countries, socio-economic inequalities influence access to and use of existing health services. People with higher incomes and higher education are more likely to access and use primary healthcare, compared to their counterparts who are unemployed and not economically active (Gao et al, 2022).

Second, pensions are not as widely available. While more than 95 per cent of people above retirement age in Europe receive some sort of pension, only

23 per cent do so in Sub-Saharan Africa (UN, 2018). In Asia, participation in contributory pension schemes is below 10 per cent in some countries (Chomik et al, 2024). A large proportion of the labour force in lower- and middle-income countries works in the informal sector; hence they cannot draw work-based pensions. Statutory age-based pensions are not available or too low to cover even the basic necessities (Barrientos, 2009). Because of such low levels of support, most older people in lower- and middle-income countries need to continue working.

Third, and as a result of the previous two points, poverty levels are concentrated in older age (Barrientos and Lloyd-Sherlock, 2002; Randel et al, 2017; Moonga, 2024). Women, in particular, tend to face greater disadvantages in older age, because of their generally lower levels of education and exclusion from formal employment, despite their continued contributions in both financial and social reproduction to their own households and those of the younger generation (Heslop and Gorman, 2002; Vera-Sanso, 2012; 2018).

## Intersectional inequalities

Throughout this research we have used intersectionality to frame our data collection and our analysis. This is a term that we have used before (Bastia, 2014; 2019; 2023; Bastia et al, 2023). We continue to engage with this term because we find it useful in helping us frame our analysis and think through how various sources of both privilege and disadvantage interact in the context within which we are researching.

Intersectionality was first coined in 1989 by Kimberlé Crenshaw, a feminist legal scholar. By introducing and coining this term, Crenshaw wanted to highlight the double discrimination that Black women faced in the US legal system. She argued that black women in the United States were doubly discriminated against: on the basis of their colour and because they were women. Under the legal system at the time, they could only claim discrimination on the basis of either race or gender. Crenshaw argued that this did not provide a just system and that it was only by taking into account the double discrimination they faced, that the legal system could provide the basis for redressing the injustices that black women faced.

The fundamental problem that Crenshaw aimed at redressing is one of framing: a problem is often not seen, and will remain invisible, unless the right framing is used. Intersectionality aims to provide such framing, so that the intersections of multiple discriminations can become visible and seen, and therefore provides the opportunity of finding redress (Crenshaw, 1989; 1991).

Since its introduction, intersectionality became popular in feminist research, first in the United States during the 1990s and more recently since the turn of the century in Europe. Intersectionality has been taken up in most social science disciplines, from sociology, politics, to geography and psychology. In some disciplines, there has been more emphasis on policy, such as in politics (Yuval-Davis, 2006; Squires, 2008). In others, more emphasis on understanding people's lived experiences, such as in geography (Valentine, 2007).

With the greater uptake of intersectionality in so many disciplines, also came a proliferation of the types of disadvantages taken into consideration. From the original focus on gender and race, today studies of intersectionality include religion, sexuality, disability, ethnicity, class, and so on. Some may argue that such proliferation weakens the original intention of the term. Others argue that once multiple discriminations are included, it focuses attention much more on individual experiences than on the social structures that produce disadvantage. More recently, some research has also used intersectionality to address the analysis of privilege.

However, while Crenshaw (1989) coined and popularised the term, intersectionality has a much longer history and a much more varied geography as well (Bastia et al, 2023). Intersectional approaches are not new within feminism and, before it was coined, it was already being incorporated into different feminist theories throughout history. In the Latin American context, writers and artists, as well as postcolonial authors, have contributed different perspectives that are quite critical of the discursive coloniality of hegemonic feminisms, since 'it cannot be assumed, neither theoretically nor politically, that gender and racial inequalities and their articulations are universal' (Viveros Vigoya, 2016: 9). Feminist scholars in Latin America started articulating gender and race, in particular, already during the 1970s (Saffioti, 1978; 1992; Vargas, 1985; Bairros, 1995; Gonzalez, 2020). Feminist voices from the Global South, identified from peripheral, community and decolonial feminisms, have broadly addressed intersectionality (Curiel, 2007; Espinosa Miñoso, 2007; Espinosa Miñoso et al, 2014; Viveros Vigoya, 2016). Other authors, such as María Lugones, have proposed that the analysis of intersectionality incorporates the analysis of the coloniality of power (Quijano, 2000), coining the concept of gender coloniality (Lugones, 2008).

In Bolivia, there is a long history of grassroots women's movements making intersectional-like claims, while at the same time rejecting the Western notion of liberal feminism (Barrios de Chungara and Viezzer, 1979). More recently, there has been an exciting proliferation of studies using intersectionality, particularly in relation to migration in the Latin American region (Magliano and Ferreccio, 2017; Gavazzo et al, 2020; Garcés-Estrada et al, 2021; Pinto Baleisan and Cisternas Collao, 2021; Reyes Muñoz and Reyes Muñoz, 2021; Ariza and Jiménez Chaves, 2022; Martínez Espínola and Delmonte Allasia, 2022).

By drawing on intersectionality, therefore, we tap into a very current debate in both the English-speaking social science circles as well as research published in Spanish, while also honouring and acknowledging a much longer history and practice of intersectional interventions that have been present in Bolivia and in Latin America more broadly.

## Diversity and heterogeneity of older 'stayers'

By using intersectionality in our research, we therefore build on this longer history of intersectional approaches, which aims to highlight inter-group differences, while at the same time being true to the feminist aim of seeking equality and justice for all. For our research, this has meant seeking to disrupt notions of homogeneity that seem to be prevalent in studies of older 'stayers'. While King et al (2017) have already argued for taking greater care in reproducing stereotypes of vulnerability for older migrants, we have taken this further and deliberately sought informants from different socio-economic groups. Given the organisation of Bolivian society, this has meant carrying out interviews in rural, urban and peri-urban areas (see Chapter 3 on the methodology). However, even within this strategy, we have then looked further into each of these areas and discovered that further dimensions of (dis)advantage were present. While, broadly speaking, urban areas are significantly better off than rural areas, and peri-urban areas are somewhere in between; there were also some areas where the local history of migration meant that some of our interviewees had been able to benefit from significant accumulation of financial capital (for example, Arbieto, which is considered a rural area). Likewise, there were some interviewees in generally speaking better-off urban areas, who lived isolated and impoverished lives.

Breaking 'transnational care' down into material, hands-on and emotional aspect of their lives also allowed us to identify cases where the problem might not have been a lack of material resources, but one where social networks have failed. These weaker networks might be a consequence of migration, though not necessarily international migration. Internal migration can also lead to weakened social networks.

While using concepts that are understood in the English language – such as gender, socio-economic status, race and ethnicity – we have qualified what these mean in the varied contexts in which we have carried out our research (see Chapter 3). We have also retained the specificity of each fieldwork context by situating our findings in the specific history of each region and sub-regional contexts (rural, urban, peri-urban).

## Conclusion

The existing literature on transnational care shows that it is possible to care at a distance. However, this care is not available to older adults equally. From an intersectional perspective, care is traversed not only by age status, but also by gender, socio-economic status, place of residence, access to state infrastructure, mainly to health services by older adults, as well as other factors such as the destinations and migratory circuits of children abroad, income levels and immigration status. As the empirical chapters will show, the interaction and tensions between the decision of children abroad to migrate or return, the support of mothers and fathers regarding this decision and their permanence in the countries of destination, and the provision of care for older people also play an important part in how transnational care is practised.

It is likely that, as in Kreager's (2006) study for the Indonesian case, in the Bolivian case, the vulnerability of older adults is not a direct and/or exclusive result of the migration of their children, but rather has to do with the intergenerational transmission of poverty and the absence of state infrastructure and public policies for this population. This is even more so the case if one considers that in countries such as Bolivia, migration is historical and part of the *habitus* of a large part of the population. Therefore, especially in certain regions, migration is a common phenomenon.

Unlike other studies such as that of Baldassar et al (2007) that describe cases in which there is clearly a functional relationship between older adults and migrant children, in the case of this study, given the methodology and theoretical approach used, we have sought informants from different socio-economic groups and places of residence. As a result, we have also found older adults who have little or no contact with their children abroad. However, despite having identified some cases of abandonment, as a general rule, children abroad carry out care actions at a distance towards their mothers and fathers.

In this book we therefore build on literature on ageing and migration and the role of ageing and older people in contexts of high migration to explore how transnational care varies across socio-economic status. We define transnational care as being made up of material concerns, including income, housing and remittances; health and personal care; as well as emotional wellbeing. By doing this, we contribute to a greater understanding of how older people fare in context of high levels of out-migration and show that the category of older 'stayers' is highly heterogeneous.

3

# Methodology

## Introduction

In this chapter we cover our methodological strategy. We discuss sampling and the decisions we have taken, and explain why. We talk about our main method – the semi-structured interview, and explain collaborations as well as the role of language in both data collection and in the process of writing across languages. Finally, we also discuss ethics and the role of care in both data collection and fieldwork.

## Data and funding

This book draws on interviews from a research project on ageing and migration in Bolivia. It is based on 100 in-depth interviews we carried out with men and women aged 60 years and over from the five regions in Bolivia (see Appendix for full list of interviews, including gender and age of each interviewee). This was a 'thin and long' project, which we started in 2013 with a pilot, funded by the Manchester Institute of Collaborative Research on Ageing, and then went on to secure further funding: a Small Grant from the British Academy and the Leverhulme (2014–2015) and finally a Leverhulme Fellowship (2019–2022).

Geographically, we started with a pilot in the region of Cochabamba (22 interviews). We then expanded to Tarija (19 interviews) and Santa Cruz (21 interviews) regions with the small grant and finally added Oruro (18 interviews) and La Paz (20 interviews) regions in the last phase (see Figure 3.1). Data collection was completed by January 2020, just before the onset of the COVID-19 pandemic. While all three projects were led by Tanja, this was very much a collaborative process, where different people and organisations collaborated at different stages of the project (more on this further on this chapter). Claudia worked as a researcher in all three projects and carried out about half of the interviews.

What remained constant was our interest to better understand the consequences that migration has for the migrants' parents.

**Figure 3.1:** Bolivian regions

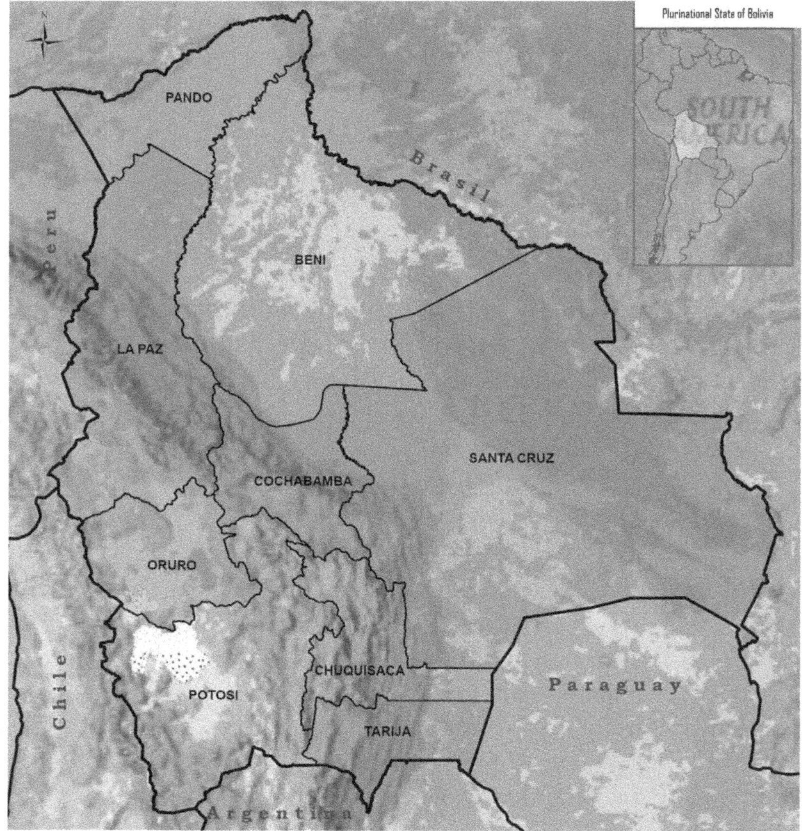


Source: Map designed by Ronald Llano. First published in Bastia and Calsina Valenzuela (2022: 83).

## Key analytical variables: residency, socio-economic background, age

As already mentioned, from the inception of this project we wanted to capture the diversity in transnational care practices. We initially took rural, urban and peri-urban as proxies for socio-economic strata, given that, overall, rural areas are generally much poorer than urban areas and peri-urban areas are somewhere in between (see Chapter 4). However, we soon realised that reality was far more complex than this. For example, in the Cochabamba region, interviews in rural areas included impoverished rural hamlets in the province of Cochabamba as well as in Arbieto, a town with long-standing links to the United States (de la Torre Avila, 2006; de la Torre Avila and Alfaro Aramayo, 2007; Jones and De La Torre, 2011). In Arbieto, we found the more diverse set of interviewees, some of whom also had entrepreneurial experiences and for whom their own migration or the migration of their children led to upward social mobility. On the other hand, some interviewees in urban areas were clearly in a very vulnerable situation, not being able to properly look after themselves or their grandchildren, even though they were receiving monthly remittances from their adult children abroad (see Chapter 6). Half-way through the writing, we therefore decided to re-code all interviewees according to socio-economic status, in addition to residency (rural, urban and peri-urban), to help us bring out our argument that socio-economic background matters when we talk about transnational care.

Defining socio-economic background in a context as diverse and fluid as Bolivia was not without its challenges. We started by deciding that we were going to take into account education and income as the basis for categorising interviewees' socio-economic background. We ended up with three main categories: low, medium and higher-medium. We felt that none of our interviewees could fit into a higher socio-economic status category. Interviewees who have not finished primary school education and did not have a stable source of income were categorised as '*lower socio-economic group*'. In this category, we included informal street vendors, subsistence farmers or those who sold excess produce at local markets for minimum profit. The majority of our interviewees, 54 per cent, were in this category. In the '*medium socio-economic group*', we included interviewees who finished high school and/or had a more profitable and possibly stable source of income, such as teachers, successful business owners (whether their businesses were formal or informal), farmers who had larger plots and invested in their agricultural businesses, whether growing specific crops (peaches in Cochabamba or quinoa in Oruro) or rearing farm animals. We had 30 interviewees in this category. In the '*higher-medium socio-economic group*' we included people who had a higher level of education (for example, finished university) as well as a secure income base (for example, through a contributory pension or continued professional involvement in their jobs). We had 16 interviewees in this category. Interviewees who fall within this category therefore benefited from the social benefits associated with formal work, including the contributory pension (in addition to the universal *Renta Dignidad*) as well as health insurance, albeit through the *Caja*. As we will discuss in the chapters that follow, these benefits make a significant difference in the interviewees' everyday lives and their wellbeing and are in marked contrast with other interviewees, who only receive the *Renta Dignidad*.

Because we recategorised our interviewees after data collection, we did not end up with an even spread across all three categories. But our sample was not evenly balanced across rural, urban and peri-urban areas even before this categorisation due to difficulties in gaining access, regional specificities and the sometimes limited time we had available to spend in the field. In any case, we aimed for data saturation and gathering examples that would be representative – from a qualitative point of view – of social realities in the varied contexts we carried out data collection, rather than equal numbers. Statistical representation was not an aim in this project.

We realise that there are significant problems with this dry categorisation of our very diverse set of interviewees. The fact that we have imposed this categorisation onto the interviewees post-data, after the data has been collected, rather than using it to select our interviewees, is an additional problem. Looking back, we should have had this discussion at the beginning of the project, rather than once the data collection was finished. However, this is the best we could do given the long and thin nature of this project and the fact that we added areas of data collection as funding became available. We still feel that it was worth going through this process as the data speaks to this categorisation *as well as* to the one that we initially worked with, that is more based on residency. However, this additional layer of analysis allows us to talk to the heterogeneity of socio-economic status that is present in different areas across the country. In fact, if we look at the categorisation of socio-economic differences together with residency, we find that while in rural areas 73.8 per cent of interviewees belonged to the lower socio-economic group, 23.8 per cent belonged to the medium and 2.4 per cent to the higher-medium. In peri-urban areas, almost two thirds (62.1 per cent) belonged to the lower socio-economic group, 27.6 per cent to the medium and 10.3 per cent to the medium-higher. In urban areas, 17.2 per cent belong to the lower socio-economic group, 41.4 per cent to the medium and 41.4 per cent to the higher-medium (see Table 3.1). Had we stayed with our initial categorisation based on residency, we would have missed out on some significant variability within those residency areas, and we would not have been able to bring out the exceptions to the averages in those areas.

The interviewees were selected based on their age (60 years and over), having one or more children abroad, and residence. There is one interviewee (see Appendix, number 46) who did not have children abroad at the time of the interview. This was because her son had died while in Argentina, but this only became clear during the interview. We felt that it would not have been tactful to exclude this interview from the sample given the circumstances. But we also wanted to include this interview as it is an important acknowledgement of the reality of migrations in the region.

**Table 3.1:** Interviewees by area of residency and socio-economic status

| Residency/socio-economic status | Low | Medium | Higher-medium |
| --- | --- | --- | --- |
| Peri-urban | 18 | 8 | 3 |
| Rural | 31 | 10 | 1 |
| Urban | 5 | 12 | 12 |
| Total | 54 | 30 | 16 |

In terms of age, we adopted a working definition of 'old age' as being 60+, given that this is the minimum age of the receipt of the universal cash transfer *Renta Dignidad*. We chose this threshold based on Law No. 369, 'General law of older people' (Ley N° 369, *Ley General de las personas adultas mayores*), which indicates that beneficiaries from this legislation are people aged 60 years old and over. The threshold of 60 years old is also used by international organisations, such as the World Health Organization (WHO, 2024). However, we also recognise that chronological age is seldom very useful in defining the later stages in people's lives. In fact, we would argue that ageing is better described as a process and recognise that people age differently and have very different experiences of ageing (Lulle, 2024). In a country like Bolivia, where fertility rates, while falling, are still higher than the regional average (2.69 versus 2.01 births per woman) (WB, 2023), it is quite common for people to become grandparents while in their 40s. Other life cycle events, which are often used in the gerontological literature as key markers of 'later life' starting, such as retiring, are not easily mapped onto the majority population given the largely informal nature of the labour market, and are only available to a minority of its population (see Chapter 5). We recognise this diversity and, in the material that follows, we try to do justice to it. However, we also felt that, given the large scope of qualitative data collection, we wanted to have some common ground in terms of some of the basic interviewee characteristics. We therefore decided to adopt the age of 60 as the minimum age for our interviewees.

We have also come across an additional problem, which is that it is not uncommon for older people not to have identity documents and/or not to know their exact age and date of birth, especially in rural areas. When we have encountered these situations, we have included an approximation based on what interviewees and their relatives and friends have told us.

## Sampling and data collection

As mentioned earlier, our project grew as we found new sources of funding. Although our methodology remained the same, research in each region ended up evolving somewhat differently.

We started with a pilot project in Cochabamba in 2013, where Tanja Bastia, Claudia Calsina Valenzuela and Maria Esther Pozo worked with Silvia Jaldín and Sahara Roque Rocabado to interview older people in rural, urban and peri-urban areas. Tanja returned to the peri-urban areas where she had conducted her PhD and her longitudinal ethnographic research on gender and migration (Bastia, 2019). She worked with Sahara, a mother-tongue Quechua speaker, with whom she conducted interviews with older residents of that neighbourhood as well as some in the city centre, using Sahara's contacts from when she worked as a nurse in one of the city centre clinics. Silvia Jaldín, who is also a Quechua speaker, did interviews in the Koari area of rural Cochabamba, with families she has known for a while. Tanja also conducted some interviews in the Cochabamba care home, Asilo Buen Pastor.

For several weeks in 2013, Claudia Calsina went daily to the municipality of Arbieto, located more than 50 kilometres from the city of Cochabamba. She carried out interviews with older adults with ties to the United States. Thanks to a colleague, Lady Montaño, who is a resident of Arbieto, Claudia was able to establish contacts with older people who had adult children abroad. In most cases they received her in their homes and helped identify others to be interviewed.

Once funding was secured for two additional areas, we started data collection in Santa Cruz and Tarija. Claudia started interviews in Santa Cruz and Tarija. However, this fieldwork proved quite difficult. Claudia travelled to Santa Cruz in August 2014, in the middle of the electoral process for the general elections that took place on 12 October of that year. On the one hand, there was a lot of mistrust on the part of the population due to the political situation, so many people did not agree to be interviewed. On the other hand, Claudia did not have institutional support nor contact with key people, family or friends who could help in the identification of potential interviewees in those regions. This situation made the work of finding interviewees even more difficult, especially when Claudia went to areas far from the city centre, where she was faced with situations of insecurity.

In the end, some of the interviews were too short to be usable and Claudia was unable to finalise fieldwork that year, so Tanja travelled to Santa Cruz on two occasions, in 2015 and 2016. During the first visit, she carried out interviews in the city centre and Plan 3000, a peri-urban area on the outskirts of the city of Santa Cruz. She used contact provided from friends of friends to identify older people who had some of their children living abroad and proceeded with checking whether they wanted to be interviewed. Somebody working at the hostel where she was staying had a relative whose children lived in the United States, and they agreed to be interviewed. Moreover, she established contact with a Spanish non-governmental organisation that ran a day centre for older people in Plan 3000 and travelled there a number of times to observe their activities and meet the people who made use of that service. Observing them at the day centre gave her the opportunity to check whether potential interviewees had any of the signs that would indicate a potentially vulnerable person – confusion, memory lapses, and so on. She approached individuals who were clearly able to understand issues around consent and proceeded to interview them if they were interested in participating in the study. Most of these interviews were carried out at the day centre. A few additional contacts emerged from these interviewees and were later followed up with home-based interviews, including one, where initially it was suggested that Tanja could interview a woman who was over 100 years old. However, arriving at the house, she found that the potential interviewee was not able to understand issues around consent, so she proceeded to interview her daughter, who also had children living abroad and was in her 70s, so fitted the profile of the type of person we were looking to interview.

In a second trip, in January 2016, Tanja sought the help of Carmen Paiva Fernandez, who has long-standing work in the lowland indigenous areas, to interview Guaraní migrants in some of the towns that lie to the north of Santa Cruz city and members of the Guarayo community in Guarayos, about a half-day drive from the city of Santa Cruz. Interviews in Guaraní were also facilitated by doña Ángela Sánchez Arambiza, of Guaraní origin herself, who travelled with us to the households and translated for those who were not comfortable speaking in Spanish.

Tanja also travelled to Tarija in April 2014 to begin the data collection there. She visited formal institutions, such as the Servicio Departamental de Gestión Social (Regional Office for Social Services), the Defensoría del Pueblo (Ombudsman) and the Pastoral de Movilidad Humana (Human Mobility Pastoral) and carried out preliminary interviews that allowed her to map the relevant institutions that were involved in providing services for older people. She also carried out a small number of interviews with residents of the older people's home, Santa Teresa Jornet, run by a religious order (Las Hermanitas de los Ancianos Desamparados). To facilitate access to interviewees we secured the collaboration of Jaina, a community-based research group. Pilar Lizarraga and Carlos Vacaflores carried out 18 interviews, mostly in rural areas of Tarija, which were complemented by a few interviews in peri-urban areas. As we were not able to return to Tarija to carry out additional interviews, our sample in this region is quite skewed in favour of lower-income, mostly subsistence farmers from rural areas.

Tanja would have continued carrying out fieldwork, but the birth of her daughter in 2016, as well as teaching and administrative commitments, did not allow for additional travel and fieldwork trips, particularly given the extensive travelling required for the methodology we decided to follow in this project. So Claudia took over data collection at this point and was accompanied by Sahara Roque, who had already helped with data collection in Cochabamba. Sahara was instrumental in identifying people to be interviewed, especially in rural areas for the regions of Oruro and La Paz.

Claudia and Sahara did various trips to the region of La Paz during the months of May, June and July 2019. Getting to the rural areas took at least three hours of travel. Although they visited some nursing homes and arranged meetings with older people organised by the Head of the Unit for Persons with Disabilities and Older People of the Municipality of La Paz, for the bulk of the interviews Claudia and Sahara resorted to contacts previously established through their relatives. Most of the interviews were conducted in the homes of the interviewees. In the case of rural areas, it was essential to stay for several days and contact people through snowballing.

Claudia and Sahara then travelled to Oruro in the months of November and December 2019 and January 2020, before the measures imposed in March of that same year, because of COVID-19. Even though Oruro is a smaller city, it took about three hours to get to the rural areas to meet potential interviewees. As in La Paz, most of the interviewees were contacted thanks to the help of their relatives. Sahara's contacts were also important, especially those related to people working in mining, which generated greater confidence and predisposition on the part of the people to participate in the study, after they understood the aims and scope of the study.

## Care in/and fieldwork

Fieldwork for this project was not easy, nor straightforward. The process was not linear and data collection was difficult to plan. The challenges of carrying out research in Bolivia for Tanja related to the distances involved as well as the methodology we decided on of talking to people in rural, urban and peri-urban areas, given work as well as caring commitments at home. The methodology adopted for this research meant that it would have been very difficult to combine childcare with data collection and it was not possible for her partner or other family member to also travel to Bolivia to support this work. The challenges of combining fieldwork far from home and care-work, particularly for women, have been well-documented elsewhere (Hope et al, 2020; Jenkins, 2020; Bastia et al, 2022a; Cox et al, 2024).

The writing process was disrupted by innumerable caring emergencies, including the most recent when Claudia had to take time off writing because of illness in her family. But we adopted a care-centred approach to both data collection (see the 'Ethics' section in this chapter) as well as analysis and writing.

## Methodology

We approached the field being aware that we were going to talk to people who might be in a very vulnerable position and who might be sensitive or triggered by the questions we were going to ask. The absence of children, albeit adult ones, is a sensitive topic. Or, at least, it can be. However, our assumptions were very much informed by a middle-class understanding of transnational care and familial relations. First, we had assumed that adult children will be missed. This was not always the case. Some children were missed but many had been migrating for a long time, sometimes for decades. Their absence was therefore embedded into the everyday lives of our interviewees as they aged.

Second, migration was not always a breaking point or something exceptional. In fact, in some of the regions, such as Cochabamba but especially Tarija, migration was – for lack of a better cliché – a way of life. Our interviewees had learnt to migrate from their parents and then, in turn, they *taught* migration to their own children (this is the term they used) while they were still small. Our interviewees continued to migrate, often spending six months in Argentina and six months in Bolivia, once they set up their own families. In the case of the rural areas of La Paz and Oruro, it is expected that, in general, the children will migrate both internally and internationally, especially if they have not studied or if they are not working in the place of origin. In some cases the children first migrated to the east of the country, such as the city of Santa Cruz, and then abroad. Parents were not involved in the decision to migrate because it was an expectation that they would migrate. So, there was no actual breaking point in parent–(adult) child relations as a result of migration. The type of breaking point was a reality for often middle-class interviewees, particularly mothers, whose daughters, in particular, had migrated abroad when in their early 20s to study or to follow their partners/husbands.

Third, because our assumption did not prove right, the migrant (adult) child was often not a very significant part of the interviewee's life. When adult children had migrated a long time ago, or they did not have a particularly close relationship with their parents, there was not any expectation of transnational care and ongoing transnational relations between the adult child abroad and the parent in Bolivia. We suggest that there was almost no expectation on the part of the interviewees to receive care, because they see that their children have their own families and need resources to support them. In fact, as we discuss in the chapter on remittances (Chapter 6), there are also cases of reverse remittances (Mazzucato, 2011). Migration in the Western parts of the country (Oruro, La Paz), and in most rural areas, is assumed as something that will happen as a matter of course, not as an exception. The vulnerability that might follow for older people is therefore almost given, in the sense that it would have happened anyway. Some parents had other children close by or in other parts of Bolivia. Some managed fine on their own. At times, we felt the interviews overall said little about transnational care and more about the state of older people in Bolivia. We made peace with this and worked with what we had.

So, there are quite a few things that we had assumed and did not prove right. One of these is also the concept of the 'family'. When approaching interviewees, we asked questions about their children abroad and they talked about their husbands and other family members. We have not provided space for a different conceptualisation of the family, such as the one used by Mihaela Nedelcu. Nedelcu approached interviewees by asking them to identify 'who is family' without assuming that these will always be kin. In a very different context – Switzerland – they received varying answers. Interviewees identified friends and neighbours as 'family' while not wanting to include sons and daughter or other kin as belonging to their immediate family group because they were distant, either geographically or emotionally (Nedelcu et al, 2023). This would have been a better approach to use as it would have allowed us to further explore how our interviewees understand 'family' and who they would include in such a category. The case of Sonia comes to mind here (see Chapter 8). Sonia is a woman in her 80s who struggled with mobility issues but was in charge of looking after her two adolescent granddaughters. The only practical help she received was from a man who lived next door, who picked up the remittances that her daughter sent from Spain and also helped with the weekly shop. It might as well be that Sonia considered this neighbour as her family now, but we did not ask that question, only recorded what he did for her (CBB12).

## Methods

Our main method for data collection was the semi-structured interview with some guiding questions. These were broadly organised around four main parts: background information on the interviewees' life history (place of birth, childhood, education, marriage, work, history of migration); the migration of their children; current situation, including questions about living arrangements, social networks, access to health services, support in times of crises, communication with children abroad, visiting practices (either way) and remittances; and attitudes towards the future.

Some interviewees, usually those who were most talkative, took control of the interview and this was fine. We let them talk about the things that were most important to them even when this was not part of the guiding questions. These interviews proved really interesting, opening our eyes to what had really mattered to our interviewees in their lives. Examples included meeting God in an evangelical church or finding beauty in growing flowers, even though the house they lived in lacked basic facilities such as a toilet, which the interviewee really missed. Allowing interviewees to lead the interview also meant that they sometimes moved *away* from talking about their absent children. This meandering still allowed us a view into their lives and thereby the lives of older people in Bolivia.

Before starting the interviews, we both sat down with Maria Esther Pozo, who was also part of the research team at the inception, for the pilot, to discuss how we were going to approach the interviews. We had wanted to adopt a biographical approach, following Wengraf's Biographic Narrative Interpretive Method (Wengraf, 2001). However, we already knew that we were going to be involving a number of interviewers and that it would not be possible for two or even three of us to carry out all the interviews, because of the languages involved as well as the fact that Tanja lives in another continent. This was a very different type of fieldwork to the one that Tanja was familiar with. She had done longitudinal and data collection involving different fieldwork sites for her PhD and her postdoctoral research. However, this had been with the same group of people, who were scattered across different cities and countries (see Bastia, 2019). Despite the length of time and the distances involved, she had been able to collect a similar number of interviews but with a smaller number of interviewees and only using a very limited number of entry points (three in total) (see Bastia, 2019). We soon realised that finding interviewees across rural, urban and peri-urban areas in five different regions, albeit within the same country, required a much larger number of gatekeepers and entry points. This was not quite doable for one person, given the amount of time it required to secure these entry points – lots of negotiations, getting to know people, hanging around, and so on – especially with a full-time academic job and family responsibilities on another continent.

We therefore settled for a relatively extensive but flexible interview schedule, which allowed us to include some comparative material to be gathered in each of the interviews, but also the freedom for the interviewee to go off piste if they so wished.

## Multilingualism

Most of our interviewees spoke Spanish but some preferred to speak in their native indigenous languages so some interviews were carried out in Quechua, Guaraní and Guarayo. As indicated earlier, we worked with research assistants who were native speakers in these languages. Most of these interviews were less in-depth than the ones we conducted in Spanish as some of the meaning got lost in the translation and having to speak through another person's interpretation of what was being said.

Both of us are fluent Spanish speakers. For Claudia, this is her native mother tongue, while Tanja grew up speaking Slovenian, Italian and Bulgarian, learnt English and Spanish in high school and then became fluent in Spanish when she spent six months in Bolivia in the 1990s. She continued to study Spanish at university and has been speaking it at home with her partner all her adult life.

All interviews were transcribed and kept in Spanish. We carried out the analysis in Spanish and Claudia wrote the first drafts of the chapters she led on in Spanish while Tanja switched to English for the writing. Given that we are also planning to publish a Spanish version of the book, we aimed to keep the Spanish writing in Spanish for as long as possible but Tanja started translating these chapters into English during the second drafting of the chapters. At this stage, it became clear that she was translating not just linguistically but also the way that meaning is conveyed in different languages.

For example, in English the argument is usually presented at the beginning of the text (essay, book, and so on) and the writer uses the piece of writing to develop the argument further, while the conclusion is meant to explain the wider relevance of the findings. In Spanish, the argument is not revealed until the reader reaches the conclusion.

Following Anzaldúa (2015), we kept some of the bilingualism in the writing of the text and include the original in Spanish, often in parenthesis, for terms that are more difficult to translate into English and for which the Spanish might provide a more nuanced understanding of the tone or context for those readers who do speak Spanish (Anzaldúa, 2015).

The translation of quotes into English was challenging and some of them might read as grammatically incorrect or, at least, awkwardly phrased. We sometimes resorted to a literal translation of the quotes to maintain the sense of the ways in which some of our interviewees conveyed their ideas when Spanish was not their main language. Quechua or Aymara speakers will often maintain the grammar of their mother-tongue, even when they speak in Spanish (Lozano, 1975; Muysken, 1984). We therefore tried to maintain some of these idiosyncrasies while translating the quotes into English.

Translating at these multiple levels took time but we felt that it was the best process given we aim to publish the book in both English and Spanish.

## Ethics

This section on ethics will cover the formal ethics clearance process as well as the ethical issues we have encountered throughout this project.

All names used in this book are pseudonyms.

In relation to the formal ethics clearance, Tanja obtained ethics clearance from the University of Manchester Research Ethics Committee prior to commencing each of the three phases of fieldwork (Ethics Decision-REF 12435; Ref: 2019–6158–10100). As part of this process, we developed a protocol for obtaining consent, which included sharing the project information sheet with each potential interviewee, allowing them time to read the information and discuss it with others and ask any questions they may have, before returning and arranging an interview, if they were interested in participating. Before beginning each interview we again explained that the interviewees' participation was entirely voluntary and that they could stop the interview at any time. We gave assurances that the information will be fully anonymised and explained that we are going to use pseudonyms in anything we are going to write on the basis of their interview. Given that a number of interviewees had not learnt to read and/or write, we sometimes had to read out information sheets and consent forms and then record oral consent on a separate digital file to the one we were using to record the interview. We felt that this was more ethical than asking interviewees to sign a form that they could not read.

Even following this protocol proved quite difficult. As already explained, we were working and carrying out interviews in places where we did not have any social capital as such – we were not familiar with the communities where we wanted to conduct the interviews and nobody knew who we were. In some of these places there was a lot of diffidence and mistrust. Although the ethics process was set up in order to give interviewees some protection against the misuse of the information that researchers collect, asking people to sign papers before an interview often created a general feeling of mistrust rather than one that was conducive to the trust-building that is needed for successful interviews to take place. Here, again, there was a significant level of translation that was required as forms and processes that were set up in the UK, largely for the UK legal, social and cultural context, had to be translated for the Bolivian realities we were working in. For some of our interviewees, particularly for those who had travelled abroad and had a higher level of education, it was easier to understand the reasons behind information sheets and consent forms. For those who had limited, if any, formal education and did not have a high level of familiarity with the formal legal system, asking them to sign a form and explaining redress mechanisms in case something went wrong with the interview was a completely alien concept and immediately set them up on a defensive note.

In some areas, such as Tarija, the long-standing commitment that Jaina has with rural communities and with some of the people they have interviewed, worked to mitigate these potentially negative dynamics. A similar thing happened with Carmen Paiva Fernandez and the research assistants that she was able to recruit in Santa Cruz.

The situation described was no different in the case of the regions of La Paz and Oruro. Thanks to the previous work carried out by Sahara and by the contacts with family and friends who helped with the identification of older adults in these regions, a process of trust was generated that facilitated informed consent. In rural areas, it was important for Claudia and Sahara to stay in the homes of people they knew in these places and stay for several days, in order to establish contacts and conduct interviews. The fact of explaining the scope of the research in Quechua, even if the interview was later conducted in Spanish, facilitated the bonds of trust and the disposition of our interviewees. Using the digital recorder generated some discomfort. However, interviewees soon forgot it was there once they started talking.

Working with people who knew the interviewees well and had their respect and trust was absolutely essential to successfully complete the data collection.

We knew from the outset that we were going to be working with a group of people who were potentially vulnerable. Our ethics agreement rightly precluded us from interviewing anyone who was not able to consent to the interview. This meant that we had to assess whether interviewees were able to understand that they were going to be interviewed, that the interview was going to be recorded and that we were going to use the interview for research. They also had to understand that they were not going to draw any direct benefit from participating in our research, other than the opportunity to have a conversation and tell their stories to some people who, in most cases, were complete strangers.

For most of the interviews, it was fairly easy to make decisions about whether the interviewee was able to give his or her consent. In some instances, it was immediately clear that this was not feasible, as, for example, with the woman who was over 100 years old, who was bedridden and could only communicate through her daughter who Tanja visited at home in Plan 3000 in Santa Cruz. When visiting older people's care homes, this became slightly trickier given there were many residents and their needs and potential disabilities were not entirely visible. In these cases, we had initial conversations with both the carers and service providers as well as the potential interviewees, to check whether they were able to understand the purpose of our visit and what an interview would entail.

In some cases, the ethical issues were more related with the interviewee's vulnerabilities, which became evident during the course of the interview. For example, this was the case when the interviewee was capable of understanding the purpose and agreed to be interviewed but during our conversation it became clear that the interviewee was in a very vulnerable situation. Sonia, mentioned earlier, who Tanja interviewed with Sahara in Cochabamba, was able to have a conversation with us but it became clear during the interview that Sonia was in significant pain because her feet were inflamed (CBB12). She was also eating food that had gone off and had not combed her hair. Sahara, who also worked as a carer for older people and is a trained nurse, offered to take her food away, comb her hair and give Sonia a foot massage, promising to bring her a cream next time she was in town.

In other cases, the interviewee's vulnerability was not unusual for the context within which the interviewee lived. For example, Irene did not have a toilet and had to use her neighbour's. Irene complained about not having a toilet but there was little we could do to redress this situation and help her given that houses in peri-urban areas often lack basic facilities (TRJ10). In all these cases, we carried information about grassroots organisations and local municipal service providers for older citizens and shared them with the interviewee, encouraging them to get in touch with them if they ever needed to.

The safety of the researchers working on this project was also of paramount importance. When Claudia started feeling unsafe in Santa Cruz, we stopped data collection and Tanja went there a few months later to continue the interviews and finalise data collection in that region. In Tarija, Pilar and Carlos worked together and carried out most of the interviews together, albeit this was a region they knew well. In La Paz and Oruro, Claudia worked with Sahara and they both travelled and did most of the interviews together, except for a small number of interviews that Claudia did on her own in La Paz city centre. Tanja did some of the interviews in Santa Cruz, including Plan 3000, on her own, but always left information at the hostel where she was staying and with her family back in the UK, regarding where she was going and when she was expected to return back to the hostel.

One challenge we encountered was that it was difficult for our researchers to be paid on time, including Claudia, who often had to face significant delays in receiving payment because of the multiple administrative steps that are required for international payments at UK universities. We understand that this is to ensure that there is proper accountancy of who the payment is going to and ensuring that taxes are paid where required. However, in practice, this leads to researchers having to wait for significant amounts of time before they receive payment for the work they have carried out. Despite these not always being large amounts in the UK context, they represent significant amounts in places like Bolivia, especially for people who do not have a regular source of income.

## Analysis

Once we had a set of interviews transcribed, we proceed with analysing them. We mostly used a deductive method of analysis, using the three pillars of transnational care we had identified from the literature (material, personal and emotional care) to start organising our material. In additional to this, we also used place (rural, urban and peri-urban) as well as socio-economic status (low, middle, higher-middle) to draw out our analysis, as well as differences in women's and men's experiences to advance a gender perspective. Although we had a large set of interviews, we decided not to use NVivo for a number of reasons. Tanja had used it before but had not found it very useful. Working across two countries, sometimes unstable internet connections, and changing jobs and starting a PhD for Claudia, would have meant that we could potentially lose access to the joint folders and documents. We therefore decided to use a spreadsheet with three main columns, one for each of the transnational care pillars, to start organising our material. We later prepared a data table that includes different variables of analysis of the 100 interviews conducted.

We started analysing the material for each region with the aim to eventually move on to having the material sorted according to place of residence and/or socio-economic status. However, as our analysis progressed, we realised that the migration realities were so different for each region that in some instances we decided to stick to this categorisation (see Chapter 4).

## Co-writing

This book has been entirely co-written. We have already discussed how we have collaborated for the data collection. Once we were happy with a preliminary set of findings, we started writing. We had already been meeting regularly to discuss transcriptions and data analysis. We continued to meet regularly over Zoom to decide on how to structure the monograph and how to divide the writing. We decided that Tanja was going to write the first drafts of Chapters 1, 2, 3, 9, 10 and 11 and the migration part of Chapter 4, while Claudia was going to write the ageing part of Chapter 4, and first drafts of Chapters 5, 6, 7 and 8. We then discussed and revised all first drafts and we each added to the chapters that the other had drafted. At this stage Tanja translated the chapters that Claudia had written in Spanish into English.

Although this seems a relatively straightforward and seamless process, in practice, it took many iterations, lots of discussion, many pauses when life's work required that our attention be focused on other priorities, such as starting doctoral training, children getting ill, grandparents passing away, getting COVID-19 or taking on new administrative responsibilities. We are at very different stages in our lives and careers and have been patient and respectful of each other's needs throughout this process. We have learnt that it is not possible to co-write a monograph ethically without having a basis that is respectful of each other's wellbeing and needs.

## Conclusion

Despite both of us having done significant amount of writing before this book, we can say that co-writing this book has been a true learning process, one that has care and ethics at its centre. We took both rigour as well as some flexibility of approach as the basis on which we built the analysis and the co-writing of this book.

Throughout these projects and the writing process, we were guided by our commitment to create knowledge that will serve the interests of older people in Bolivia and other places in the Global South and contribute to the literature on migration as well as the one on gerontology.

Undoubtedly, the intersectional approach has made it possible to capture the diversity in transnational care practices, and it was also fundamental in the understanding that there is no single experience of migration that unites all the older adults interviewed.

In the next chapter, we outline the context within which we carried out our research, particularly in relation to both ageing trends and migration flows in Bolivia. We also give a brief introduction to each of the regions, given the high levels of difference we found in each of the regions.

4

# Migration and older age in Bolivia

In this chapter, we lay down the foundations for understanding the empirical analysis that is included in the chapters that follow. We first review the history of Bolivian migrations, tracing the long history of regional migrations as well as diverse internal migration practices already present during the colonial period. We then focus on more recent regional, South–South as well as South–North migration flows. Here, we highlight the fluid nature of migrations, as they respond to the various crises that have been experienced both in Bolivia as well as in some of the main destinations, where Bolivians have been migrating to, such as Argentina. As will become evident, towards the end of the 20th century, but especially more recently in the 21st century, Bolivians have diversified their migration streams to include a number of new destinations in Europe as well as South America. In addition, they also consolidated regional migrations that had already started in the previous century. While doing this, they also increased the reach that migration had internally. While migration as a livelihood strategy used to be concentrated in quite specific places in Bolivia (see, for example, the section on Tarija in this chapter), by the end of the 20th century all regions in the country were involved in migration, from Pando to La Paz.

In this chapter, we also present the background to the situation that older people experience in Bolivia, including a general overview of key indicators to a more specific review of public policies that are relevant for older people. Bolivia has a quite well-developed framework for looking after its older citizens. It is the only country to have a universal cash transfer for older people in Latin America (Müller, 2009; Barrientos, 2024). However, in practice, as we show in this book, older citizens continue to experience difficulties accessing even the most basic services.

We finish with a brief overview of each region. This regional approach might not be obvious to those not familiar with Bolivia. We adopted it for a number of reasons. First, this was a practical response to the nature of the available funding, as explained in the previous chapter. Although our focus throughout has been on bringing out how residence in rural, urban and peri-urban areas leads to different transnational care practices, it also became apparent as our data collection progressed that migration takes very different forms and indeed has a very different history in each of the regions we have worked in. As will become evident further on in this chapter, some regions, such as Tarija, cannot trace a beginning of their migration history given translocal migration is deeply embedded in their history and widely practiced throughout the rural areas. For other regions, such as Santa Cruz, on the other hand, transnational migration is relatively recent and therefore, more narrowly concentrated in specific areas.

Bolivia is organised territorially in nine '*departamentos*', the literal translation of which is 'departments', but which in this book we will call 'regions'. Regions are in turn divided into provinces, municipalities and indigenous territories (*territorios indígena originario campesinos*). All regions benefit from relative autonomy since 2010, because of the Law of Autonomies and Decentralisation (Ley N° 031, *Ley Marco de Autonomías y Descentralización 'Andrés Ibañez'*). This law was approved with the intention of distributing political and administrative functions of the state in a balanced and sustainable way within the whole national territory. However, in practice, this does not happen. This law is part of a set of laws that advocate the plurinational character of the Bolivian state that has governed the country since 2009 with the approval via referendum of a new political Constitution of the state.

A regional approach, or at least an awareness of the regional make-up of the country, also makes sense given the decentralisation process, which means that regions have relative autonomy to promote their own policies. This relative autonomy is evident, for example, in the policy that only the region of Tarija introduced to support its older population with a monthly food basket (see the section on 'Tarija' in this chapter).

Finally, each region has quite different culture and geography, as is often the case in many countries. In Bolivia, regions tend to differentiate themselves in terms of climate and topography, and many have quite distinct indigenous cultures, which go hand–in–hand with different languages. Although Spanish is spoken throughout the country, Quechua, Aymara and Guaraní are also recognised as official languages, by constitutional mandate. It is beyond the scope of this book to provide an exhaustive review, but we end this chapter with a brief description of each region for those readers who are not familiar with the Bolivian context.

## Bolivian migrations in context

Bolivian history has been characterised by mass migrations. It was colonised over 500 years ago, a result of the Spanish arriving in Latin America. Through the colonial period, the indigenous inhabitants of this land were resettled into *haciendas*, with men being required to spend significant periods of time in indentured labour in the mines, while women had to provide domestic service to the landowners. The *hacienda* system persisted after independence and was only dismantled with the agrarian reform that followed the national revolution of 1952 (Klein, 1995; 2003). Internal migration continued to be used as a key element of nation-building, with the mass migration of people from the highlands to the lowlands, with the aim of finishing the internal colonisation that was never achieved during the colonial period (Nobbs-Thiessen, 2020).

Migration and seasonal, cyclical movements are also part of the ways in which indigenous people have historically organised their livelihoods. The indigenous agricultural system was organised on the basis of spreading risk across vertical ecological zones (Murra, 1972; Isbell, 1979; Van Buren, 1996). This diversification was the foundation on which Andean political systems were built (Regalsky, 2003). Within this system, indigenous communities kept land at different ecological zones so they could cultivate tubers in the highlands, vegetables such as sweetcorn in the valleys, as well as tropical fruits and vegetables in the lowlands. This allowed indigenous communities and households that relied on subsistence agriculture to spread risks associated with agricultural production as well as to maximise the variety of agricultural products they could grow. This system required households to distribute their family members across different ecological zones and spend part of the year in different geographical regions. Modern migrations can be understood as a modern adaptation of these traditional livelihood systems, as households diversify their risks by tapping into different labour markets (Bastia, 2019). While risk-diversifying strategies have been covered in the literature of the New Economics of Labour Migration theory (Stark and Bloom, 1985), exploring the history of indigenous ways of organising livelihoods in Bolivia also leads to the same suggestion: that households spread risks across ecological zones (in the past) and different labour markets (in the present) to maximise their economic viability and mitigate against recurrent economic crises. That some of these moves take place across international borders, while others take place within national borders seemed almost irrelevant to some of our interviewees, particularly in those regions with a long history of transnational migration.

During the last half of the 20th century, Bolivian migration has been characterised by two main types of migration flows: one regional, mostly cross-border, and the other transoceanic (Hinojosa, 2010). Regional migration has mostly involved migrating to neighbouring countries such as Argentina, Brazil and Chile (Garcés-Estrada et al, 2021). Migration to the United States picked up during the 1960s and 1970s, while Spain and Italy emerged as preferred destinations after the turn of the millennium, a shift that was also characterised by a strong feminisation of Bolivian migrations (Román, 2009; Hinojosa, 2010; Parella, 2011; Bastia, 2019). However, Bolivians have been migrating to neighbouring countries since their inception. Bolivians were already recorded in the first Argentinean Census in 1869, while Bolivians have also migrated for work to Chilean mines throughout the 20th century (de la Torre Avila, 2006).

Latin American migration flows have been responding to a number of more structural changes related to unequal levels of economic development, exchange rates (particularly the Argentinean peso parity with the US dollar throughout the 1990s), migration policies, demographic transitions and more meso-level factors related to the development of migrants' social networks. The fact that relative levels of poverty persist and continue to be the basis of significant inequalities between countries in the region is a strong driver of cross-border migrations. The strengthening of migration controls in the United States following 2001, the ageing of the European population with the concomitant increase demand in the care sector, as well as the development of social networks of migrants who had arrived in previous decades all contribute to continued strong migration flows within the region as well as from Bolivia to North America, Europe and other destinations in the Global North (Yépez and Herrera, 2007: 22). Adding to these, the social imageries of success that circulate among migrant social networks add to people seeing migration as a way out of the relative levels of poverty and persistent high levels of inequality that characterise many Latin American societies.

Overall, it is estimated that at least 708,000 Bolivians live abroad, representing 6.8 per cent of the total population (IOM, 2011). In 2012, Argentina was the primary destination for Bolivian migrants (38.2 per cent), followed by Spain (23.8 per cent) and Brazil (13.2 per cent), while Chile and the United States attracted 5.9 per cent and 4.2 per cent of Bolivian migrants respectively (INE, 2012).[1] In 2019, according to the United Nations South American Observatory on Migration (OSUMI), Argentina continued to be the primary destination for Bolivian migrants (48.2 per cent), followed by Spain (17.2 per cent), the United States (10.6 per cent), Chile (9.2 per cent), Brazil (5.9 per cent), Peru (2 per cent) and Italy (1.8 per cent) (OSUMI, 2019).

There is broad agreement that these figures are likely to be underestimated, given more fluid border crossings within the region. The last Census in 2012 also showed that 11 per cent of all households had a member living abroad (INE, 2017a). Over a quarter of these households are in the region of Cochabamba, one of our research sites. Despite the relatively small size of its population of almost 12 million, the incidence of migration in the country is quite high and means that migration can have a large impact on family members and neighbours who have not migrated.

The different migration streams also have specific characteristics in relation to the types of jobs that migrants engage in. The historic migration to Argentina was characterised by cross-border migrations from the southern Bolivian region of Tarija to the northern regions in Argentina. This was very much a rural to rural migration: rural farmers from Tarija migrating seasonally to seek work on the more labour-intensive plantations in the north of Argentina. We can still see the remnants of this type of migration in many of the interviews we carried out in Tarija. With the mechanisation of agriculture in Argentina during the 1980s, and the increased demand for services in the capital Buenos Aires and other cities, migrants started migrating further south, to the capital but also other cities, including the southernmost city, Ushuaia (Sassone, 1989). With this geographical shift of migration flows also came a diversification of types of jobs that migrants engaged in, as well as an expansion of the Bolivian regions that started participating more intensively in migration flows. While traditionally international/cross-border migration was mainly taking place in the regions of Tarija, Oruro and Cochabamba, migration as a livelihood strategy expanded to every region of Bolivia.

In relation to Argentina, the main destination, Bolivians who migrated to Buenos Aires entered three main areas of work: agricultural production in Greater Buenos Aires, aimed at supplying the City of Buenos Aires with fresh fruits and vegetables; the garment sector; and petty trading (Bastia, 2007). In the agricultural sector, they started working as day labourers but over time bought land and used their own social networks to supply the sector with Bolivian migrants (a process that was very well documented by the sociologist Roberto Benencia [Benencia, 1997; 2003; Benencia and Karasik, 1994; 1995; Benencia and Gazzotti, 1995]). A similar process took place within the garment sector: Bolivians initially found work in garment workshops owned by Koreans and, over time, some started their own garment workshops, sometimes in their own homes, using family and friends to recruit workers (Bastia, 2007; Bastia and Montero Bressán, 2018). Petty trading was particularly attractive to women, who found it difficult to combine childcare responsibilities with work in the garment workshops (Bastia, 2019).

While the agricultural sector mainly employed men (albeit, often with their families), petty trading mostly involved women. Both men and women found work in the garment sector. A process of feminisation of migration, which started from the 1980s onwards, meant that what had traditionally been a very male-led migration, slowly became feminised, so that by the turn of the century, women often became the lead migrants in the new migration to Spain (Hinojosa, 2010; Bastia, 2011; 2019).

Migration from Bolivia to Europe took off following the Argentinean crisis of 2001. With the end of the 'convertibility plan', which pegged the Argentinean peso to the US dollar, and the political and economic crisis that followed, Argentina stopped being a very attractive destination for Bolivians. The United States also increased migration restrictions around the same time, following the events of 11 September 2001. At the time, Spain allowed Bolivians to enter the country as tourists until 2007, when it introduced a visa for Bolivians. During that five-year window, Spain, as well as Italy, became the main destinations for Bolivian migrants, particularly in the years preceding the introduction of the visa (Yépez et al, 2011; Parella et al, 2014; Yépez and Marzadro, 2014). In contrast to previous migrations, though, this migration was very much led by women, who mostly found jobs in the domiciliary care sector, as live-in carers for older people or sometimes as domestic workers (Bastia, 2015). Their partners sometimes followed and found work in the agricultural sector, if they migrated to a rural area, or the construction sector, if they migrated to an urban area, but it was not very long before the housing bubble in Spain burst and many migrant men found themselves unemployed (Baby-Collin and Cortes, 2014). Given high levels of irregularity (Parella et al, 2014) and their relatively recent arrival, the crisis hit them hard as a result of decreased levels of employment, precarious living and housing conditions, and increased levels of xenophobia and rejection by the mainstream society (Baby-Collin and Cortes, 2014). Although Bolivian women experienced high levels of unemployment (13 per cent), men's levels of unemployment were much higher (35.9 per cent) (Ioé, 2012; Baby-Collin and Cortes, 2014). A number of voluntary return programmes were introduced by both Spain and Bolivia, but the uptake has been low (Parella Rubio et al, 2014). However, as a result of the crisis in Spain, Bolivian migrants reactivated their long-standing migration to Argentina and diversified their regional migrations to Brazil and Chile (Baby-Collin and Cortes, 2014).

In relation to Chile, also a significant destination for Bolivians, Bolivians have been migrating to work in Chilean mines since the 19th century (de la Torre Avila, 2006). However, this migration stream intensified from the turn of the century as a result of the reactivation of the Southern cone migration streams following the crisis in Spain (Baby-Collin and Cortes, 2014). Chile experienced relative stability in economic and political terms in the decades following the return to democracy. This meant that, despite relatively high levels of inequality and low public social spending, Bolivians have been attracted to what they sometimes perceive as 'the Chilean dream' (Ryburn, 2016). This has led to a steady increase in the number of Bolivians living in Chile, from 24,116 in 2009 to 47,100 in 2015 (Ryburn, 2018). However, despite the allure of perceived prosperity, Bolivians in Chile experience high levels of social marginalisation as well as economic exploitation, particularly for those who are unable to regularise their stay (Ryburn, 2016; 2018).

Likewise, Bolivian migration to Brazil, despite recent intensification, dates back to at least the 1950s, when the first wave of migrants was made up of skilled Bolivian health workers, a stream that then intensified during the 1980s when Bolivians started taking up employment in the garment sector (Souchaud and Baeninger, 2009; Baby-Collin and Cortes, 2014). By the 1990s, the garment sector became pretty much the only economic niche available to Bolivians in São Paulo (Miranda, 2017; 2019). This migration circuit (Simon, 1995) grew out of Bolivians migrating specifically from the city of El Alto to São Paulo, in what Miranda (2019) describes as cycles of migration. Bolivian migrants mostly of Aymara origin capitalised on their pre-existing experience with textiles, going to work in garment workshops in São Paulo and then returning to El Alto, closing one migration cycle, before reopening another when needs arise. In this sense, this circularity challenges ideas of a return movement, given that another migration cycle is always possible once one cycle closes (Cortés, 2004; Miranda, 2019).

As in Argentina, Bolivian migrants in Brazil also experience marginalisation, discrimination and high levels of economic exploitation, with long working days and low pay, in what some have described as 'slavery-like working conditions' (Montero Bressán and Arcos, 2016). Having said this, Miranda (2017) rightly points out the tension between coercion and consent, albeit based on institutional and ideological elements that put some workers in a disadvantaged position vis-à-vis their employers.

These broader movements between countries are made up of quite specific sub-national migration streams, linking specific regions in Bolivia to specific destinations (Baby-Collin and Cortes, 2014). On the basis of careful analysis of quantitative data, Baby-Collin and Cortés (2014) find that 50 per cent of the Bolivian migration to Spain is made up of migrants from Santa Cruz and Cochabamba. Migration to Argentina is mostly made up of migrants from La Paz and Cochabamba; however, it has much greater incidence in the valleys in Tarija, Potosí and Chuquisaca. Migration to Brazil mostly originates from La Paz. And most Bolivians migrating to Chile come from Oruro. Geographical proximity explains some of these patterns, but they are also related to labour market insertion, the types of jobs available at destination and the skills that migrants might already possess before migrating, such as pre-existing sewing skills of Aymara migrants from El Alto for garment work in Brazil.

Migration to the United States intensified during the 1970s and 1980s. Although the United States has generally attracted more highly skilled migrants of middle-class backgrounds, there has also been a significant migration to the United States from some rural areas, such as Arbieto, which we covered in our fieldwork (de la Torre Avila, 2006; Jones and De La Torre, 2011). The largest concentration of Bolivians in the United States is in the Washington, DC area, from where migrants continue to maintain close links to their rural areas of origin (Yarnall and Price, 2010; Strunk, 2015; Price, 2016).

Given this long and complex history of migration, it is not surprising that migration was also quite common among our interviewees, including inter-regional migration. Out of the total, 79 per cent of our interviewees had migrated and, of these, 62 per cent migrated internally.

## Older people in Bolivia

Despite relatively high rates of economic growth, Bolivia continues to be one of the poorest countries in Latin America. It has an average gross domestic product per person of just over US$3,414 per annum (WB, 2022).

The ratio of the older generation in Bolivia has increased in the last few decades. According to Census data, in 1976, 6.4 per cent of the population was over the age of 60, which increased to 6.5 per cent in 1992, 7 per cent in 2001 and 8.7 per cent in the last Census in 2012. While Bolivia is still a youthful country, estimates indicate that 11.5 per cent of the population will be over the age of 60 by 2030 (INE, 2015; 2017b). Moreover, older people are among the poorest groups in society.

According to the post-Census study, *The State of the Situation of Older Adults in Bolivia*, carried out by the National Institute of Statistics (INE) in 2019, the composition of the older population by area shows that a greater proportion of older people live in urban areas (58 per cent) compared to rural areas (42 per cent). This is broadly representative of the overall population, 67.5 per cent of which lives in urban areas and 32.5 per cent in rural areas. However, older people make up a greater proportion of the rural population (11.3 per cent) as compared to the urban population (7.5 per cent). In some of the regions, the majority of the population over the age of 60 lives in rural areas, such as in Potosí (72.3 per cent), Chuquisaca (61.1 per cent) and Oruro (50.1 per cent); while in other regions, we find that the majority of the population over the age of 60 lives in urban areas, such as in Santa Cruz and Beni, with 79.6 per cent and 74.0 per cent, respectively.

Another important piece of information is the old–age dependency index, which measures the percentage ratio of older adults to the potentially active population. According to this indicator in the region of Potosí, for every 100 people between 15 and 59 years old, there are about 20 older adults, with a value of 19.6 per cent, followed by the regions of Chuquisaca, La Paz and Oruro, which are regions with a considerable population of older people, mainly in rural areas (INE, 2019).

The ratio of older adults to children and adolescents under 15 as measured by the ageing index remained at around 18 per cent until 2001, and then increased to about 28 older adults per 100 children under 15 in 2012. In rural areas, the ageing rate rose to almost 34 per cent in 2012 from a level of 17 per cent in 1976, an aspect that could be linked to internal migration or out-migration from rural areas. According to historical census information from the INE (2019), the western regions (La Paz, Potosí and Oruro) present an expulsion trajectory, with emigrants of potentially active ages, which in some way allows us to understand the population restructuring of these regions, especially in rural areas (INE, 2019).

In the last 20 years, the activity status of older people accounts for an increase in the labour participation of older adults, either because they have a job or because they are looking for one. According to data from the 2012 Census, of the total number of older adults amounting to 878,012 people, the economically active population reached 203,832 women aged 60 and over and in the case of men 283,536. Likewise, older people remain more economically active in rural areas with 10.1 per cent economic activity rate compared to 4.2 per cent in urban areas (INE, 2019).

With regard to the employment situation, the labour insertion of older adults is mainly self-employed or independent, with 128,420 women and 173,231 men aged 60 or over respectively at the national level. In rural areas, about 71,832 women and 105,661 men aged 60 and over are self-employed.

Regarding data on poverty, according to the INE (2019) in 2012, there was a higher percentage of households with older adults in indigence (27.1 per cent) and marginal poverty (36.8 per cent), 18.8 per cent with moderate poverty and 15.2 per cent on the poverty line. In this context, it should be noted that women aged 60 and over are more likely to experience poverty compared to men in urban and rural areas. Of the total 7,833 marginalised older people in rural areas, 4,542 were women and 3,291 were men. In urban areas, of the 409 older adults living in marginalised areas, 248 were women and 161 were men.

Despite improvements in relation to public policies related to older people in Bolivia, the situation of this group of people is characterised by vulnerability, precarious living conditions and difficulties in accessing health services, particularly for those in rural areas. Bolivia continues to have the lowest life expectancy in the whole region: 66.7 years for men and 71.9 for women, worse only in Guyana (65.4 and 72.2 years, respectively) (UNDESA, 2020). While women benefit from longer lives, this is often accompanied by greater vulnerability given women's lower socio-economic conditions compared to men. The higher male mortality as age increases is evidenced in the masculinity index that expresses the relationship between the number of men per 100 women. In all regions there are more women than men, except Pando and Beni (INE, 2019).

Women in Bolivia continue to experience high levels of violence, including some of the highest levels of feminicide in the region, 1.3 feminicides per 100,000 women in 2023, according to the latest figures (CEPAL, 2024). The National Institute of Statistics has begun to gather data on the prevalence and characteristics of violence against women (Encuesta de Prevalencia y Características de la Violencia contra las Mujeres), since 2016. These indicate that on average, 71.5 per cent of the women in Bolivia have experienced or continue to experience violence from their partners. This includes women who are 60 years old or older: 42 per cent of them said they were experiencing violence because of their age and their gender. Of this group of women, 12.8 were experiencing physical violence, 9 per cent economic violence, 56 per cent psychological violence, for example, they were not talked to or were not taken into account. Over half, 54.3 per cent, were left alone or abandoned, 51.1 per cent said that they were made to feel like they were a hindrance, 47 per cent were shouted at, insulted or offended, 37.4 per cent said that they have been denied help, including when they were ill or were not bought medicines. These are significant findings, given that they support some of the testimonies we have gathered as part of our research.

## Public policies

Pensions cover only 20 per cent of the older population in Bolivia, with a slightly higher percentage in the main cities (27 per cent) (see Table 4.1). Of those who receive pensions, only one in five are women (Escóbar de Pabón, 2012) (see Table 4.2). This gender disparity in access to contributory pensions is a regional as well as global phenomenon (Barrientos, 2024).

**Table 4.1:** Beneficiaries of the *Renta Dignidad* according to contributory pension status, selected regions, 2020

| Region | Total | Receiving contributory pension (*rentista*) | | Not receiving contributory pension (non-*rentista*) | |
|---|---|---|---|---|---|
| | | Total | Percentage | Total | Percentage |
| *Bolivia* | *1,111,879* | *172,568* | *15.52* | *939,311* | *84.48* |
| La Paz | 352,759 | 66,080 | 18.73 | 286,679 | 81.27 |
| Cochabamba | 200,862 | 33,655 | 16.76 | 167,207 | 83.24 |
| Oruro | 65,294 | 15,439 | 23.65 | 49,855 | 76.35 |
| Tarija | 59,787 | 5,981 | 10.00 | 53,806 | 90.00 |
| Santa Cruz | 214,921 | 27,475 | 12.78 | 187,446 | 87.22 |

Note: People who have received the *Renta Dignidad* to date at least once. Updated 31 January 2021. According to the place where each beneficiary is registered.

Source: Own elaboration based on data from the Authority for the Supervision and Control of Pensions and Insurance.

**Table 4.2:** People in receipt of retirement pensions by sex and selected regions, 2020

| Region | Total | Men | | Women | |
|---|---|---|---|---|---|
| | | Total | Percentage | Total | Percentage |
| *Bolivia* | *163,490* | *115,377* | *70.57* | *48,113* | *29.43* |
| La Paz | 61,593 | 44,236 | 71.82 | 17,357 | 28.18 |
| Cochabamba | 32,537 | 22,021 | 67.68 | 10,516 | 32.32 |
| Oruro | 10,935 | 8,795 | 80.43 | 2,140 | 19.57 |
| Tarija | 6,987 | 4,777 | 68.37 | 2,210 | 31.63 |
| Santa Cruz | 31,703 | 21,808 | 68.79 | 9,895 | 31.21 |

Source: Pension and Insurance Control and Control Authority

Contributory pensions are not universal and are linked to the type of job that the pensioner carried out. They are therefore only available to those who have worked in the formal sector. However, at the time we carried out data collection, everyone over the age of 60 also received a monthly cash transfer called *Renta Dignidad* (Dignity Payment), of Bs200 for those who were also receiving a contributory pension, or Bs250 for those who did not, equivalent to about US$28 and US$36 per month. These have more recently increased to Bs300 and Bs350, respectively, which is equivalent to about US$43 and US$50. For many interviewees, particularly those living in rural areas whose livelihood depends on agriculture, the *Renta Dignidad* makes a significant contribution to their wellbeing (Vargas and Garriga, 2015; Godfrey-Wood and Mamani-Vargas, 2019).

This public policy dates back to 1994, the year in which Law No. 1544, Capitalisation Law, was enacted in the government of Gonzalo Sanchez de Lozada (Müller, 2009). Article 6 of this provision authorised the Executive to transfer the state-owned shares in mixed economy companies that had been capitalised free of charge for the benefit of Bolivian citizens residing in the country and who had reached adulthood as of 31 December 1995. Delimiting the beneficiaries to those who had reached adulthood on this date meant that the benefit would be time-delimited and not available in perpetuity. Whereas, in 1996, Article 3 of Law No. 1732, the Pensions Law, established the destination of capitalisation resources, indicating that the resources derived from state-owned shares in capitalised enterprises be transferred for the benefit of Bolivian citizens specified in Article 6 of the Capitalisation Law. These resources would be used to pay a life annuity called *Bono Solidario* (*Bonosol*) from the age of 65 and to pay for funeral expenses.

The payment of the *Bonosol* was first made in 1997, establishing its annual value of US$248 per beneficiary and funeral expenses at US$211 (Gamboa, 2006). In 1998, during the government of Hugo Banzer Suárez, this policy was replaced by the *Bolivida*, while in 2002, through Law No. 2427, the *Bonosol* Law, the *Bolivida* was eliminated and the annual amount of the *Bonosol* was set at Bs1,800 and the amount of funeral expenses at the sum equivalent to 50 per cent of the amount set for the *Bonosol*.

Pensions and cash transfers are, however, only some of the public policies that affect the lives of older people. This group of people are equally affected by a number of other policies, which we review in the following.

Although there has been significant progress in terms of public policy aimed at older persons in Bolivia, it is still insufficient since it lacks an intersectoral perspective and coordination between the different levels of the state is weak. In general, care services policies are mainly focused on early childhood care and education services, which do not respond to the needs of the population we have focused on in this book.

The legal framework related to older people in Bolivia is extensive and goes back to 1998, when Law No. 1886 of Rights and Privileges included a number of discounts and privileges in favour of older people aged 60 and over. Since then, there have been laws promulgated almost every year, which included benefits and support for people in this age group (see Box 4.1). The current Constitution, approved in 2009 (Section VII, Articles 67, 68 and 69), frames the rights of older people, recognising the right to a dignified older age, with quality of life and human warmth. Under the Constitution, the state needs to provide a life-long income in older age, as well as public policies for the protection, attention, recreation, rest and social occupation of older people. It also prohibits and sanctions all forms of maltreatment, abandonment, violence and discrimination of older people.

There is also a specific law related to older people, Law No. 369, the General Law of Older People (*Ley General de las Personas Adultas Mayores*), approved in 2013, whose main objective is to regulate the rights, guarantees and responsibilities of older people, as well as the institutionalisation of their protection.

According to Article 5 of this law, the right to a dignified old age is guaranteed through:

- The Universal Payment for Older Age (*Renta Universal de Vejez*) within the non-contributory framework of the integral pension system (*Sistema Integral de Pensiones*).
- A holistic development, without discrimination and without violence.
- The promotion of personal freedom in all their forms.
- Access to social housing.
- Provision of sufficient food that guarantees conditions of health, giving priority to those older people who find themselves in situations of vulnerability.
- Recreational practices and social occupation, with the provision of infrastructure, equipment and resources necessary for their sustainability.
- The development of conditions of accessibility that will allow older people to use the infrastructure and services offered by public and private institutions, public spaces, media and systems of communication, technology and transport.
- Their integration into productive economic development, according to their capabilities and possibilities.
- The recognition of the authority, knowledge, experience and expertise, acquired throughout their lives.
- The implementation of specific information programmes about the rights of older people and the promotion of technical, alternative and higher level training.

**Box 4.1: Legislation relevant to population over the age of 60 years old**

Law No. 1886 of Rights and Privileges (1998): Includes a number of discounts and privileges in favour of people age 60 and over.

Law No. 3791 of the Universal Income for Older People and Funeral Expenses (2007): Establishes the Universal Income for Older People (*Renta Dignidad*), within the Non-Contributory Social Security Framework, including funerary expenses.

Supreme Decree No. 0264 (2009): 26 August is declared the 'Day of the Dignity of Older People in the whole Territory of the Bolivian Plurinational State'.

Law No. 065 of Pensions (2010): Establishes the administration of the Integral Pension System.

Law No. 145 of the General Service of Personal Identification and General Service of Driving Licences (2011): Establishes that the Identity Card is a public document that carries the obligation of having it issued and renewed, and it needs to be given in a life-long format to all Bolivians at 58 years of age (so there is no longer a need to renew ID periodically from this point onwards).

Law No. 165, General Transport Law (2011): passengers that have a disability or special needs (older people, boys and girls, the infirm, pregnant women if relevant) and their accompanying person have to receive preferential treatment.

Law No. 378, Law of Universal Income for Older People (2013): modifies the total amount to be paid through the Universal Income for Older People (*Renta Dignidad*).

Law No. 475, Law of Access to Integrated Health Services (*Servicios de Salud Integral*) (2013): Establishes the basis for the universalisation of the integral attention in relation to health.

Law No. 562, Law of the Aguinaldo[2] of the Universal Income for Older People (*Renta Dignidad*) (2014): beneficiaries in receipt of the income will receive the *Aguinaldo* as part of this payment.

Ministerial Resolution No. 1028 (2014): Approves the distribution of the nutritional supplement 'Carmelo', an instant product in powdered form, made up of concentrated protein from milk, cañahua and/or amaranth cereal, rice and/or sweetcorn, and hydrolysed collagen.

Law No. 721 (2015): People who have worked in the Metallurgic Mining Sector and the Cooperative Mining Sector can access a Solidarity Pension for Older People within the Integral Pension System.

Law No. 953 (2017): An increase of Bs50 to the *Renta Dignidad*.

Law No. 1196 (2019): Modifies the total amount to be paid under the Universal Income for Older People (*Renta Dignidad*) to Bs4,550 for those beneficiaries who are not in receipt of an income under the Long Term Social Security System and Bs3,900[3] for those beneficiaries who receive an income under the Long Term Social Security System.

The Council for the Sectoral Coordination 'For a Dignified Old Age' was set up within the framework of the Law No. 031 Law Framework of the Autonomies and Decentralisation 'Andrés Ibáñez', including the setting up of the Day of the Dignity of Older People in Bolivia, the 24 August 2014. The Council is a consultative body, that proposes and liaises between the government of the central state and the autonomous government, for the coordination of sectoral matters. The Council's responsibilities include the elaboration and implementation of plans, programmes and projects for the benefit of older people; to promote the development and institutional strengthening necessary for the defence of the rights of older people; to promote the realisation of multidisciplinary research in all areas that would allow the knowledge of the life conditions of this age group; to promote the opening and functioning of centres that would welcome older people in situations of vulnerability, in either a temporary or permanent manner; and to establish mechanisms of protection of the rights of older people.

More recently, in 2018, the Ministry of Justice and Institutional Transparency approved the Multisector Plan of Integrated Development for Older People 2016–2020, which considers five strategic points:

1. Health for older people.
2. Security of income and social occupation.
3. Institutional strengthening.
4. Older people in situations of vulnerability.
5. Education for older people.

In the case of the region of Tarija, since 2013, people over the age of 60 who have been resident in the region for a minimum of five years receive a 'food basket', which consists of a monthly delivery of food products produced in the region and basic non-perishable foods.

We can see from this review of public policies that Bolivia has a well-developed framework of support and attention for older people. This shows that there is concern for this population from the government at the national level as well as some regional governments. However, as we will show, in practice many older people struggle to access even the most basic of services, because the institutions that are supposed to be providing these services experience resource constraints, but also because the decentralisation policies, while aiming to improve coordination, in practice allow different institutions to relay responsibilities on others. In the absence of agreed strategies, municipalities can say that certain responsibilities should fall onto the regional governments, while these can relay responsibilities on the national government. The overall consequence is that, while seemingly comprehensive and progressive on paper, the legislation does not always translate into material changes for older people in Bolivia.

## Diverse family formations

Bolivia is made up of a significant percentage of people who identify with one of the indigenous populations (*grupos originarios*), while the majority are of mixed origins. According to the latest household survey, 26.5 per cent of the population declared to belong to one of the Indigenous or Afro-Bolivian communities (*Nación o Pueblo Indígena Originario Campesino o Afro boliviano*), with significant differences according to areas surveyed: 17.6 per cent of the urban population compared to 47.8 per cent of the rural population. These are not fixed ethnic or racial categories but rather subscribed to, or ascribed by others, on the basis of language, beliefs and everyday practices. While the Spanish language was imposed during the colonial period as the main lingua franca and continues to be used today as the main medium of communication in national institutions and schooling, Quechua, Aymara and Guaraní have been recognised as official languages and are also widely spoken but so are a number of other languages, which are not recognised as official languages. This diversity also translates into diverse cultural practices and social forms of organisation, which includes variety in family formations.

While the nuclear family with a main male breadwinner is the idealised norm promoted by both the Catholic and the newer evangelical churches, in practice, family composition varies. According to the latest household survey (*Encuesta de Hogares* 2021), 43.2 per cent of households are nuclear (nuclear complete), 16.4 per cent have one person, 14.2 per cent have one parent (*monoparental*), 12.1 per cent a nuclear couple and 10.4 per cent an extended household (INE, 2021). In urban areas, most of the households correspond to what under the Census data is referred to as a 'complete household' (that is, includes father, mother and children) (44.9 per cent), followed by single-parent households (16.1 per cent) and single-person households (14.7 per cent). In rural areas, the households with the highest percentage are 'complete' nuclear households (39.4 per cent), single-person households (20.3 per cent), followed by households with a nuclear couple without children (17.9 per cent).

In terms of women's propensity to head households, 82.3 per cent of single-parent households are headed by women, as well as 40.5 per cent of single-person households and 37.9 per cent of extended households. It should be noted that in single-person households headed by women, the heads of household are characterised by older women who live alone, reaching 54.4 per cent. While in single-parent households, 53.8 per cent represent women between the ages of 30 and 49.

In terms of the demographic characteristics of the population and the distribution by number of people within the household, at the national level 50 per cent of households have up to three people per household. The distribution by area shows that 68 per cent of households are located in urban areas. In rural areas, one- and two-person households have higher percentages (20.3 per cent and 25.2 per cent respectively) and in urban areas, households with three or four people are more frequent (21.5 per cent and 22.3 per cent respectively).

In this section we have captured information mainly from survey data, which uses quite standardised definitions of household composition, based on the assumption that households are formed of usually heterosexual couples who live in nuclear households. There are multiple other types of household formation. In our fieldwork we also came across different types of household formation – for example, multiple households sharing the same plot of land and co-existing in systems of reciprocity, despite the fact that they might cook separately, as was the case among the Guaranís who settled on the outskirts of Santa Cruz (see Chapter 5, section on Housing).

## Ageing and migration in the five regions

Rural areas suffer from severely unequal land distribution dating back to colonial times, which has only marginally improved since the agrarian reform of 1953. Land fragmentation continues to pose a significant challenge for small-scale farmers (Cortés, 2004). Most of our rural interviewees mentioned that the migration of their children was not desirable but had the unintended positive consequence that land did not fragment any further (CBB14, CBB15, CBB21, CBB22) or that it lay fallow and therefore regenerated, because the parents who stayed did not have the capacity to cultivate all of it (CBB22).

Rural areas are also significantly poorer than urban areas. Despite decreases in poverty rates since 2000, 36.4 per cent of the population continues to live in poverty – 48.1 per cent in rural areas and 31.5 per cent in urban areas; while 11.1 per cent live in extreme poverty – 23 per cent in rural areas and 6.1 per cent in urban areas (INE, 2021). It is not surprising, therefore, that many of our rural interviewees suffered from some extreme forms of material vulnerability.

### Cochabamba

Cochabamba sits in a valley at the centre of Bolivia. It has an estimated population of 2,117,112 people, of which 11.06 per cent are over the age of 60 (INE, 2023).

Cochabamba has a long and varied history of migration. While over the last couple of decades, migration in this region has intensified and experienced a marked and rapid process of feminisation, the history of transnational migration from this region goes back to the 19th century, when men from rural areas used to migrate to work in the Chilean mines (de la Torre Avila, 2006). In contrast to some of the other regions, many of our interviewees from Cochabamba had a history of migration, both internal and international. Some had worked abroad for part of their lives, while others migrated to the Cochabamba region from other areas, particularly mining towns, when they were younger.

As is common in other lower and middle-income countries, half of our interviewees continued to be economically active well into the later stages of their lives (Barrientos, 2006; Lloyd-Sherlock, 2010; Escobar, 2014). Interviewees living in rural areas generally continued to work the land. Only half of our interviewees received remittances, although some of those who received no financial help from their migrant children received clothes and shoes (especially from the United States). For some, the *Renta Dignidad* was the only regular and reliable source of income, used to pay for basic everyday living expenses: electricity and water bills or the monthly grocery shop. The *Renta Dignidad* was absolutely essential for some interviewees in rural areas, where the migration of younger people had more negative economic consequences.

Among those not engaged in paid work or income-generating opportunities were women who had caring responsibilities. Over one-third (36 per cent) of our interviewees were looking after grandchildren at the time of the interview. About two-thirds of these (62 per cent) received remittances to help them with the additional expenses, but the remainder received no financial support from their children abroad. They, therefore, had to support grandchildren with their own income or pension. Some of these were living with other family members, but some were living on their own.

Where children migrated had significant consequences. At the time of the interviews, Argentina was facing an economic crisis so currency controls and lack of jobs negatively affected remittances. The Argentine peso was losing value vis-à-vis the boliviano and the US dollar. Moreover, to send money via official agencies, migrants had to show where they had earned the money they were sending. This posed particular difficulties for those working in the informal sector or those whose migration status was irregular. Jobs were also more difficult to find. This made it more difficult for migrants in Argentina to send remittances back to their families, which was a lesser problem for those who had gone to the United States, Europe or Brazil.

Because of this varied history of migration, it is difficult to generalise about the consequences that migration has for the migrants' parents. Migration in Cochabamba included migration for education and/or professional work, regional migration to Argentina for unskilled work, particularly garment work, and women migrating to Spain and Italy, most of whom ended up working in the care sector, as domiciliary carers for older people or as domestic workers. Interviewees in rural areas generally experienced the migration of their children in a negative way, given it precluded further studies and more prestigious career options. Yet at the same time, migration was acknowledged as a necessity, given the lack of sufficient available arable land or suitable jobs. Migration from urban areas was generally more recent (last couple of decades, as opposed to having a longer history of migration) and for better paid work in Europe and sometimes professional work, both regionally and in the United States. Some migrants' parents benefited materially from the migration of their children. Others, however, experienced high levels of vulnerability, despite receiving significant financial remittances from their children, because they were socially isolated and could not access their usual sources of support.

Migration from this region therefore highlights the potential that migration has for securing a comfortable ageing, where resources, communication and travel allow it, but also the high levels of vulnerability that migration can bring to older people when the basic elements of a healthy and robust social support network are missing.

## Santa Cruz

Santa Cruz lies in the eastern part of Bolivia and is part of the central axis that contributes major economic development to Bolivia, together with Cochabamba and La Paz. It is the largest region in Bolivia, covering 34 per cent of the national territory. Population projections indicate that this region has a population of 3,425,399 and that 8.73 per cent of these are over the age of 60 (INE, 2023).

Santa Cruz has a relatively long-standing history of internal in-migration from rural areas, attracting internal migrants from both lowland as well as highland areas, but in relation to international migration, its history is more recent than some of the other regions. It was only around the turn of the millennium, during the early 2000s, when a significant number of women took advantage of the opportunities that were then available in Spain and started engaging in international migration. International migration from this region was still so incipient, that we struggled to identify people who had migrated internationally directly from rural areas. Cross-border, international migration in this region was very much an urban experience and people tend to migrate from rural areas to Santa Cruz, and then abroad from there. There were very few, if any, direct experiences of international migration from rural areas, in contrast to the other regions where we carried out fieldwork.

Here, we were also able to tap into the experiences of some of the indigenous groups that inhabit this region who also participated in international migrations. Some of our interviewees from peri-urban areas belonged to the Guaraní community, while others were Guarayos, from a town north of the city of Santa Cruz.

## Tarija

Tarija is located in the south of Bolivia and is the region that has the closest ties with Argentina. It is estimated that the population of this region will reach 601,214 inhabitants and that 10.71 per cent of this population will be over the age of 60 by 2022 (INE, 2023).

Its historic migration links between the south of Bolivia and the north of Argentina, so well documented in Alfonso Hinojosa's early work (Hinojosa Gordonava, 2000), were also very strongly reflected in our interviews. Unlike the other regions where we did our research, there was no diversity here in migration streams – everybody whose children were abroad, their children had migrated to Argentina. Moreover, over half (11/20) of the interviewees themselves had experience of migration to Argentina, often from a very young age. Interviewees in this region talked about their children 'learning' migration (see Chapter 9, this volume) in typical seasonal migration journeys that involved the whole family migrating to Argentina to work as sharecroppers, '*mita-mita*', a system of renting land by paying the landowner with half of the harvest. Alternatively, they worked for a '*patrón*' (landowner) for six months of the year and then returned to Tarija for the other half of the year to cultivate the plots they had there.

Some interviewees started migrating from a very young age. Hernán, for example, who was 67 years old at the time of the interview (in 2014) said he started going to Argentina when he was 12 years old, with the '*patrón*':

> I went with the *patrón*, they used to take me [to Argentina] until I was able to get my documents and then I went with the *Corregidor*,[4] that's how I used to get taken, because I was still a minor. ... The *patrones* do what they like, sometimes they pay you, sometimes they don't, they shout at you (*le putean con todo*). Or when I was little and I wasn't

very strong, the others were older and they wanted me to be equal to them in strength, and the truth is we suffered. Our children at least, since they went with me and they have been able to learn to work and once they were old enough (*han tomado estado*), then they went on their own. (TRJ15)

Here he also implies that, this way, he spared his children the suffering that he had endured.

Girls were often 'sent' by their parents to work in people's homes as domestic workers for better-off families. Emiliana's mother had given her and her sisters away to work as domestic workers. Her employers took her to Buenos Aires for six months. She then stayed also in other places but did not go back after she married. She married 'badly', to a violent man who also did not support the family. When asked about dreams, she describes how much violence she suffered, as if to say that there was no space in her life for dreams (TRJ13).

This region also had some more progressive policies to support those aged 60 and over. Besides the national *Renta Dignidad*, the regional government started a 'family basket' programme (*Canasta Alimentaria para las Personas de la Tercera Edad por una Calidad de Vida Digna*, Regional Legislation W72, introduced in 2013, and revised in 2021). This was aimed at every person over the age of 60 and included basic produce grown in the region and non-perishable foodstuff. It was distributed monthly in the region of Tarija, with some differences in specific provinces, and only to those who had been resident in the region for at least five years. Although the policy was welcomed, some of our interviewees mentioned that the foodstuff included was quite 'useless'. Sometimes receivers did not know how to prepare the food, as it was not something that they would usually consume (for example, Quaker instant porridge). Some of the food required refrigeration and many households did not have a fridge. Some mentioned that the food often ended up as 'dog's food' because they had no way of preserving it and they would rather give it to their dogs than see it go to waste.

The Tarija region also had a special health programme to support people aged 60 and over.

### La Paz

The region of La Paz covers 12.2 per cent of the Bolivian territory, with its capital and the seat of the Plurinational State located at an altitude of 3,632 metres above sea level. La Paz has just over three million inhabitants, of which 12.12 per cent are above the age of 60 years old (INE, 2023), which confirms the demographic dividend that the region is expected to benefit from until 2050.[5]

During the last inter-censual period La Paz has been losing its demographic weight at the national level, despite being still the second most populated region in Bolivia after Santa Cruz. The latest Census (2012) suggests that La Paz is losing some of its population and it is expected that this trend will continue. The tertiary economy predominates, with an increase of people employed in the service sector.

In La Paz we carried out 20 interviews in urban and peri-urban areas of the municipalities of La Paz and El Alto, and in rural areas in the municipality of Santiago de Callapa, located in the Altiplano (eastern part of the Cordillera Central).

## *Oruro*

The region of Oruro is located in the central Altiplano and covers around 4.9 per cent of the total national territory. Its climate is semi-cold to cold, with an average of 8.3°C to -8.0 °C during the winter months of June and July. The population is estimated at 551,116, which represents 4.73 per cent of the national population (projection for 2020). The population structure indicates a higher proportion of young people of working age, while the population of 60 years and over (who might also be working, despite their age), represents 10 per cent of the total population of the region (INE, 2023).

Oruro is characterised for its tradition based in mining. Of note here is the exploitation of metal sources, such as tin, zinc, silver, wolfram and gold, as well as non-metal ones, such as salt, gypsum, borax and ulexite. Other sources of production include livestock raising, including camelids, sheep and cows, and agriculture, such as the production of quinoa, among other Andean produce.

For this study we carried out 18 interviews in urban, peri-urban and rural areas, including in Huari, Quillacas and Challapata, small towns that are important centres for agricultural production and trade.

During the last few decades, Oruro has been experiencing a process of demographic shrinkage, due to the slow rate of population growth, migration (temporary and permanent) towards other regions of Bolivia as well as other countries, particularly Chile. Most interviewees had a history of internal migration, and some had also migrated internationally.

Bolivian migration has a long history, given that it has been practised since pre-Hispanic times and because a fundamental characteristic of these migration flows is their structural character. Although many more conjunctural factors influence these migration flows, there is evidence of a sustained growth in Bolivian migration flows, which go hand in hand with a diversification of destinations. For the children of our interviewees in Oruro, destinations included Argentina, Chile, Brazil, Spain, Italy, the UK and France. In our interviews, regional migration to Argentina and Chile is usually characterised by agriculture and garment sector work, migration to Italy and Spain for work in domestic service and care of older people, and, to a smaller extent, for professional jobs in Brazil, Spain and France.

## Conclusion

In this chapter we have shown that Bolivia is still in the early stages of the ageing process but that it will soon move to more advanced stages of population ageing. Migration is both a historical practice, as well as a strategy that has been taken up more recently by a larger number of people across all regions of Bolivia as a response to the political and economic crises that the country experienced in the second half of the 20th century. These diverse migration streams and practices, which have emerged over time, all play a part in the ways in which ageing is experienced.

We also reviewed Bolivia's legal framework as it relates to older citizens. Although Bolivia has a well-developed legal framework for older people, as we will see, the implementation of this framework is not without its challenges.

The overview of regional characteristics help explain why we partly retain this regional focus in our analysis.

In the next chapter we will start moving towards presenting some of our findings related to the first analytical pillar, the financial and material resources that underpin transnational care.

# Financial and material resources

## Introduction

The first analytical pillar that we approach in these empirical chapters refers to financial and material resources, to understand the situation of our interviewees and how their children's migration might have had an impact on these. In our interviews, we asked about accommodation, working practices and how older people manage their livelihoods, including those who practice subsistence agriculture. In this chapter we focus on these founding elements of the stayers' lives to better understand how they meet their economic needs.

The migrants' parents' material subsistence is clearly key to their wellbeing. Contrary to some of the higher-income countries where previous studies of transnational care have been carried out – such as Australia – Bolivia has a very weak national social and economic infrastructure. Pensions are only accessible to those who have worked in the formal sector, which comprises a minority of the labour market: in 2015, 78 per cent of employment in non-agricultural employment was informal (DTUDA, 2021). Despite improvements in the legislation that relates to older people as well as the introduction of a cash transfer, the *Renta Dignidad*, that anyone aged 60 years old and over can claim, formal social security and health infrastructures remain extremely weak. Contributory pensions, which were nationalised in 2010, cover only about 15 per cent of the population (DTUDA, 2021). As already discussed in Chapter 4, most people, including our interviewees, have to continue working in order to make ends meet and cover even a basic level of subsistence. In fact, Bolivia has one of the lowest rates of unemployment in the region given weak coverage of unemployment schemes (DTUDA, 2021).

In this chapter, we cover housing, businesses, pensions and savings, access to land and its ownership, as well as subsistence agriculture as the fundamental elements that shape the material resources on which the migrants' parents rely to secure their material wellbeing.

We begin by laying out the housing conditions of our interviewees to help the reader situate the interviewees' living conditions.

## Housing

Most of our interviewees own their own homes: 79 per cent of the people interviewed have their own home, and in some cases, interviewees had more than one property, especially in the case of Oruro and La Paz. The percentage of home ownership is highest in rural areas, where 90 per cent of our interviewees owned their own home compared to 72 per cent in peri-urban areas and 69 per cent in urban areas. Data on housing tenure at the national level show that 63.4 per cent of the population own their own homes, with a higher percentage of own home tenure in rural areas (81.09 per cent) compared to urban areas (55.33 per cent) (INE, 2020). In rural areas, interviewees also had access to land suitable for cultivation, the largest areas being found in Oruro.

Our interviewees placed high importance on home ownership, beyond the quality of the materials of the house; for example, one interviewee said: '[I]t is our own, it is our own, but it is a humble house, made of *adobe*, we cannot even add another room now since it's so expensive to build another room' (CBB4). In that same vein, another one mentioned: '[T]he house is my own, because to the extent of my possibilities, I have built it myself on the land that I have inherited from my parents' (CBB15).

However, of the people interviewed, almost a fifth do not have their own home: 2 per cent lived in *anticrético*,[1] 6 per cent rented, 7 per cent lived with their children and 6 per cent lived in a care home. This is a lower rate than at the national level, where 15.3 per cent of the population rents and 2.9 per cent lives in housing in *anticrético* and mixed contracts.[2] As would be expected, the percentage of people living in rented property or in *anticrético* is lower in rural areas (4 per cent in rented and 0.24 in *anticrético* and mixed contract) compared to urban areas (20.5 per cent in rented and 4.1 per cent in *anticrético* and mixed contract) (see Table 5.1).

To illustrate the commitment of the interviewees to have their own home, some testimonies are shared in the following. Beatriz is a 66-year-old woman, who sold sports balls for a living at the time of the interview. She had worked as a caregiver for older people in Italy for 13 years and returned to Oruro because her husband had died. One of her daughters then left for Italy, where six of Beatriz's brothers also resided, and another daughter left for Chile. She did not receive remittances or any other additional income from them. The *Renta Dignidad* was her only income. She said that all her relatives migrated due to lack of work. Sometimes she thinks about returning to Italy but recognises that at her age it is already difficult. However, she wanted to continue working to have a house. She said tearfully: 'My dream I tell him, I would like to have my little house, I don't have a house, that would be my dream' (OR10).

The desire to own their own home was echoed by other interviewees: 'I don't suffer from anything, my only dream is to buy a house of my own, nothing else' (TRJ5), while another one mentioned that she asks God to have a house to avoid paying rent, 'I would like to have my little house, I tell God that, I say: "My God give me a little house to avoid paying rent"' (SC14).

**Table 5.1:** Households by area, selected regions and housing tenure, 2019 (%)

| Region and house tenure | Rented | Own[a] | *Anticrético* or mixed[b] | Assigned for services | Ceded by kinship | Other[c] |
|---|---|---|---|---|---|---|
| *Bolivia* | *15.33* | *63.40* | *2.90* | *2.92* | *15.20* | *0.26** |
| *Urban* | *20.49* | *55.33* | *4.11* | *1.83* | *17.92* | *0.32** |
| *Rural* | *4.01* | *81.09* | *0.24** | *5.30* | *9.22* | *0.14** |
| La Paz | 11.76 | 70.52 | 2.82 | 1.81* | 13.07 | 0.02* |
| Cochabamba | 18.97 | 60.79 | 3.16 | 1.73 | 15.20 | 0.15* |
| Oruro | 12.52 | 66.16 | 2.53* | 5.54* | 12.41 | 0.84* |
| Tarija | 16.55 | 57.55 | 3.00 | 1.91* | 19.73 | 1.26* |
| Santa Cruz | 20.16 | 55.09 | 3.31 | 3.57* | 17.65 | 0.22* |

Note: [a] Includes homes that are in the process of payment. [b] Includes housing in *anticrético* and rent. [c] Those not included in the above categories. * Coefficient of variation greater than 20 per cent, use as reference data.

Source: Own elaboration based on data from the Instituto Nacional de Estadística, *Encuesta de Hogares,* available https://www.ine.gob.bo/

For those interviews that were carried out in the interviewees' homes, we noticed that the type and comfort of the houses in which the interviewees lived varied considerably. Some homes were very precarious. Some complained that their houses were still unfinished and that they did not have money to add basic services, such as a bathroom: 'I need a bathroom, as I want to have a bathroom ... I have to bathe there in the corner tying the dog ... if I have to go to the bathroom, I have to go to the ravine, don Daniel has a bathroom, I go there' (TRJ10). This is not an unusual situation for people living in lower-income households in peri-urban areas in Bolivia. In fact, it is estimated that, in Bolivia, 10.80 per cent of households do not have a toilet, although in urban areas the percentage is much lower (0.94 per cent) compared to rural areas (32.62 per cent) (INE, 2020). So, this example is not that unusual but it is clearly challenging for somebody who is in their 80s to be managing without a toilet close by.

We have identified other similar cases in Santa Cruz, where, although 57 per cent of our interviewees owned their own house, for the most part, the houses are of very poor quality. For example, Marina and Dolores (SC8 and SC15) both lived in Plan 3000, a peri-urban area on the outskirts of the city of Santa Cruz. The houses they lived in were very basic structures, with leaky roofs. They did not have money to make repairs. Marina lived in a poorly constructed log cabin. Although she was receiving the *Renta Dignidad,* she continued to work in a garment workshop because she needed to support herself and her husband who was 76 years old and sick. On the other hand, Dolores was of Guaraní origin, and lived in a house that her grandchildren

**Table 5.2**: Households by area and quality of housing, 2019 (%)

| Area and quality of housing | Low | Medium | High |
| --- | --- | --- | --- |
| Bolivia | 3.00 | 35.05 | 61.95 |
| Urban | 0.67 | 22.58 | 76.75 |
| Rural | 8.09 | 62.39 | 29.53 |

Source: Own elaboration based on data from the Instituto Nacional de Estadística, *Encuesta de Hogares*. available https://www.ine.gob.bo/

built for her. Her daughter, along with her family, as well as her grandson with his wife and children, lived on the same plot of land. Each family cooked on their own as they lived in separate households, but the close proximity enabled them to have a very strong sense of community and tight family relations. Dolores was receiving the *Renta Dignidad* and monthly remittances from her daughter in Spain to buy food and meet basic needs. The grandson she lived with was also contributing to the household expenses.

Ernestina, who was also living in Plan 3000, also found herself in very precarious accommodation that was built of bricks with a metal roof, set off from a communal yard where each family member cooked. Although she did not comment on the quality of her house, during the interview, rats came and went from a space between the walls of the room we sat in and the metal roof that covered it, to look for food in the closet. Ernestina did not comment on the rats either, which suggested that this was normal (SC13).

Regarding the quality of housing, according to the National Institute of Statistics (INE) data (2021), 66.47 per cent of households in the country are of high quality (up from 61.95 per cent in 2019) (see Table 5.2). The quality of housing is defined in the INE through an index composed of quality of material, habitability and access to basic services. However, high quality housing is more common in urban areas, where 79.7 per cent of homes are of high quality, than in rural areas, where the majority, 55.36 per cent, are of average quality (see Table 5.3). Although this would suggest that even in rural areas, the quality of housing is acceptable, the way in which housing is assessed is highly questionable, given, for 2019, only 12.87 per cent of households in rural areas had running water, while 16 per cent of these households did not have access to electricity.

Some people interviewed had enjoyed a better financial situation during their working lives, but then lost their homes or plots of land, either because they separated from their partners or because they had borrowed money. Marina, mentioned earlier, for example, together with her husband owned a large plot of land, which they cultivated, but they lost everything they had. Her husband convinced her to lend the savings to her mother, but she never paid them back. Her husband also mortgaged his land to pay his brother's

**Table 5.3**: Homes by apartment area and building materials used in walls, ceilings and floors of the dwelling, 2019

| Area, region and building materials used in walls, ceilings and floors of the dwelling | Material on walls (%) | | | | Material on roof (%) | | | | | Material on floors (%) | | | | | | |
|---|---|---|---|---|---|---|---|---|---|---|---|---|---|---|---|---|
| | Brick, cinder blocks or concrete | Adobe or rammed earth (tapial) | Wood | Other[a] | Calamine or 'plancha' | Tiles (cement, clay, fiber cement) | Reinforced concrete slab | Straw, cane, palm or mud | Other[b] | Earth | Parquet or machihembre | Wooden planks | Cement | Mosaic, tile or ceramic | Brick | Other[c] |
| Urban | 87.79 | 9.43 | 2.46 | 0.32* | 47.28 | 36.56 | 15.92 | 0.22* | 0.02* | 4.45 | 10.22 | 0.82 | 41.22 | 41.49 | 1.63 | 0.18* |
| Rural | 38.32 | 51.43 | 7.83 | 2.42* | 69.74 | 17.74 | 3.09 | 9.32 | 0.10* | 35.34 | 2.01* | 3.46* | 46.18 | 10.62 | 2.34 | 0.04* |
| La Paz | 69.39 | 28.90 | 1.49* | 0.22* | 83.46 | 3.36* | 12.07 | 1.06* | 0.05* | 14.60 | 24.53 | 4.14 | 52.55 | 3.61 | 0.19* | 0.37* |
| Cochabamba | 76.33 | 19.72 | 3.56* | 0.40* | 52.09 | 25.83 | 20.61 | 1.47* | 0.00 | 13.91 | 0.49* | 0.35* | 45.76 | 39.16 | 0.21* | 0.12* |
| Oruro | 36.24 | 61.59 | – | 2.17* | 86.55 | 3.17* | 2.47* | 7.81 | 0.00 | 12.60 | 13.04* | 0.25* | 34.18 | 27.62 | 12.32 | – |
| Tarija | 82.54 | 15.00 | 1.29* | 1.18* | 52.67 | 19.21 | 26.98 | 1.06* | 0.08* | 9.53 | 0.08 | 0.00 | 48.75 | 41.32 | 0.23* | 0.09* |
| Santa Cruz | 89.57 | 3.47* | 5.38* | 1.59* | 19.96 | 71.60 | 7.02 | 1.38* | 0.04* | 8.73 | – | 0.49 | 28.48 | 59.04 | 3.27 | – |
| Total Bolivia | 72.29 | 22.59 | 4.14 | 0.98* | 54.32 | 30.66 | 11.90 | 3.07 | 0.05* | 14.13 | 7.65 | 1.64 | 42.77 | 31.81 | 1.86 | 0.13* |

Note: [a] Those not included in the previous categories, such as: partition or *quinche* [a structure made of cane or wood filled in with mud], stone, cane, palm or trunk, cardboard, cans, waste materials or others. [b] Those not included in the above categories such as: roof built with boards, planks, waste materials or others. [c] Those not included in the above categories such as carpet or upholstery, stone, cane. * Coefficient of variation greater than 20 per cent, use as reference data.

Source: Own elaboration based on data from the Instituto Nacional de Estadística, *Encuesta de Hogares*. available https://www.ine.gob.bo/

hospital bills, so they also lost the land. She now lives in a wooden hut with a leaky roof, which she built on her daughter's land:

> He [husband] had mortgaged the land. He had borrowed 5,000 pesos from a man. I didn't know any of this. When my brother-in-law died, the man came and said: 'Give me the money or the land will stay with me', and I said to him: 'And why is the land going to stay with you?' 'Because your husband has left it to me as a pledge.' 'What do you mean, he has given in pledge, if he hasn't told me anything.' 'Ah, that's your husband's problem if he hasn't told you, I have the paper and the payment.' Oh my, we fought, we separated for almost a year. From that time, we don't have the land anymore. The other man kept the land. We lost everything. (SC8)

Some interviewees sold their houses before moving to a nursing home. Eduardo used to have a big house and a piece of land, but he sold it before moving to a nursing home. He now lives on his savings: 'I sold my ranch for $30,000 and with that I support myself, I always try not to spend, so that it will not end [laughs], because if it runs out …' (SC1). He gives part of his *Renta Dignidad* to the nursing home, and in return he can live there, which is a common arrangement for nursing home residents who do not have an alternative income. They give him food, do his laundry, but unlike most residents, Eduardo also helps serve meals, cleans the floor and does odd jobs. He does not receive remittances from his daughter and would not want to anyway, because, he says, he values his independence (see the next chapter).

Consuelo, 72 years old and a native of Vallegrande, studied to be a primary school teacher, but she was not able to work as a teacher after she got married because her husband did not let her. She had eight children, two of whom were from her husband's previous marriage. Her youngest was living in Peru and she had left three of her five children with Consuelo. At the time of the interview, Consuelo was looking after her grandchildren with the money she received from her children. However, she did not receive any money from her daughter who lived in Peru and also did not have any information on her whereabouts. Although she had her own house in a central area of the city, her economic situation was precarious. Her late husband sold his business to invest in agriculture but lost everything:

> First, we had a business, and then he became enthusiastic about agriculture. So, he was focused on that, and he invested everything we had into agriculture. But the fields did not produce *Mamita* [my dear – to the interviewer], the field was finished, we threw in lots of money but didn't harvest anything. We lost everything except for this house, but I don't even have money to fix it. (SC4)

Consuelo's story illustrates the responsibilities that some of our interviewees take on with regards to the care of grandchildren (discussed in Chapter 8), including when interviewees lose contact with their children. It also highlights the additional difficulties that women encounter, across socio-economic groups, in relation to gendered inequalities and restrictions to their freedoms. Many have had to curtail their working lives once they got married because of jealous husbands. Their lack of paid work when they were younger then has repercussions for their economic wellbeing and curtailed independence in later life.

Dual residency was also common in some regions. Some interviewees maintained two houses, one in a rural area and one in a city, which sometimes happened to be in different regions, to support their practice of cyclical migration and the maintenance of productive roles and social obligations that come as part of their membership of specific communities. For example, in the regions of Oruro and La Paz, some interviewees maintained dual residency, where people had been born in that region, usually in rural areas. They then migrated to other regions of Bolivia but then returned sporadically to their communities of origin, not only to fulfil social and productive roles, but also to maintain productive businesses. As an example, Albina, a 63-year-old woman born in Santiago de Callapa, lived with her husband in their own house in Santiago de Callapa but they also had a house in Cochabamba in the Villa Pagador neighbourhood. This district is characterised by being an area of migrants mainly from Oruro, where they dedicate themselves to the garment sector. However, they return to Oruro, where they were interviewed, at least every two months, because they have to take care of their land dedicated to growing potatoes, quinoa and raising sheep. They also return to attend mandatory community meetings: 'We come to work on the fields, ploughs the land, make *chuño*,[3] pick potatoes, always – yes, you cannot leave the land. Sometimes I come every month, every two months' (LP14). There has been an increase in the demand for quinoa worldwide, which means that those people who were already engaging in growing quinoa were making sure that they could continue growing it and expanding its cultivation, particularly given the government has also been promoting its cultivation (Vassas Toral, 2016).

However, the extent to which migration leads to improvement in housing for the migrants' parents was questionable. We found that children's migrations only very exceptionally led to the improvement of their parents' housing situation and this only happened in some contexts. One of these examples is Basilia, who we interviewed in Guarayos, in the region of Santa Cruz. Basilia was 77 years old at the time of the interview. Her daughter had migrated to Spain. Basilia spoke in Guarayo, which was then translated by one of her other children. Basilia used to work making hammocks and also washing clothes but has since stopped working. Her daughter had migrated to Spain ten years prior to the interview and had not been back since. However, she had been sending regular remittances since she left, which enabled Basilia to build her own house (SC18). We discuss remittances in more detail in Chapter 6.

It is clear that in the majority of the cases, migration does not play a prominent role in the interviewees' housing situation. The interviewees' housing largely reflects their own socio-economic backgrounds and only in a handful of cases has migration played a role in improving the housing situation of the interviewees.

## Income and businesses

Despite sometimes having an advanced age and/or multiple health problems, many older adults interviewed do not stop working. Paid work is often the only way in which they can guarantee their subsistence. The only universally available social security payment is the *Renta Dignidad*, and the family basket, which is only available in Tarija. Very few of our interviewees (6 per cent) had jobs in the formal sector and were able to benefit from a contributory pension.[4] The *Renta Dignidad*, although almost universally welcome, was not enough to cover even the most basic needs in either rural or urban areas, so unless interviewees were able to draw on their children's remittances, they were forced to work. As has been documented elsewhere, older adults in countries with little state support have to continue working in order to earn a living (Barrientos, 2006; Vera-Sanso, 2012; ADB, 2024).

The majority of our interviewees continued working: 73 per cent of the people interviewed in this study still performed some kind of paid work to ensure their own maintenance: 41 per cent of these are women and 32 per cent men. The greatest majority of those who work (92 per cent) did so in the informal sector. And, as would be expected, the propensity to work reduces, but does not disappear, as the age group increases. Of the ones who were working, 41 per cent were in the 60–69 age category, 23 per cent in the 70–79 category and 9 per cent were 80 years old and over.

These findings broadly represent national trends, where according to preliminary results of the Continuous Employment Survey (ECE) of the INE, in the fourth quarter of 2019, in urban areas, the economically active population reached 3,959,000 people, of which 3,768,000 people were employed. Of these, 22.6 per cent have trade as their main activity, 14.4 per cent are dedicated to the manufacturing industry and 9.9 per cent work in accommodation and meals, while 4.83 per cent were unemployed. Although the largest proportion (43.6 per cent) of employed persons are between 36 and 59 years old, 9.2 per cent (about 348,000) are people aged 60 or over, of which 57.47 per cent are men and 42.54 per cent are women.

In this section we highlight professional work in urban and peri-urban areas, as well as informal trading, running one's own business and transport. In rural areas, subsistence agriculture and informal trade were most common (which we discuss later in this chapter). In line with feminist approaches, we also understand care as being part of 'work', but we do not include it in this section, because it does not bring financial and/or material resources to the interviewees. Instead, we discuss it in the chapter on care (Chapter 8).

Felisa did not know her exact age, but she said she was over 60 years old. She lived in a very vulnerable situation. At the time of the interview, she had problems with her documentation, which is why she was unable to collect the *Renta Dignidad*. She commented that she did not receive remittances, as her son had gone missing, and to guarantee her subsistence she sold vegetables in an informal market stall (see Chapter 10).

Gladys, who was 67 years old at the time of the interview, was in a similar situation. Gladys used to live in a very remote place. She used to live off the land, growing sugar cane, tomatoes, potatoes and sweetcorn. She moved to Tarija five years before the interview for health reasons and now lived in a peri-urban area at her son's house with four of her grandchildren. She cleaned the market for Bs200 (US$29) a month, received the *Renta Dignidad* and the 'food basket' that was available to people over the age of 60 in Tarija. Her son in Argentina sent her a little money from time to time, with people they know. She sometimes received help from her evangelical church or borrowed money from her neighbours. She also sold second-hand clothes but did not have a stall in the market. She paid for a space on the floor. She was in a very precarious economic situation, but said that she usually has food and a place to sleep, highlighting the low expectations that some of our interviewees had about their basic needs (TRJ5).

The occupations and jobs carried out by the people interviewed varied from working as a doorman in a nursing home and receiving 'in kind' payment through the provision of accommodation and food, public servants, having their own businesses, and providing administrative support to various associations. Some interviewees continued to work the land – both for their own subsistence and for sale in large quantities as in the case of quinoa – as well as raising animals. Others took very precarious jobs that paid little or in kind, such as Efrain (SC10). For example, Efrain, who was 93 years old at the time of the interview, washed dishes in a restaurant in the evenings in exchange for his evening meal. Others, usually women, did the laundry or worked in garment workshops. Some, but very few, continued to migrate seasonally to Argentina (TRJ14). But all of the women interviewed also continued to provide unpaid domestic and care work for their partners and other family members, unless they were prevented from doing so because of physical disabilities.

In La Paz, which is the region with the largest presence of the public sector at the national level, three men and one woman continued to be employed in public service: Victor, a 75-year-old man, despite having retired as a soldier, continues to work in a public institution which depends on the national government, while also owning a restaurant in El Alto. Three of his four children migrated abroad: in Mexico, the United States and Colombia (LP1). Two interviewees were university professors at public universities (LP2 and LP20), and one worked as a public servant in the National Health Service (Caja Nacional de Salud) (LP19). As indicated earlier, these were the exceptions and most interviewees had more precarious backgrounds.

However, work was important not only in terms of providing an income but also as the basis for one's identity and sense of self, giving meaning to everyday life. In some cases, older adults continued to work despite having their economic needs met through pensions or by being supported by their children. Victor, mentioned earlier, said his youngest son, who migrated to Colombia four years ago, constantly asks him: 'Why are you working? You shouldn't work, what are you missing? Well, it's the habit son and if I don't work, I die, I die, I tell him' (LP1). In the same way, Walter, aged 72, owns a carpentry shop in which he continued to work because according to him, work is his therapy:

> My hobby is to work and work only, I cannot be without working, I start to just lie down, I do not know why but I can't, I can't, I can't. I have my three houses, I have my lot of stalls at the fair, I have a large estate (*patrimonio*), but I could just quit right now, but I can't. (SC7)

Some were, however, unable to work due to health problems or had difficulty in moving about. Some stopped working because they had other economic income that allowed them not to work. Alfredo, who was 75 years old, was bedridden at the time of the interview and unable to walk. He indicated that before his health problems he was still working as a driver (OR3). Similarly, 63-year-old Diana, was not able to work because she had an ictus (*derrame cerebral*) four years prior to the interview (SC12, see Chapter 8). As a result of these health problems, she could not work. Similarly, 74-year-old Amilcar no longer worked because he had silicosis, or 'the mine disease', which makes it difficult to breathe: 'I am so close to dying. [If I get] a cold, puff [I'm gone]!' (OR6). Amalia, who used to sell fruit, after having gone through surgery said: 'I don't do anything anymore, I'm already very tired, plus I'm a little sick' (CBB17).

As with the housing, we found that the income base of our interviewees also changed little as a result of their children's migration. We found variety in the situations of our interviewees, which largely reflected their levels of education and socio-economic backgrounds. Some were able to retire and not work, but if they did so it was on the basis of their own savings or pensions rather than because their children's migration opened up these opportunities for them. The majority had to continue working because there was little else to fall back on, while some, usually men, also continued working because this gave them a greater sense of self and wellbeing. For these interviewees, work was a pleasure rather than a necessity. Their children's migration rarely had implications for their working lives, given, as we will discuss later on in this chapter, remittances were seldom regular and reliable. Hence, even when their adult children abroad sent remittances, they were either not sufficient or not regular enough (or both) for the migrants' parents to stop working altogether.

## Pensions, savings and *Renta Dignidad*

Statistics from the Pension and Insurance Control Authority indicate that only 163,490 people gained the right to payments from contributory pensions by 2020 in the whole country, where the total population was 11.94 million (APS, 2024). Of these, 70.57 per cent were men and 29.43 per cent women. However, affiliation to the contributory pension scheme increased significantly in the last couple of decades, from 633,152 in 2000 to 2,373,688 in 2019 (DTUDA, 2021), so the situation of older adults in Bolivia in the future is likely to improve significantly. We also know that of the 1,111,879 beneficiaries of the *Renta Dignidad* in 2020, only 15.52 per cent were also in receipt of a contributory pension. This is very similar to our interviewees, where 14 per cent were in receipt of payments from a contributory pension scheme.

As mentioned earlier, not all interviewees were in a precarious situation. Eloy, for example, while living in a rented room, kept a room of his own in the family home he left to his wife. He said he had his large TV and a sofa, as well as everything he might need. He received a pension of Bs4,000 (US$579) as well as the *Renta Dignidad*. He also continued to work at the local radio station and taking solar panels to remote places so that people can charge their batteries. He felt he had everything he needed: 'I don't need anything. I earn 4,000 bolivianos without doing anything' (SC20).

Hernan, who spent all his working life in Argentina, but 'coming and going' as is typical for the rural areas of south Tarija, also managed to access the retirement pension in Argentina. He said: '[P]eople praise me, since people say: you have helped raise the boys, you have put the hard work, until I have reached 65 years and by law it is your obligation to retire. That is why they have retired me. Retirement is 4,000 [Argentinean] pesos.' At the time of the interview, this oscillated around US$290 (TRJ15).

Another case that draws attention is Gonzalo, who used to work as an engineer for Yacimientos Petrolíferos, the state oil company. He also worked in the construction sector in Argentina for 20 years. He received a contributory pension of Bs2,500 (US$361) and had only limited expenses – around Bs700 (US$101) monthly to cover his food and lodging in a nursing home. Also, at the time of the interview, he was in receipt of the *Renta Dignidad* (Bs200 or US$29, the reduced rate because he was also receiving a contributory pension). He had built houses for each of his seven children, although only two were still alive at the time of the interview. But he felt he did not get the love and attention he expected in return:

> In Salta I have a daughter, but it's like I have an enemy. … She has taken advantage of all my salary. I have given her a house, but she sold the house … for half of what the house cost. They offered her 200,000 dollars, 250,000 dollars. She sold it for 80,000 dollars. … She didn't give me a penny. (TRJ19)

His only son lived in Bolivia but he said his son does not visit him, although the nuns who ran the home where he lived disagreed:

> I only have one son who lives in a province called Paracaya. He hasn't come to see me for almost a year, not for a moment. And I have a grandson in the province of Argentina on the border. … They should come to see me, they don't come, I have to go to see them at great sacrifice because I can't walk. (TRJ19)

The limited mobility was Gonzalo's great frustration. He felt very limited by the fact that he was unable to leave the care home on his own and had asked various people for help in getting about and into town for a stroll or for a meal.

Although all of our interviewees should have been receiving the *Renta Dignidad*, only 93.1 per cent did. Some did not receive it because of lack of documentation, as in the case of Felisa, mentioned earlier, who at the time of the interview did not have an identity card (OR8). This is a common problem, particularly in rural areas where births are not always registered.

In general, the *Renta Dignidad* payment for older adults is perceived as a help, especially for those who have no other income. Some buy medicines not provided by insurance, treats or sweets, or alcoholic beverages such as *chicha*.[5] However, the amount is not enough to cover even the basic necessities for anyone, so most of our interviewees continue working.

## Land

Land tenure was particularly important in rural areas, because it is linked to the growth of food, which is used for consumption as well as to sell and generate an income. However, land also had particular importance in peri-urban areas, where interviewees sometimes bought plots of land to build houses for their children.

In rural areas, the migration of children was associated with some benefits and also some problems. Interviewees mentioned that their children's migration meant that there was less pressure on the land given that there are fewer younger people in the rural communities and therefore more land available for those who have remained in their communities of origin. However, for the parents themselves, the emigration of their adult children often represents a problem, if there are no adult children left behind to help with agricultural production.

The primary problem in rural areas related to migration is the lack of sufficient labour to cultivate the land. Luciano, a 75-year-old man from Koari, Cochabamba, explained:

> We perceived that migration allows people to achieve more of their dreams than if they stay in the area of origin, since being here, [the children, the community members] were going to continue working without much hope for their lives. Even the land to continue cultivating is not enough. The fragmentation of farmland is a product of the necessary inheritances. (CBB14)

His dream was to be able to raise animals, such as pigs, cows and sheep, and sell them to earn extra money. But the price of animals had dropped, so he could not make any profit selling them. However, the fact that his children were abroad worked as a buffer, as they help him when he needs money, but those who are nearby do not. Although Luciano did not give more details, from the interview it can be inferred that those who live nearby did not help, because Luciano and his wife already received help from their children abroad, when they visited.

Migration often contributed to increasing the vulnerability of interviewees in rural areas. Rural areas suffer from severely unequal land distribution dating back to colonial times, which has only improved marginally since the 1953 land reform. Land fragmentation continues to be a major challenge for smallholder farmers (Cortés, 2004). Most older adults in rural areas mentioned that the migration of their children was not desirable, because they missed out on their children's help and the migration usually did not involve professional work, which would have been the desirable path from a social mobility perspective. However, an unintended positive consequence was that the land did not fragment because fewer children remained locally to inherit the land, or that it laid fallow, because parents were sometimes unable to cultivate it without their children's help, and, as a result, it regenerated.

Martin, who was interviewed with his wife, cultivated land for his livelihood in the Cochabamba region. The couple were both happy that their children had left because the land they had was increasingly tired and fragmented – split into smaller plots after each generation inherited it. They had land higher up in the mountains, but there are no roads to reach them. They equate staying with surviving or getting by, while leaving – migrating abroad or to places like Santa Cruz – implies at least the possibility of progress. They mention people who came from 'outside' and stole things, but they organised as a community, caught them and physically punished them.[6] They did not come back. They did not see any improvements for themselves as a result of their children's migration, but they saw some improvement for their children, because they bought cars and plots: 'Although sometimes they send us money, it is not enough, because we continue to work hard to survive. Our farmlands are miles away in the hills and roads are not opened. Even our lands are increasingly fragmented and tired' (CBB22).

Some interviewees already distributed land among their children to avoid inheritance conflicts later on. None of the interviewees who gave up their lands in inheritance reported conflicts, except Juliana, who lives on her own land, but this is not extensive. Juliana had a disagreement with her 50-year-old daughter who had lived in La Plata, Argentina, for about 30 years. Her daughter wanted to claim an inheritance about five years ago: '[S]he is like a dead daughter!' Juliana said (TRJ16). Juliana said her daughter should have been sending money to support the granddaughter that Juliana was raising and instead claimed money. So they were not on talking terms at the time of the interview. There was another daughter who lived nearby, and this daughter's grandchildren visited her frequently. They got along well.

When giving away their inheritance, most interviewees stipulate that children cannot sell the land until the parents die.[7]

> I have nothing, I am almost attached to the children, but the commitment was that the children cannot sell the land until we leave [die, pass away], or where are we going to live? They are small pieces, they already wanted me to distribute them, I have distributed it, I have agreed with my wife. (TRJ14)

Ignacia, a 73-year-old woman, who had her own house, as well as approximately half a hectare of cultivated land and another piece of land in Rujero, also in Tarija, commented:

> On land I have a fourth hectare and then my daughter has bought another fourth and there I also work, so between the two pieces I have half a hectare … everything, then in Temporal [a local area] I have in

> Rujero, but sometimes I cannot go to sow and it is far, I get fatigue,
> it doesn't keep up the value … in Rujero I have sheep as well. (TRJ8)

She had been producing organically for about ten years but needed to do all the work herself because her husband was an alcoholic. He drank and slept all day. If she needed help in the field, she had to pay for it. She had a stall at the Tarija market on Saturdays and needed to have all the vegetables ready the day before. She had a long walk from her house to the road. She had to carry everything herself and make several trips. She said it was very hard work. She was receiving the *Renta Dignidad* and also participated in *Prosol*, a Community Solidarity Programme, which aimed to redistribute income from the natural gas sector for the benefit of indigenous and peasant communities in the Tarija region (Tarija, 2024). She used to have animals, but at the time of the interview she only had chickens because she could not do everything – cultivate the land and take care of the animals – herself without help. She was receiving some remittances from her daughter in Santa Cruz. Her son was living in Bermejo, but he did not contribute anything. Rather, he often asked for money. Her other son, who was in Argentina, died when he was 20 years old because of an illness. She said that her neighbours scolded her: 'They scold me, "You don't have to work like that, your children are already grown up", they tell me, but when you don't work, you miss it. It is never enough.' So, she keeps working (TRJ8).

In peri-urban areas it was common for interviewees to buy plots of land for their children. Marisa, who was 69 years old and was living in a peri-urban area on the outskirts of Cochabamba, bought a plot of land next to hers and was building a house for her daughter, with the money that her daughter was sending her from Spain. She had also borrowed money from the bank for the building work (CBB10). Paulina, who lived in the same neighbourhood, was living in her daughter's house, which was built with money that her children saved when they were in Argentina. But she also bought plots of land for all her children – she had five children, four of whom were abroad, in Argentina, Spain and the Middle East (CBB13).

Buying plots of land in peri-urban areas is seen as a safe way of investing savings, given that land prices usually rise significantly in a relatively short period of time. Typically, people will also build additional floors to their own homes, which they will then rent out and secure an income for when they are no longer able to work (see Bastia, 2019).

## Growing food

In this section we begin our analysis by region, given regional differences in food production, but then move on to highlight socio-economic differences.

In the rural areas of the highland region of the country, such as Oruro and La Paz, older adults work in the cultivation of quinoa and the raising of camelids and sheep. When we started our research, the cultivation of quinoa had positioned itself as one of the most important productive enterprises in the Oruro region. According to the Instituto Boliviano de Comercio Exterior, in the ten years leading up to 2013 Bolivian exports of quinoa grew 26 times its value and nine times its volume, reaching 25 destination countries and bordering a value of 80 million dollars (Erbol, 2013). Quinoa exports totalled US$1,237 million for 408,000 tons of quinoa between 2000 and 2021. Oruro is the main region that exports quinoa. The region received US$64 million for the sale of 26,000 tons of quinoa in 2020 (IBCE, 2021).

The growing demand on the international market has caused the agricultural frontier of this crop to expand to non-traditional areas such as Huari. It is estimated that in the southern part of Oruro there are about 2,500 permanent quinoa producers. These reside regularly in this area and fulfil social and productive roles. In rural areas of La Paz, there are producers called residents. These have dual residence, both in La Paz as well as in other Bolivian regions, but they own land for the production of quinoa, so they return periodically to their communities and work with the help of their children in Bolivia and bought-in labour.

Another important productive potential in the highland region is the raising of cattle, especially camelids[8] and sheep. In the words of Maria, a 64-year-old woman from Quillacas: '[W]hen my children were little, those times the quintal was 60–50 Bs. ... That's why, [at the time] we almost didn't sell any, we just used to eat it ... llama's meat was despised, but now llama meat is expensive, they say it is healthy' (OR1).

In the rural areas of the regions that make up this study, the average number of children of the people interviewed is 5.6, quite a bit higher than in cities (4.1) or peri-urban areas (5). During an interview, the wife of an interviewee in Oruro said that older people used to say that the ideal number of children is 12. So, what happens if some emigrate? Do the interviewees see it as risk diversification? But how do they meet their labour needs? Does this emigration at least decrease the pressure on land?

In the case of Oruro, we found that most of the people interviewed live with their partner and at least one of their children. By keeping at least one of their adult children at home or nearby, they can overcome the difficulties involved in the cultivation of quinoa and the raising of animals. They continue to work in a relationship of reciprocal help because despite some physical difficulties due to age they have stated that they also help their children.

One of the interviewees, Benito, was a farmer. He had had seven children and at the time of the interview lived with his wife and youngest son. One of his daughters migrated to Argentina and the other sons live in different regions of Bolivia. He was receiving the *Renta Dignidad*, but not remittances. He had his own house and land suitable for planting quinoa in which he worked with his son. During the interview he said:

> I am almost no longer working; I am in poor health. … This is how I help my son a little. I grow small things for myself, it is not like before, before I grew lots of things, with that I have also supported my *wawas* [children] through their studies. (OR14)

Benito arrived home for the interview after a long day of work in the quinoa field driving a large truck:

> We bought that car. … We have shopped around with my son, so here we are. … Now there is no time, for him to go to work, here you have to *barbechar* [prepare the land to improve the yield], you have to be planting, fumigating, everything has to be done, so that it produces otherwise, it doesn't. (OR14)

Arturo, a 64-year-old man dedicated to quinoa agriculture and raising llamas and sheep, lives with his wife and one of his children. He was receiving the *Renta Dignidad* and also has a pension for having worked in a mining cooperative. He had his own house in Oruro and Quillacas. More than 20 years ago, four of his 12 children migrated to Mendoza, Argentina. He said that they no longer wanted him to work, but that he cannot be without it:

> My children, they no longer want me to work … 'No daddy, what are you going to be working for if you have your income'. I just cannot be like this. If I were young, I could do anything, I can raise animals here, but that's work for younger people. But at my age, you cannot even get them to graze because. … You can't even get them to graze, that's just the way it is. (OR15)

In Oruro, only one of the interviewees expressed his difficulties in working the land, Bernardo, 63 years old, a native of Huari, who was a widower. His wife died with cervical cancer about ten years prior to the interview. He was living with his youngest son who was studying at the university, which is why he did not help him with the cultivation of quinoa. When Bernardo was eight years old, he suffered a serious accident while working in the mine, and as a result, he had a physical disability that prevents him from walking properly:

> Well … I am also disabled from my health, which is why I sow quinoa, but there are others who want to share the sowing (*sembrar partido*).[9] It

> works for me, because I have a bad foot, so they sow the land. I cannot work because it is better not to mistreat this body. (OR12)

Bernardo commented that the people who plant on his land give him 20 quintals (100kg) of quinoa in return for lending them the land. At the time of the interview the price ranged around Bs500 (US$72) per quintal. Bernardo said that this amount, which totalled around Bs10,000 or US$1,447 plus the *Renta Dignidad* was sufficient to cover his costs for the year. He did not receive remittances from his daughter in Chile. His main concern was to have some capital to continue working the land. He needed money not just to buy the seeds but also to pay day labourers, trucks, tractors and water. He wanted to dedicate himself to raising sheep and thus help his son financially to complete his university studies (OR12).

In the case of La Paz, except for a man with dual residence who lives mostly with his daughter in El Alto, the people interviewed in rural areas only live with their partners. Their children migrated not only outside the country, but also to other regions in Bolivia. Although the municipality of Santiago de Callapa, located in the southern highlands has soils suitable for the livestock of camelids and sheep and conditions for the production of quinoa and other Andean cereals such as *cañahua*, people focus on subsistence agriculture, unlike Oruro, where interviewees grow quinoa to sell.

One of the interviewees, Teófilo, an 83-year-old man, had three children. Two died and another migrated to Brazil more than 20 years ago. He mentioned: '[S]ometimes when it snows there is nothing. … There are no young people, only older people, and so they do not show up for meetings for anything … only a few come. Some are professionals, but they do not come' (LP11). Among lower-income interviewees, there often was a stronger sense of community, which also included responsibilities such as attending regular meetings and sponsoring *fiestas*. When younger people who had migrated were not honouring these responsibilities, parents complained. For them it was morally wrong that those who left to go to the university do not come back to the community, not even to attend meetings, which are compulsory for all households. In addition, we can infer that the young people's absence and reluctance to get involved also means that they do not take up leadership responsibilities (*cargos de autoridad*), which in communities is mandatory or, at least, expected.

In Aymara communities, a '*cargo*' is the space where a person performs functions in favour of his or her community (Carrillo Chambi, 2015). In general, these responsibilities are assigned for a period of one year on a mandatory and rotating basis, that is, all members must exercise the position of authority, with the prior acceptance of the community. Its objectives are to provide service to the community and to legitimise the right to land. All the community members throughout their agrarian life follow an ancestral itinerary called '*thaki*' or path. Therefore, when a person exercises leadership by providing service to the community, s/he fulfils his or her *thaki*, thus obtaining prestige, social capital and respect from the entire community (Carrillo Chambi, 2015). In these practices there is always an element of restraining individual freedoms for the collective wellbeing, and the expectation is that all who are deemed to belong to a specific community, contribute to the continuity of the practices (Godfrey-Wood and Mamani-Vargas, 2017).

In the case introduced earlier, Téofilo did not receive remittances or retirement income, but was engaged in agriculture and raising some cattle. However, his main income was the *Renta Dignidad*: 'We are going to collect [the payments] and my old lady is barely holding. ... She is only just about walking. We pick ours up on the same date.' He commented that they raised their granddaughter (of one of his sons who died) as a daughter of their own. She visited them frequently: '[W]e are like her parents ... she watches over us, she is in La Paz, she comes sometimes once a week, sometimes after a month, she comes to see us.' At the same time, Teófilo, despite his health and mobility difficulties, begun his workday at five in the morning: 'Four, no, five sometimes ... when there is a lot of work, we get up early' and helps his granddaughter with her farm:

> I like to work, we are taking care of the farm, we have to take care of cattle. ... Now age does not do us any favours. In vain we are wanting to work on the land, by the way they do not know how to work the land, my granddaughter is trying to work on the farm, but I am ploughing it with an ox, and then I will do [sow] something. (LP11)

Interviewees from medium and higher socio-economic groups had more individual understandings of belonging so they often had fewer expectations of reciprocal care and community involvement.

Tarija is quite unique given most interviewees from rural areas engaged in the coming and going modality of migration when they were younger, spending part of the year in Tarija and the other part in Argentina. In this region, most of our interviewees based their livelihood on their land, mainly to guarantee their daily food, and in some cases also to sell some of their produce. They also dedicated themselves to raising animals such as cows and chickens and, sometimes, they sold animal products such as eggs and milk on the local market. Graciela has a garden and indicates that she grew different foods: '[W]e grow a little bit of everything to eat; a little we eat, a little we sell' (TRJ9). Guillermo said: '[W]e do not sow much, only little we sow, just to maintain ourselves' (TRJ14). Hernán commented that he no longer has land because he gave it to his daughter for her to work. On his plot he has an orchard:

I do not have land. What we have above in Carichamayo we have given to our daughter to work. Here I have only my plot and I don't use all of it, I have a little vegetable patch [*huertito*]. … We grow vegetables for our own consumption … we put onion, lettuce, chard. (TRJ15)

Hilda lived in the house that she built with her husband, on the land that her husband inherited from his mother. They began to emigrate to Argentina when they were both young, newly married (15–16 years old) and used to spend six months in Fraile and six months in Tarija. They were receiving the food basket from the region of Tarija, the *Renta Dignidad* and Hilda also worked in the public works organised by the community while the husband took care of the land and the six cows he owned. They also sold some vegetables in Tarija. Their children usually helped them when they were in Tarija, but like their parents, they also came and went every six months. Therefore, Hilda and her husband had to fend for themselves for at least half of the year (TRJ17).

Ezequiel was 71 years old at the time of the interview. He lived in Guerra Huayco and commented that, for more than 20 years, his two children migrated seasonally to Perico, a city in the province of Jujuy, Argentina. They used to be in Santa Fe, but it was too far. They were worried that if something happened to him, they would not be able to see him. Instead, the distance between Guerra Huayco and Perico is approximately three to five hours. Both he and his children are engaged in agriculture. His children usually rent land in Perico and plant different vegetables, while Ezequiel used to travel to Entre Ríos to grow beans, take his cows to graze in different places and even grew potatoes in another town near Palos Blancos: '[S]o we just go around planting, sometimes we sell well, we get 4000, 5000Bs and then again we buy potatoes, guano, fertiliser' (TRJ11). He worked in the modality called *a medias*, where he would look for neighbours who have land that they are not using and ask them if he can plant on that land and then split the harvest halfway with the landowners, as explained earlier. Ezequiel did not want to live in the city, he said, 'as here there is egg, chicken, in the countryside you can live because there is everything. In the city you cannot live because there isn't any free land. I have four hectares to plant as I want' (TRJ11).

Gloria had a son who was working in the vineyards in Mendoza, Argentina. She mentioned that together with her husband they help their children by taking care of their crops:

But right now they come at the time of sowing sweetcorn, they come to sow, they leave having planted sweetcorn and they leave a worker [*peón*] to look after them. … I also go with my husband to see their land, when we have to throw soil to sweetcorn or potatoes, we go with the *yunta* [pair of oxen], we work them and they only come for the harvest. The second daughter has come and left her plot already planted and she went again when it was time to take the sticks out from the tomato plants. (TRJ7)

In the case of Santa Cruz, there was only one interviewee who usually dedicated himself to agriculture, Elmer, a 79-year-old man, interviewed in Plan 3000, who was originally from a Guaraní area and used to plant sweet potato, cassava and bananas when he lived in Isoso. He only moved to Santa Cruz shortly prior to the interview, to access better healthcare (SC17; see Chapter 7).

In the case of Cochabamba, there are particular places within the rural areas of the region of Cochabamba where migration has led to greater social mobility. Interviewees in Arbieto, some of whom were over 80 years old, benefited from their own migration and that of their children, to different destinations such as Venezuela, Argentina and the United States. As other studies have documented, the long-standing link between Arbieto and the United States has generated new investment opportunities in agricultural products at the local level, particularly peaches, leading to greater differentiation in the rural population (Jones and De La Torre, 2011). Some households have benefited more than others. One of our interviewees, Ricardo, 83 years old, illustrates this well when he talked about the investments he has made in his own peach production and innovation in rabbit farming:

[W]e were making a cooperative to send rabbits abroad and then we were wanting to go to Ecuador to bring other breeds and cross with our own, thus competing with the Faculty of Agronomy in terms of rabbit breeding, this as it is called classified breed. ... And that's just when he left, so I stayed. (CBB1)

Ricardo could not expand the business any further because he needed his son's help to run a bigger business. His two sons have professional jobs in Argentina and the United States. They send him some remittances, which he invests in the rabbit business and in innovation in the cultivation of peaches and other vegetables:

[S]ometimes I produce this pumpkin, so I make produce or rescue from the old customs let's say, from how it was sown before, I do not sow with chemicals, I have made a production based on [organic farming] and I see results in large potatoes. I have also brought potatoes from other places that are not grown any longer here. Before there were about 60 varieties of potato, so all that, we as farmers have not known how to take care of [these heirloom varieties] and as for the peach the same … we had 15 varieties of peach now we are simply preserving the *Gumucio reyes*. (CBB1)

Ricardo benefited from his son's migration through the remittances that he received. However, at the same time, the fact that they were not close by limited his capacity to expand his business because he could not draw on their help. Their support of their father's business promoted their own social mobility but also led to greater social differentiation in rural areas.

Juana and Juvenal (CBB4 and CBB5), who live in the same town, also dedicate themselves to the cultivation of peaches. Juvenal, mentioned before, said: 'I am currently in the field because, I am with this as it is called, I am with peach plantation, I also work, I produce sweetcorn, potatoes, I dedicate myself to the field' (CBB5).

## Conclusion

These experiences show that, for some parents, their children's migration leads to the accumulation of financial capital, which in turn leads to social mobility and the securing of their financial and social position. These include those parents who have adult children who have secured their migration projects through skilled migration routes, found professional jobs either in South–South regional migrations to Argentina and Brazil or through South–North migration to the United States, and can reap some of the benefits of their children's migration projects; and those who move for unskilled work but to a variety of destinations and from a relatively secure financial base, as examples from peri-urban areas show, where migrants have sent remittances, which have been invested in plots of land and/or house construction. Migrants who can access more lucrative migration flows also pass on some of these benefits to their parents, but this depends on migration destinations, documentation and access to travel. They are a minority. However, most parents see little difference in their own income or housing resulting from their children's migrations. Remittances are low or irregular (see the next chapter). For some rural areas, children's migration means that parents are missing out on agricultural help. Negative consequences also related to sadness and depression, which we discuss in Chapter 9.

The next chapter focuses on remittances in more detail to explain the relative lack of economic impact that the children's migration has on the parents' lives.

6

# Remittances

## Introduction

Remittances have received a lot of attention in the migration literature and we were clearly interested in finding out about financial transfers between the adult children abroad and their parents in Bolivia. There was some reluctance among the interviewees to provide details about money received from their children, even though we asked questions related to this topic after having built some trust with them. Nevertheless, for the most part, we have been able to collect some information on remittances, particularly whether they are sent and how they are used by the receivers.

While, for younger people, remittances can be a disincentive for work or study, for older people they can only be beneficial, especially in contexts of weak infrastructure. Of the total number of people interviewed, 44 per cent received some remittances. Although we had assumed that remittances will decrease with the time the adult children will have spent abroad, some evidence shows that this does not actually occur, and that time has little impact on the amount or regularity of money remitted (Brown, 1998). For our sample, there are additional variables that we need to take into account, related not only to how long it had been since the interviewees' children migrated but also where they migrated to, the types of jobs they held and whether the children had already set up their own families.

There might often be an assumption that older adults would want to receive remittances from their adult children abroad. However, we have come across a number of people, across socio-economic groups, who firmly resisted receiving remittances from their children. Their reluctance stemmed from a sense of personal pride, but also because they were concerned about their children having to make sacrifices in order to make savings and being able to afford sending them remittances, even more so when they had their families with them in the destination countries. There was a sense among some interviewees that given the sacrifices involved in working abroad, any benefits should be enjoyed by the children and their families, if they had one.

In this chapter, we focus on whether adult children sent their parents remittances, how they used them, instances where remittances were resisted as well as reverse remittances, that is, when interviewees themselves sent remittances to their children abroad.

## Not receiving remittances because they are not sent

For adult children, setting up their own families was often perceived as a pivotal moment for the people we spoke to, as it indicated that the adult child would now have additional responsibilities and also potentially different allegiances. Many interviewees made references to 'they now have their own family' as an obvious explanation as to why they were not receiving any remittances. This was the case for Guillermo, for example, a 64-year-old man, who lived in a rural area in Tarija:

> No, they almost do not help us at all, because you know that they already have their children, they already have to see to their needs. In addition the children are studying, they ask for one thing, they ask for another, you need a lot of money, there in Argentina at least, all their children have grown up there. They are already finishing high school. … They ask them for a lot of money, 2,000, 3,000, 4,000 Argentine pesos.[1] Sometimes they do not have that money and they have to borrow it. It's difficult. Very rarely they would send some money to their mother, sometimes to me, but very rarely, almost never. (TRJ14)

Hilda, also from a rural area in Tarija, similarly said: '[T]hey are already apart; they no longer help us. They have to support their wife, their children' (TRJ17).

This 'being apart' is a key element on the basis of which parents explain the reasons why their children might not be sending them any remittances. Once adult children establish their own families, the parents feel that they no longer have any claims on their potential financial contributions. 'He doesn't send [any money]. He has five children. … Before he used to send at least Bs100, he always used to send. Now, he says, he doesn't earn anything, just enough to eat' (TRJ4).

> No, not anymore, they also already have a family and being like that they can no longer help us financially. My eldest son already has four children. My daughter who has lived in Argentina for years, I think she has three children, the youngest has two. They don't give us money anymore. We have some money from working and the government gives us the *Renta Dignidad* once a month. That's the income we live on. (CBB15)

Some, like Carmen, a 61-year-old woman from La Paz, said they have not asked for money from their children because they know of their needs abroad:

> [A]h. … Now that she is just starting. … I have not asked her yet, because she also has to take care of her home, she has to have her own

savings, because I always recommend that, to have her own savings for the future because it is going to be a lot of money for her girl to go to college. So, from now on both of them are saving for their girl. (LP19)

The multiple and regular crises that some of the countries of destination for these migrants undergo (Argentina, Brazil, EU countries), also add to the difficulties that migrant children have to face and this has repercussions for how much money they can remit, or whether they can remit at all.

Adela, a 62-year-old woman from El Alto, traded clothes in a fair market also located in El Alto. She had four children and her eldest son migrated 12 years prior to the interview. Due to the economic situation in Argentina and because sometimes he does not have a job, Adela was not receiving any remittances. She commented:

No, he hasn't sent me. On that account, I would say the situation in Argentina is bad. He says that they are going through a rough time. Sometimes he doesn't even have a job, four years back he didn't even have a chance to get a job. And I was already living with my partner. (LP7)

Here Adela was suggesting that she also needed less support and had less of a claim on her children's support because she was in a relationship.

In terms of help, there is no help from the children, what are we going to say. The children sometimes give a little bit, say 100 Argentine pesos, which are about 50 Bolivian pesos [US$7.22]. But only sometimes, because the situation over there [in Argentina] is fierce. They rent land over there and this year they lost everything. They had hail and have lost everything. They owe money. They usually lend money from the bank over here [in Bolivia] and rent land over there, but now they are owing money to the bank. It's the same with my sons-in-law, they have borrowed money from the bank to rent land there, and now the lands are expensive, and they have lost. Well, some years it's worth it, but when there are disasters like that, they cannot gain anything. (TRJ14)

This example illustrates the powerful transnational connections that exist between origin and destination, through the borrowing of money in Bolivian banks to rent land in Argentina.

Migrants going to Brazil do not seem to fare much better – a combination of slower economic growth and increased competition from co-nationals:

The country is a little bad now, isn't it? It is [wages] very low. There are lots of Bolivians, lots. My youngest daughter is also there. She travelled earlier this year with the intention of staying for three years. She recently said that [the Real] has dropped a lot, to Bs40 she says. There just isn't a lot of work. There is no way of making a living. Everything is really expensive. Before it wasn't like this. Now everything is just too expensive. She says she will just come back at the end of the year. She will come back. (LP14)

The difficult economic situation in countries of destination also leads to changing practices in relation to whether migrants remit. For example, Mercedes, who is 60 years old and lives in a rural area of Tarija, has two children in Argentina: one of them has five children and the other one son. The latter used to send remittances (Bs100, equivalent to US$15) from time to time, but the situation in Argentina then deteriorated so he cannot send any money (TRJ4).

Sometimes the children's migration does disrupt more supportive relationships and older adults stop receiving support when their adult children leave for abroad. Efrain, mentioned earlier, was 93 years old at the time of the interview. His son used to give him money when he was in Santa Cruz, but he left for Argentina seven years prior and has not been in contact since he left. His situation was quite precarious given that his (ex-)wife returned after 28 years and wanted to kick him out of the house, as apparently the plot of land where they were living was in her name. They also had tenants. He was receiving the *Renta Dignidad* and did the dishes in a restaurant at night to earn money for food and bills (SC10). Everything about this interview pointed to a very vulnerable situation for this interviewee but a fuller story emerged when we interviewed his much younger ex-wife, who described how her parents had given her to him when she was still just a girl, while he was already around 50 years old. She suffered abuse and violence from him, then left when she had a stroke (*embolia*) and was hospitalised (SC13). She had returned to the house only shortly before the interview to find that Efrain was still living in the house.

After coming across this story through this linked interview, which happened quite by chance, we wondered about the extent to which the vulnerability and abandonment we witnessed in some of the older men were linked to a more complex history of parental abandonment, violence and abuse on the part of these men towards their spouses and their children. For example, another interviewee from Santa Cruz, Edson, also interviewed in Plan 3000, had recently separated from his wife after 44 years of marriage and in the process lost all the assets he had: houses, garment workshop, cars and a minibus. He had to move out of his family home and ended up renting a room on his own. He worked in a garment workshop to make ends meet. He was also receiving the *Renta Dignidad*. His son, who had left his own son in Bolivia, was in Spain and used to send remittances to his mother, but not to him (SC11). Overall, we have witnessed that children abroad tended to have a closer relationship with their mothers than their fathers (see Chapter 10).

Some of these men might not be receiving support from their families because they were 'absent fathers', or men who were violent towards their partners and children and are then 'abandoned' by their children when they grow up. Many of the personal histories we have encountered are complex and because we usually interviewed only one person in the relationship, we only have information from one point of view. In instances where we did interview couples separately, the full complexity of their relationship came to the fore, when disparate opinions and experiences were expressed on their life courses.

It is striking that in many cases the ageing parents who have financially supported their children not only do not receive remittances but they are also taking care of their grandchildren, supporting them with their own incomes. For example, Juliana was receiving *Prosol*,[2] *Renta Dignidad* and had received the food basket five times. However, although her two children abroad brought her something when they visited her – usually once a year – she did not receive any remittances. At the time of the interview, she was selling gasoline in a small shop that she had installed in her house. Her husband brought the gasoline to sell. That was their only income, in addition to some vegetables that they grew mainly for their own consumption. She said she also had to pay to support the grandchildren to go to school and that she planned to send them to Argentina with their mother so they could go to school there. She said:

> They do not help me, rather I have to support their children! ... I have to pay for school, I have to look after them. ... Every time they go to school, I give them two *pesos* for their lunch. ... Money! Money! The boys always ask. They ask and they don't care if there is money or if there is none, but I've had enough. (TRJ16)

A similar situation is that of Consuelo, who had a daughter in Peru, but her daughter was not sending her money, although Consuelo was taking care of some of her daughter's children (15, 17 and 19 years old). Consuelo had no retirement pension, and her only income was the *Renta Dignidad* (SC4).

As this section illustrates, there are many instances where parents were not receiving remittances, even in cases where they needed them to cover basic needs or were looking after grandchildren.

## Receiving remittances

As mentioned earlier, almost half (44 per cent) of all interviewees received some remittances. However, the amounts they received were not very large and they were usually quite sporadic as well. One interviewee, whose daughter was in Spain, received US$200–250 every six months or so (SC13). Alvaro, a 64-year-old man, had eight children. Two of his daughters had migrated to Spain about 15 years prior to the interview: 'Well, yes, they send me … economically also for my expenses, for my vice … although this I am sending you … this they say, any little thing you're going to buy, they send me, they don't forget' (OR4). Alvaro's experience reflects his socio-economic background, in that he is using remittances not to cover basic expenses – such as food or medicines – but to buy himself treats. His two daughters in Spain – one in Madrid and one in Algeciras – were sending him approximately 30 to 50 euros (US$31–52) a month. This is not a great amount but it is much greater compared to some of the amounts mentioned earlier by people who live in rural areas and are of lower socio-economic backgrounds. Even for Alvaro's situation, the amount is sufficient to make a difference in his everyday life. Amanda, a 76-year-old woman, had two children (out of seven) who had migrated to Italy about six years prior to the interview. Her eldest son sent her remittances of about Bs300 (US$43) three to four times a year through her sister in Bolivia (OR5).

Martina, a 70-year-old widow, whose eldest son had been living in Virginia, United States, for 20 years, commented that although her son sent her money sometimes, she relied more on the *Renta Dignidad*: 'I just pick that up, because my son also sends me sometimes, although he has no obligation' (LP4).

Others received money for very specific things, usually food, payment of basic services, and to guarantee access to health and medicines. In the case of rural areas, remittances are also used to pay labourers and expenses related to the cultivation of the land: 'They send me, but I also have to do something so that nothing is missing. I already have to pay a labourer, I already have to pay for the care of my plants, I already have to pay to sow, to raise my harvest' (TRJ2). Some interviewees use this money, even if they are small amounts, to pay for food: 'He sends me sometimes, as I have other relatives, from my brother I have another older brother … his son is called Edil, his children are in Argentina … what he sends is just to pay for food' (TRJ5).

The amounts sent, even if small, are always appreciated, even by those interviewees who do not necessarily need the money, because it allows them to buy themselves some treats:

> He sends me everything, he sends me parcels from there, everything he sends me, when he comes he gives me money. … My children do not give me much, they give me about a hundred pesos (Bs100, or US$14), but since I do not drink, I do not even chew coca [*acullicar*], I buy some soft drinks, I buy fruit juice, yogurt every day and that's what I spend the money on. (TRJ6)

Remittances, rather than being regular, are used to mark special occasions, such as birthdays, and to show appreciation and love for the parents, as for Juvenal, who was from a medium socio-economic background:

> Yes, there are times, they send me 100 dollars a month, but especially for those as it is called, for some special day, for teacher's day, for my birthdays like that, more special, if that's what they send me for. ... Here there are *fiestas* sometimes. We prepare a barbecue, like that. We also use it to buy things for the peaches, it's expensive to fumigate, for that too. (CBB5)

Poorer interviewees, such as Gloria, save the money for emergencies:

> Yes, because there are times when I get sick and they always send me money, a little, a little each. ... I always have it stashed away and if I need it, I spend it and if not, I don't. When I get sick, I have this my little money to take out and I go to the doctor. (TRJ7)

As we discuss in the next chapter, health is a major concern for the migrants' parents we interviewed and poorer as well as better-off interviewees often spend remittances – if they receive them – on paying for better medical services and for medicines. Better-off interviewees, such as Celia, whose children have professional jobs in Peru and in Australia, pay for her broadband, private health insurance and for her to travel to visit her children and grandchildren abroad (SC21).

Sometimes children will alternate sending money to their parents, as in the case of Florentino, of higher socio-economic background:

> Every month they send money for the family, they send. But to me they take it in turns: she sends me once, then my son does. Every two months I have some money in my account, if it is not one it is the other. But I receive almost every month, from one or from the other. ... I use the money to go to the barber when it arrives on time, in cafes, in polishing shoes, in other special treats that one has. (CBB20)

In some cases, in which situations of vulnerability stand out, children abroad play a key role in contributing to the economic solvency of their parents. Edgar lost everything in a fire and moved to Santa Cruz three years prior to the interview to have surgery. He was receiving the *Renta Dignidad* but had no retirement pension. His children, who were in Santa Cruz as well as those abroad – gave him money for his medical expenses and daily needs, although recently he had been refusing to receive money from one of his daughters who was abroad, because he felt that life abroad must be difficult for her: 'They need it more. ... For me, they need it the most' (SC9).

In rare cases, ageing parents built their own houses with the money their children sent from abroad. This was the case with Basilia, mentioned in the previous chapter, who used to work making hammocks and was interviewed in Guarayos (SC18); as well as Paulina, from a peri-urban area in Cochabamba, who had saved the money that her children sent her from abroad, and bought plots of land to build houses for each one of her children (CBB13). However, these were exceptions, rather than the rule.

## But only when needed ...

Given the difficult situations that many of the countries of destination experienced in the last couple of decades, with regular economic and political crises, already discussed earlier, many parents expressed reservations in relation to receiving remittances, and often only accepted remittances if they were absolutely necessary for their survival. Interviewees were aware that their children often did not tell them everything that they were going through, as a form of protecting them from worrying (Sampaio, 2020) (see Chapter 10). When they accepted remittances, they often did so reluctantly.

Florencia, who lost everything she had to debt, and whose daughter had to travel to the United States to help her mum pay for the debts, explained: '[O]nly God knows what sacrifices she goes through to send me what she earns and that makes me sad. I ask her [for money] at the very last moment, when I can no longer bear it, I ask her' (CBB19). Remittances sometimes allow migrants' parents to buy household items that they would otherwise not be able to afford, such as fridges, which are not common in rural areas: '[W]hen I ask for money, they send me money, they even bought me a fridge about ten years ago, there I keep my groceries, the meat' (TRJ11).

Ignacia, who was 73 years old, said: 'He helps us sometimes when my husband gets sick, he helps. My daughter also sends us fruits, fruit boxes and things like that. A little bit of money' (TRJ8), illustrating how 'in kind' gifts were the norm for interviewees from lower socio-economic backgrounds but that interviewees can also rely on monetary help when the need arises.

Graciela said she was receiving some remittances from her son in Argentina, but she said he was quite far away to be able to send the money quickly when they need it, such as to pay for the doctor in a medical emergency. The daughter, on the other hand, whose child Graciela raised, did not send money, not even for her son (TRJ9).

## Resisting receiving remittances

Some interviewees were quite comfortable financially, so they refused to receive remittances from their children abroad. Julian, for example, whose daughter lived in Chile and worked as a journalist, was receiving a pension, the *Renta Dignidad*, as well as fees for administrative functions he performed in various associations. His daughter used to send him some money for small personal expenses, but he had recently refused to receive this money because she had health problems, and he said he did not really need the money (SC6). Eduardo, similarly, who lived in a nursing home, did not receive remittances from his daughter and would not have wanted to anyway: 'I, from that point, I support myself, I do not bother anyone, no, no, no, I am completely independent' (SC1). Similarly, Alejandro, said:

> No, I have made the decision to tell the two [children] that they are in another country, in Spain they are both. I have indicated that they have to develop their lives to look for their dreams and forget a little about the father, who happily has enough [financial] means or at least the necessary means to develop his life. (CBB16)

Alejandro's testimony illustrates a more middle-class understanding of family relations, where children are expected to be independent of their parents. Similarly, Walter, who also has the financial means to support himself and continues to enjoy working in his carpentry workshop in Santa Cruz, helped his daughter settle in the UK and refuses to take money from her even now that she has a job (SC7).

Other explanations given for not receiving remittances included life being expensive in the country of destination, 'No, we don't want to bother them, because how will they make ends meet? Because life there is very expensive. Life is very expensive there, that's why no, we always tell them no' (CBB4), or adult children being undocumented and out of work (SC5).

There was sometimes a temporal element to the parents' attitude towards receiving their children's remittances and financial contributions. Some considered remittances a form of help that they did not need right then but that they considered they might be able to accept when they were older. Miguel, for example, 61-year-old man from El Alto, was a public transport driver and a father of four children. His eldest son had been in Argentina for 15 years. He was receiving the *Renta Dignidad*, but no remittances: 'At the end of the year when he visits, he buys us something. He tells me "I'll send you money", but no … I don't want to. Maybe when I'm older and maybe yes, I'm going to ask him' (LP6). Or Arturo:

> When I'm going to be older, they're going to send me, not now, I can [afford to support myself]. … This year I have taken on the role of *pasante* [sponsor][3] and have spent for the *fiestas* here in August, with the *morenada*.[4] I have put in money. There are two fiestas, and they have supported me, they have helped with the money. (OR15)

While this quote suggests a contradiction ('they are not going to send money now' at the beginning of the quote and 'they have helped with the money' at the end of the quote), the purpose of the money is quite different – at the beginning he is referring to money that is sent for his own needs, while at the end of the quote he is referring to money that his children have sent to help with the *fiesta* sponsorship.

Based on these last testimonies, it can be seen that older adults – especially under 70 years of age – who do not have mobility difficulties or health problems, do not perceive themselves as old. Many continue to work, either as self-employed or in paid jobs, and are active in civic and social organisations. There is therefore an expectation and a hope that parents will be able to draw on support from their children abroad, when they get older: 'I believe that when we get older, they have to take care of us. They always tell us that this is their dream, although what sustains our lives now is agricultural work and our effort in tilling the land' (CBB14).

These testimonies show us that socio-economic status and age both mediate the receipt of remittances. Having enough money meant that interviewees were less likely to be asking for remittances and more likely to be refusing them if their children abroad offered to send them. This means that their children can keep more of their money and there is less pressure for them to be sending remittances. Overall, this would suggests that the current practices can be leading to greater inequalities as better-off migrants face less pressure to support their parents financially compared to those whose parents have lower incomes or no pension.

## Gifts

Money was not the only thing that children abroad sent. Sometimes they took responsibility for paying for specific things like nursing home fees (TRJ18 and CBB9), internet or private health insurance (SC21) or they bought their parents gifts: 'He does not always send me money, but he always brings some gift, but not money, clothes' (OR1).

Eulogia, a 64-year-old woman from Santiago de Callapa, sold groceries and sweets in different trade fairs. She had her own house in Santiago de Callapa as well as in Patacamaya and was finishing building another house in La Paz. Her intention was to leave a house for each of her six children as an inheritance – she had nine but three died. She was receiving the *Renta Dignidad* and said that her two daughters who migrated always brought her gifts, biscuits and new things from Brazil when they visited: 'They often send me things. ... They don't spend much, they send clothes ... biscuits, they have different style of biscuits in Brazil, isn't it?' (LP9). Similarly, Ignacia said: 'My daughter also sends us fruits, fruit boxes and things like that. A little bit of money' (TRJ8).

Bonifacio, a 62-year-old man from Santiago de Callapa, was working as a driver, although he also had other responsibilities, such as taking care of the church in the community. He earned other income, in addition to the *Renta Dignidad*, from selling sheep that his wife raised. He had five children. His youngest daughter, who was in Buenos Aires, Argentina, did not send him remittances:

> Of course they treat me to meals. I cannot deny that. 'Daddy I will pay', she says. 'But I will pay'. 'Not daddy I will pay, we will eat.' Well, that is, *cariño de las wawas* [children's love]. I do not want to stop her from showing her affection either. (LP10)

Those migrant children who have higher incomes often sponsor their parents' visits. So parents of higher socio-economic status are able to visit their children abroad without having to incur any expenses. Inés' daughter, for example, was not sending remittances but she had sponsored two of the last trips her mother made to visit her:

> [H]er husband told her – once when she was asking me for money – why do you ask your mother, I am your husband, ask me [laughs] and since then I have stopped helping her. She has a profession now. The last two times I have travelled, she paid for it. When I was there, she paid for everything. She took me on a tour and was happy that I went, she was working, and I went shopping. I mean, it's a joy that I am able to go and since she earns money, she's paid for everything, so it's a benefit [*retribución*, referring to it being the daughter's turn to help her mother] that I still have, right? (LP05)

We discuss visits in more detail in Chapter 10.

## Reverse remittances

It is clear from some of the examples we have included so far that remittances do not only travel to the country of origin. As Mazzucato showed, remittances also flow from the country of origin to the countries of destination (Mazzucato, 2011). In fact, some of our interviewees have also sent money to their adult children abroad or sponsored their first trip. However, this was almost exclusively a practice of those interviewees from higher or medium socio-economic background (all except our first example).

Genoveva, to make a living, sold food in the town where she was living, in the Cochabamba region. Her children emigrated to Spain, Italy, Argentina and Paraguay. She was living with her husband, who had been sick for the past eight or nine years and was not working. They did not own their home and had to pay rent. Her job as a street vendor was her only income. The children were not sending remittances and she had borrowed money, with interest, she stressed, to help her children migrate: 'I sent him money then, for his ticket. I had to borrow myself with interest, for his ticket. They do send me, but I have also given him' (CBB3).

Others, like Antonio, a 70-year-old man from La Paz, had closed a very prosperous business of his own, collected the *Renta Dignidad*, did not receive remittances, but said that he continued to help his two children – one was living in Santa Cruz, Bolivia and another in Brazil. When he travels to Curitiba, Brazil, he pays for the tickets and the stay, for himself and also for his ex-wife. Although his son occupies a managerial position, Antonio said that he still helped him financially, particularly in relation to his grandchildren: 'And I can tell you that so far in some way I help them. … Because they are, they are my children, I cannot get lost, and now I have two grandchildren' (OR18).

In the case of professional migration, some older adults interviewed have financially helped their children to study abroad. For example, Arminda during the interview said that her daughter was able to pay for her studies with the rent that she was collecting from the house that Arminda owned in Buenos Aires: 'No, no, I never sent money to my daughter, my daughter has always been able to pay for her expenses herself with the rents of my house in Buenos Aires' (CBB7). Although she stressed that she has never sent money for her daughter, arguably, the money from the rent of her house in Buenos Aires is her own but she was allowing her daughter to use it instead.

Néstor, a 64-year-old man who was a surgeon, was receiving a pension, but also continued to work as a university professor. Two of his sons were studying in France and Italy. Néstor helped financially his son in Italy because he did not have a full scholarship: '[N]o, what is he going to send me [laughs out loud]! I send him money, because he also has three daughters' (LP2).

Similarly, Marta helped her daughter study in Brazil:

For my daughter's expenses I used to send her US$500 per month for two years, I used to send it every three months, for her specialism. Because they didn't go to work, but to study. In total I sent US$12,000 for her specialism. I used to send the money with my in-laws, because they used to travel to Brazil every three months, because they have three shops of yarn. (CBB18)

Inés, a 61-year-old woman, who was still working as an administrator at a private university, commented that she helped her only daughter financially while studying abroad: 'I helped her, because the scholarship she had was not a comprehensive scholarship, right? They paid for the entire study, and I had to pay for everything that is related to her stay: food, housing, so I sent her money until she got married' (LP05).

Pedro, a 68-year-old man, who worked as an educational psychologist in an institution located in El Alto, had three children. One of his daughters had been in Chile for nine years. She migrated after getting married: '[S]he met a young man from Chile, and he took her just to Chile.' At the time of the interview, this daughter was studying:

[T]hey have validated her grades. Here she had to do some paperwork. Here she was studying psychology, we had to go to the embassies to validate her studies, I sent that over, right? And they have accepted her there at the university. She has half a scholarship I think but I had to send her from here about 3,000 dollars to pay for the entire career, they are there now. My daughter is studying. (LP18)

Others like Alberto, a 76-year-old man from El Alto, who had his own tire patching business, received the *Renta Dignidad*, but not remittances. He commented that he helped his children financially. He had seven children. He was sending money to three of them who migrated to Brás, Brazil: 'Rather, I send them money. They shout: "Send me some money!" … Because they ran out of money, they took it from the bank and then I had to pay. But what am I going to do, they are my children right?' Alberto also helped his grandchildren in Bolivia:

[T]hey do not want to work these young grandchildren. Two are studying at the university, I have to give them money for their bus fares … it's terrible, clothes, shoes, food, I'm helping him out, if it wasn't for me, what would he do. They don't have enough money, my son works in the transport sector, he has a minibus and traffic is so bad. (LP15)

It is indicative that all these interviewees, who have sponsored their children's migrations or supported their studies financially, are from a medium or higher socio-economic background, except for Genoveva (CBB3), who was mentioned at the beginning of this section. Most parents from lower socio-economic backgrounds are not able to sponsor their children's migrations or further studies.

Building on the previous section, then, the evidence shows that children of parents of medium and higher socio-economic backgrounds not only are not required to send remittances but they also receive support in the form of reverse remittances, from their parents. This is particularly the case when the children migrated for the purpose of furthering their education, given its relationship with social mobility. Although not all these parents were professionals, those who are would also expect their children to have professional jobs.

## Upward social mobility?

As we have seen, in most cases, the migration of children had not had positive consequences for the migrants' parents. Very few received significant remittances. As Hilda mentioned, regarding the economic changes resulting from migration: 'Not us. For them, of course, they are doing well' (TRJ17). Similarly, Guillermo said that there were no changes in his life after the migration of his children: 'At least I have continued working until the last moment. Now I can no longer work, so now we look for a little thing and another to be able to support ourselves' (TRJ14).

For others, migration opened new opportunities for individual social mobility, such as continuing education or practising the profession. In turn, these successes often had positive consequences for migrants' parents as well. Parents could consolidate their financial position and help manage their children's investment, as discussed in the previous section. Migrants' success stories are sometimes also reflected in personal satisfaction and their contribution to emotional wellbeing (see Chapter 10).

The examples of migration that lead to social mobility and benefits, particularly material, for the people interviewed, were located in some rural areas of the region of Cochabamba, but mainly in urban and peri-urban areas. Marta, a 63-year-old woman living in the city centre, reflected on her daughter's migration: 'For me as a mother it is good, because I had always wanted my daughter to emigrate, to get her specialisation so that she realised her potential as a professional. That's why I'm satisfied, because my daughter has fulfilled her mission to do her advanced qualification' (CBB18). Her only daughter went to Brazil for graduate studies in dentistry and stayed there to open a private practice with her husband. When they bought a flat in Cochabamba, they asked Marta to manage the rents. Marta was collecting the rent, making sure that everything was in order. She was also lending money and charging interest and had savings from the restaurant business she had been running for 25 years. Therefore, this is a relatively wealthy family, with an established family business. The daughter participated in a regular, safe migration for what would generally be considered skilled migration, that produces positive material results. She was in a comfortable financial position, but, as will be seen later, her emotional wellbeing suffered.

We found some examples of 'entrepreneurial spirit' that was linked to sometimes significant improvements in the material basis of interviewees and their families' lives. However, to be able to categorise this as 'social mobility' we would have expected to see some identifiable improvement in either education or income basis (or both). Unlike urban areas, where most of the migrants from better-off families who were able to find professional work came from, migrants from rural and peri-urban areas were mostly employed in jobs considered 'less skilled'. However, women, in particular, were often engaged in managing their children's assets.

Grandmothers in urban and peri-urban areas often embodied this 'entrepreneurial spirit' and were active in managing remittances on behalf of their children and investing them (for a longer history of women's role in local markets see Calderón and Rivera [1984]). Some of the people interviewed complained of loneliness and lack of help. However, they were the driving force behind migrants' projects and continued to support them in various ways. Paulina, for example, was initially sad to see her children leaving, but she was doing well at the time of the interview. A woman born in the mining town of Llallagua, she was 60 years old at the time of the interview. She had given birth to nine children, three of whom had died at a young age. Her husband had also died within a few years of their marriage. She did not go to school and worked in the mines for much of her life. At the time of the interview, two of her surviving sons were in Argentina, one in the Middle East and one in Spain. Paulina lived with her two grandchildren and did not worry about her children abroad. When asked about her son, she said: 'Okay, he sends me money. I saved it and bought a piece of land in his name.' She felt better since her children left: 'I feel better, I built the houses for my children, and … I bought land for my children. … My daughter, after building her house, she left but left me my grandchildren. … I feel better now because she left me with my grandchildren' (CBB13).

Paulina got a lot of satisfaction from having invested her children's remittances by buying land and managing the construction of houses for them. These activities require considerable capacity to interact with lawyers, negotiate financial transactions, receive remittances and keep them safe, pay sellers, deal with architects, builders and various professionals.

The picture that emerges from this interview and others like this one is that women invest their children's remittances and assume new care responsibilities. While for some, this responsibility may be seen as a burden, for others it is a blessing. They engage in strategies to ensure the material wellbeing of their children. Although many have not had the opportunity to attend school, they live in a close-knit community with strong social networks, so they do not suffer from social isolation. They are all widows, but they also have a small but regular income, receiving private pensions from their husbands' jobs in mining. Their children have migrated in search of unskilled jobs, but to a variety of destinations, including Chile and Argentina but also Spain, Italy and the Middle East.

Similar examples of social mobility also exist in towns such as Arbieto, where parents receive remittances from their children abroad, which they invest in the peach business. The absence of their children means that what they can do in practical terms is sometimes a bit more limited, because the children are not there to help them. However, they often help when they visit, while at the same time financing business expansions via remittances and joint investments.

## Conclusion

With regard to remittances, although almost half (44 per cent) of the people interviewed receive them, the amounts and modalities vary widely. Most of the older adults interviewed provide for themselves. Added to this is the concern of mothers and fathers about the economic crisis and the difficulties faced by their children to guarantee their support as migrants in some destination countries, especially those in the region.

According to the older adults interviewed, remittances are sporadic and the amounts are not high. However, regardless, they are very grateful to receive them. When they receive remittances, they use them to purchase food, pay for basic services, access to healthcare, especially privately, as well as the purchase of medicines. Many also save up these remittances as an emergency fund, while in rural areas, remittances are in some cases used to pay labourers and other expenses related to agricultural production and animal husbandry.

But we have also found cases of reverse remittances, where the parents have financially contributed to their children's migration projects and lives abroad, directly supporting them regarding the decision to migrate, as well as taking care of their grandchildren, even without receiving remittances. Particularly parents of higher socio-economic groups, whose children wanted to migrate and study abroad, not only supported their children in their decision to migrate but also paid for their travel and their studies. In other cases, parents sent money to their children because of the debts they have acquired in the destination countries or because starting a family meant that they had higher expenses. However, only parents from higher and some from medium socio-economic backgrounds were able to help their children in this way.

In this chapter we found that the children of interviewees who are of lower socio-economic background tend to engage in less lucrative migration journeys, which sometimes involve circular migrations but in other instances migration without the intention of returning. As we will see later on, some of these migrants are not able to visit their parents, because of undocumentedness and lack of funds. Community is more important for this group of interviewees, which also implies additional costs, but greater and sometimes stronger social support networks, as we discuss in Chapters 8 and 10.

The children whose parents are of middle- and higher-middle socio-economic backgrounds tend to have more individual trajectories of social mobility. They engage in safer migration trajectories and have more lucrative jobs abroad. For them, there is less pressure to remit given their parents are more likely to have access to professional jobs with more secure income, pensions and the social security benefits that go hand in hand with formal professional jobs. These parents are more likely to refuse remittances even when these are offered so the adult children abroad are able to keep more of their earnings for themselves.

7

# Health

## Introduction

Health and care represent the second pillar of our analytical framework. In this chapter, we analyse how older people whose adult children live abroad organise and manage their care needs. Looking into detail into hands-on care needs and how older people or their family members, whether in Bolivia and abroad, try to meet those needs allows us to explore the care dimension of transnational care. In the original framing of transnational care, Baldassar et al (2007) found that migrants whom they interviewed in Australia supported their parents' care needs in several ways. Some travelled regularly to offer support. Others travelled to meet specific emergencies as they arose. Still others facilitated financial support to family members who were geographically close to their parents and were then able to provide hands-on care for their parents or employ others who would fulfil that need (Baldassar et al, 2007).

In our sample, we found only very few interviewees who had their care needs fulfilled in this way. Most of the divergence is due to the very different context within which our study took place. Not only were our interviewees living in a country whose infrastructure – in terms of both financial support and healthcare provision – is much weaker, but many of our interviewees' children were also differently positioned in relation to the global migration regime as well as labour market insertion. Many of our interviewees' children, especially those from poorer backgrounds who had migrated to the United States or Europe, were not able to move freely across borders. They also had poorly paid jobs that did not provide them with the means of sending regular remittances, as discussed in the previous chapter, and thereby supporting their ageing parents' care needs.

However, it is also interesting to note that we found very few interviewees who actually needed hands-on care. As Vera-Sanso et al (2023) argue, in resource-poor countries very few people actually make it to what Laslett (1987) terms the 'third age' or 'fourth age'. In this framework, the first age is characterised by dependence on one's parents, the second age is characterised by independence and earning, the third age one of health and independence as people retire, and the fourth age by dependence, ill health and death (Laslett, 1987). As already illustrated in the previous chapter, most of our interviewees were in a situation where they could not cease working so they continued working the land or engaging in paid or unpaid work. But what was to some extent surprising was that there were very few who were being looked after by other people, whether paid carers or family members. As Vera-Sanso et al (2023: 384) argue, '[a] large proportion of the world do not experience a third age. Instead, they move from a long second age straight into a short fourth age', the exception being better-off interviewees who were still relatively healthy and had financial security.

This reality was also reflected in our data, where very few of our interviewees found themselves in that fourth stage of dependency, being looked after by family members or, more unusually, paid workers or in care homes.

As far as health problems are concerned, a large percentage of the people interviewed (47 per cent of the total) indicated having age-related problems and ailments, which were more common among women than men: 54 per cent of women reported having health problems. Some of these problems were visible at the time of the interview. They ranged from restricted mobility, generalised pain, osteoarthritis and arthritis, as well as hearing and visual problems. Other diseases, such as diabetes, the sequelae of embolism and depression were also mentioned. In the case of those who lived in highland areas such as La Paz and Oruro, they tended to mention problems related to the heart, polycythaemia vera[1] and in some cases pulmonary silicosis related to prolonged exposure to silica dust in previous work in mining.

We begin this chapter with an overview of access to healthcare given that, in most of the interviews, this emerged strongly as an important area of our interviewees' lives. Given readers might not be familiar with the Bolivian healthcare system, we review the infrastructure available, both in terms of hospitals and health posts as well as support services for older people, including how these services are accessed by those who need it. As we will see, while on paper at least, the legislation might provide generous offerings of not just standard but integrated support for older people, in practice these services are difficult to access for the majority of the population or deemed unsuitable, as many of our interviewees attest. When the state infrastructure fails, families usually step in to provide the required care. We conclude the chapter by discussing the role that traditional medicine as well as churches and spirituality play in helping support interviewees' health needs.

## Access to healthcare

The Bolivian health system is organised in three main types of healthcare provision: the private sector, short-term social security provision and the public sector. According to the 2020 Household Survey, at the national level 52.19 per cent of the population is covered by the public sector, 17.80 per cent by the short-term social security provision (also known as the *Cajas de*

**Table 7.1:** Population registered or affiliated to health insurance, by area, selected regions and sector, 2020 (%)*

| Area, region and sector | Public health services[a] | National health service (*Cajas de salud*) | Private and others | None |
|---|---|---|---|---|
| *Bolivia* | *52.19* | *17.80* | *0.53* | *29.48* |
| *Urban* | *39.67* | *23.05* | *0.72* | *36.56* |
| *Rural* | *81.66* | *5.44* | *0.09* | *12.80* |
| La Paz | 52.83 | 19.12 | 0.42 | 27.62 |
| Cochabamba | 55.00 | 17.25 | 0.46 | 27.29 |
| Oruro | 50.53 | 24.61 | 0.20 | 24.66 |
| Tarija | 67.06 | 17.70 | 0.24 | 15.00 |
| Santa Cruz | 36.67 | 17.55 | 0.94 | 44.85 |

Note: * For 2019, Law No. 1152 aimed to expand the beneficiary population that is not covered by short-term social security, by offering free healthcare, with the aim of working towards a Single, Universal and Free Health System. In its Regulatory Decree (D.S.°N°3813) in Article 3 it mentions 'Universal and Free Health Care, based on Health Products, will begin to be provided progressively from the first day of March 2019'. [a] Public health services include the Unified Health System and Health Insurance of Departmental or Municipal Autonomous Governments.

Source: INE (2020). The 2020 Household Survey considers expansion factors based on the 2020 population projections.

*Salud*), 0.53 per cent by the private sector and 29.48 per cent is not covered by any of these (see Table 7.1).

As already mentioned in Chapter 4, the Bolivian state, as part of its Law No. 475, Law of Provision of Services of Integral Health of the Bolivian Plurinational State, of 2013, establishes and regulates the integral attention and the financial health protection of older people who are not covered by the compulsory short-term social security provision.[2] Similarly, the Law No. 369, General Law of Older People, signed in 2013, in its Article 5 establishes the right to a dignified older life, while guaranteeing through the provision of sufficient nutrition to support conditions of health, while giving priority to older people and those who find themselves in a vulnerable situation. Despite this, the testimonies of older people we have interviewed describe a health system that is characterised by its precarity and inaccessibility, particularly in rural areas.

Some of the data from the National Institute of Statistics (INE) and the Ministry of Health and Sports supports our findings. In 2020, Bolivia had 4,133 health establishments. Most of these health establishments are health centres (*Centros de salud*, 2,525) but there are only 32 specialised institutes in the whole country (see Table 7.2). Each health centre services 2,825 people, while hospitals service 35,173 people. Hospitals include basic hospitals, general hospitals and specialised institutes. At the national level, the average

**Table 7.2:** Health facilities, selected regions and type of facility, 2020

| Region | Total | Centre with particular characteristic[*] | Health post | Health centre | Basic hospital | General hospital | Specialised institute |
|---|---|---|---|---|---|---|---|
| *Bolivia* | 4,133 | 72 | 1,204 | 2,525 | 250 | 50 | 32 |
| La Paz | 825 | 27 | 79 | 661 | 33 | 10 | 15 |
| Cochabamba | 642 | 14 | 208 | 348 | 53 | 15 | 4 |
| Oruro | 239 | 2 | 98 | 125 | 11 | 3 | – |
| Tarija | 294 | 4 | 35 | 227 | 23 | 4 | 1 |
| Santa Cruz | 723 | 14 | 212 | 390 | 92 | 9 | 6 |

Note: [*] Centres with particular characteristics include the blood bank.

Source: INE (2020) National Institute of Statistics based on data from the Ministry of Health and Sports.

**Table 7.3:** Hospital beds and inhabitants by hospital beds, selected regions, 2005–2020[*]

| Region | Hospital beds | People per hospital bed |
|---|---|---|
| *Bolivia* | 16,226 | 720 |
| La Paz | 4,264 | 703 |
| Cochabamba | 2,902 | 709 |
| Oruro | 548 | 992 |
| Tarija | 1,040 | 560 |
| Santa Cruz | 4,691 | 704 |

Note: [*] The populations used for the year 2020 are projections based on the 2012 Census 2020 revision.

Source: INE (2020) National Institute of Statistics, based on data from the Ministry of Health and Sports.

is 1.1 beds per 1,000 inhabitants, the lowest ratio in the region except for Venezuela (0.8 beds per 1,000 inhabitants), compared to 1.6 beds in Peru, two in Chile and five in Argentina (WB, 2024). Of the regions that make up this study, the most critical situation is found in Oruro, which has 548 hospital beds, which translates to 992 people per bed (see Table 7.3 for information by region).

Despite the different ages, a large number of people interviewed said that they do not require medical attention. A typical answer to the question: 'Where do you go when you get sick?' was: 'I've never been sick' or 'I don't need medical attention' or 'I've never been in a hospital'.

Pedro, for example, who lives in a peri-urban areas of La Paz, said he does not get ill: 'I don't know, I don't know, to get sick, only once did I get sick as a child, nothing more. ... Nobody believes me, I'm 68 years old right now, nothing hurts, not even my feet, nor my body, I think the advantage is not having smoked or drunk' (LP18). Others argue that they never get ill because they eat healthy, natural and unprocessed food, such as Braulio, a 67-year-old man from Quillacas, Oruro who said:

> We have grown up with this … with grain, quinoa, *cañahua*. … Sweetcorn, all those, but until now I don't feel pain, I don't go to the hospital because I don't get sick … sometimes I get sick with the flu and that's understandable, right? Sometimes a cough grabs me … but first [the most important thing] is to eat something natural, just like that, my teeth (he showed me) are healthy, I continue to eat roasted sweetcorn, broad bean,[3] I am perfectly well. (OR13)

Clearly, this does not mean that they do not get sick. We need to distinguish answers given regarding ailments as some people indicated that they do not go to the doctor, but this is not to say that they do not get ill. As we will see in this chapter, many self-medicate or use natural or traditional medicine. This could be a choice, but it may also be a choice that many of our interviewees make because they either cannot access Western medical services or they deem them unsuitable to meet their medical needs. Many of our interviewees felt that they cannot access dignified healthcare and therefore look for other ways of treating their ailments.

To exemplify, Bonifacio, who was 62 years old at the time of the interview, looked healthy. He did not have medical insurance and commented that he has never been to the hospital. This is not unusual, given health facilities are scarce (see Table 7.4) Even when he had a fracture a few years back, he stayed at home. Bonifacio is from the rural area and did not have many economic resources. However, in addition to this, in his worldview, even a fracture – that to us authors would require access to a hospital – for him could be cured at home and, indeed, he did just that. Sometimes he goes to the health post of the town but only to ask for some pills:

> I do not have insurance, I do not … I don't know about that part, thank God, I've never been to the hospital. When I broke [my arm], I didn't go to the hospital either, it's all this part, I haven't entered the hospital. I stayed at home, they cured me at home, I've been calm, now I'm driving. (LP10)

Women who found themselves in a similar situation often mentioned that they might have needed medical attention during childbirth but highlighted that the countryside provides rich offerings of medicinal herbs for a range of illnesses. Maria, who lives in a rural area in Oruro, highlights the point we made previously, that many of our interviewees who live in rural areas

**Table 7.4**: Inhabitants by health facilities, selected regions, 2020[*]

| Region | Inhabitants per health facility[a] | Inhabitants per first level care establishment[b] | Inhabitants by hospital[c] |
|---|---|---|---|
| *Bolivia* | *2,825* | *3,072* | *35,173* |
| La Paz | 3,631 | 3,906 | 51,647 |
| Cochabamba | 3,204 | 3,608 | 28,565 |
| Oruro | 2,276 | 2,417 | 38,849 |
| Tarija | 1,981 | 2,189 | 20,799 |
| Santa Cruz | 4,565 | 5,358 | 30,847 |

Note: [*] The populations used for the year 2020 are projections based on the 2012 Census 2020 revision. [a] All establishments of the Health Services Network. [b] Health posts and centres. [c] Basic hospital, general hospital and specialised institute.

Source: INE (2020) National Institute of Statistics, based on data from the Ministry of Health and Sports.

mentioned not getting ill and not 'needing' the hospital. 'No, I don't get sick, no, I don't. … We take *mates* [herbal infusion]. … There are lots in the countryside. … For colds, for cough, for everything there is in the fields. … Maybe that's why I don't get sick' (OR1).

These practices are not confined to rural areas. Monica, 61-year-old woman from the city of Oruro, has a similar attitude of avoiding doctors whenever possible:

> I tell them nothing hurts, no, nothing, I suffer from migraines, for example, and I take my pill and that's it, it's very difficult [rare] for me to go to a doctor. It would have to be an extreme, an extreme situation. I almost don't go; I usually don't go. … I have managed without for many years, with God's blessing. (OR16)

Some simply buy some 'tonic' or vitamins at the local pharmacy (SC2 and SC10), which is surprising, especially considering their age. Efrain, who is 93 years old, does not go to the hospital and only buys a tonic at the pharmacy. He walks daily to stay in shape and takes care of his diet (SC10).

To contextualise this last point, it should be noted that at the national level in Bolivia – beyond having some medical insurance – when people have health problems they seek medical attention in different establishments: 61.6 per cent go to public health facilities, 20.2 per cent access their short-term social security, 16.5 per cent to private health facilities and 9.7 per cent resort to their private health provision even when they might not have private health insurance. In addition, 44.8 per cent resort to homemade solutions, 46.8 per cent self-medicate and 17.8 per cent turn to traditional medicine. This figure is also similar when compared by region (INE, 2012) (see Table 7.5).

**Table 7.5**: Population by place where you go when you have health problems, selected regions, 2012 Census

| Region | Population | Caja de salud (cns, cossmil, others) (%) | Private health insurance (%) | Public health establishment (%) | Private health facility (%) | Traditional doctor (%) | Home-made remedies (%) | Pharmacy or self-medication (%) |
|---|---|---|---|---|---|---|---|---|
| *Bolivia* | *10,059,856* | *20.2* | *9.7* | *61.6* | *16.5* | *17.8* | *44.8* | *46.8* |
| La Paz | 2,719,344 | 21.2 | 10.0 | 53.7 | 14.9 | 19.7 | 48.8 | 49.8 |
| Cochabamba | 1,762,761 | 17.6 | 10.2 | 62.5 | 21.9 | 15.3 | 48.7 | 53.9 |
| Oruro | 494,587 | 22.4 | 9.0 | 58.9 | 13.0 | 19.0 | 50.5 | 47.7 |
| Tarija | 483,518 | 24.3 | 10.3 | 71.9 | 17.9 | 26.6 | 45.9 | 48.2 |
| Santa Cruz | 2,657,762 | 19.0 | 10.2 | 64.6 | 19.2 | 12.2 | 35.5 | 44.4 |

Source: INE (2012).

**Table 7.6:** Access to health social security by socio-economic status

| Access to health social security | Low | | Medium | | Higher | | Total |
|---|---|---|---|---|---|---|---|
| | No. | % | No. | % | No. | % | |
| Yes | 4 | 7 | 18 | 60 | 9 | 56 | 31 |
| No | 50 | 93 | 11 | 37 | 7 | 44 | 68 |
| N/A | 0 | 0 | 1 | 3 | 0 | 0 | 1 |
| *Total* | *54* | *100* | *30* | *100* | *16* | *100* | *100* |

In our sample, of the total number of people interviewed, only 31 per cent have access to some health insurance (see Table 7.6), and this is quite a bit higher for men (39 per cent) than for women (25 per cent).

However, there is often a divergence between the type of insurance that interviewees have and where they actually access their health services, just as it happens on the national scene. Of the total, 27 per cent of our interviewees use the public health system, 22 per cent use the *Caja de salud* (short-term social security they are entitled to from having retired, so this is mostly men living in urban areas and the middle and upper middle class); 17 per cent use the private health system (either because they are insured or they pay separately for the services they access), while 6 per cent use traditional medicine and 8 per cent never access any of the health services (see Table 7.7).

As with other indicators, there are differences between the areas of residence and socio-economic status, given that those who live in urban areas and those who belong to middle- and upper-middle-class socio-economic strata have greater access to some kind of health insurance.

While in urban areas 48 per cent of the interviewees do not have access to health insurance, the percentage increases to 62 per cent in peri-urban areas and 86 per cent in rural areas. In urban areas, 34 per cent of our interviewees use the private health sector, which decreases to 14 per cent in peri-urban areas and 7 per cent in rural areas. Only 7 per cent of our interviewees use the public health provision in urban areas, but the proportion increases to 24 per cent in peri-urban areas and 43 per cent in rural areas. This is also due to the long distances they must travel to access any health facility, whether public or private.

The consequences of not having insurance, coupled with mistrust of the health services, mean that some older people are forced to just bear illness and pain (see Table 7.8 for type of ailments experienced by older people in Bolivia).

In the case of those who access short-term social security, the *Caja*, widespread mistrust prevails, due to the quality of care and because the

**Table 7.7:** Where interviewees sought health services by socio-economic group

| Health provision | Lower | | Medium | | Higher | | Total |
|---|---|---|---|---|---|---|---|
| | No. | % | No. | % | No. | % | |
| Care home | 3 | 6 | 1 | 3 | 0 | 0 | 4 |
| Self-medication | 1 | 2 | 0 | 0 | 0 | 0 | 1 |
| Traditional medicine | 4 | 7 | 2 | 7 | 0 | 0 | 6 |
| Does not attend | 4 | 7 | 1 | 3 | 3 | 19 | 8 |
| Does not specify | 11 | 20 | 2 | 7 | 0 | 0 | 13 |
| Pastor (evangelical church) | 0 | 0 | 1 | 3 | 0 | 0 | 1 |
| Private | 8 | 15 | 6 | 20 | 3 | 19 | 17 |
| Public | 19 | 35 | 6 | 20 | 2 | 13 | 27 |
| *Caja – Seguridad social de corto plazo* | 4 | 7 | 10 | 33 | 8 | 50 | 22 |
| Foreign social security | 0 | 0 | 1 | 3 | 0 | 0 | 1 |
| *Total* | *54* | *100* | *30* | *100* | *16* | *100* | *100* |

supply of medicines is very limited. This is why, among those we have interviewed, even if they have this medical insurance, they still resort to private hospitals or buy medicines on their own. For example, Humberto, a 72-year-old man interviewed in Challapata, said: '[I go] here at the *Caja*, but they don't provide a good service … It's a pain [*macana*], so I just buy medications, yes, with that I'm calm' (OR2).

Paulina, introduced in the previous chapter, who was 60 years old and lived in a peri-urban area of Cochabamba, suffered from 'embolism' and said that her head does not work properly, but that she would not go to the *Caja*: '[Y]ou cannot go to the *Caja* because they do not even want to give you a tablet. I have [health] insurance, but it's in vain' (CBB13).

Julia has insurance through the oil sector health insurance. However, she said: 'But it is also so bad that particularly sometimes I take care of myself. … They don't give you expensive medicines … I have to buy them' (LP3).

Even Gonzalo, 90 years old, from Tarija, lives in a care home, which also includes the provision of medical care, but he chooses to pay to see a doctor privately, because he is not happy with the medical service he was given. He prefers to accept the expenditure and see a doctor privately (TRJ19).

Lucia offered a very vivid view of the *Caja*. Lucia had health insurance, but she did not want to use the *Caja* either: 'I'm insured, there I go, but I don't want to go to the *Caja*. It might be that even if I am healthy, they might kill me' (CBB11). She described how they did not let her daughter eat when she was in hospital for cancer, possibly because it was before the operation or because it was end-of-life care. However, in any case, her testimony

**Table 7.8**: People with some permanent difficulty and type of difficulty, selected regions, 2012 Census

| Region | Total | People with some difficulties | | Total | Type of difficulty | | | | | |
| --- | --- | --- | --- | --- | --- | --- | --- | --- | --- | --- |
| | | Women | Men | | Sight, even if they wear glasses or glasses | Hearing, even if you wear hearing aids | Talking, communicating, or conversing | Walking or climbing steps | Remembering or concentration | Unspecified |
| *Bolivia* | *342,929* | *174,683* | *168,246* | *398,284* | *188,036* | *59,454* | *37,452* | *68,073* | *29,550* | *15,719* |
| La Paz | 108,859 | 54,546 | 54,313 | 125,382 | 63,217 | 18,689 | 9,053 | 21,890 | 8,777 | 3,756 |
| Cochabamba | 54,502 | 28,022 | 26,480 | 63,343 | 28,903 | 10,068 | 5,632 | 11,696 | 5,317 | 1,727 |
| Oruro | 18,638 | 9,351 | 9,287 | 21,733 | 10,989 | 3,613 | 1,428 | 3,405 | 1,301 | 997 |
| Tarija | 18,212 | 9,528 | 8,684 | 21,410 | 8,970 | 3,501 | 2,619 | 3,425 | 1,773 | 1,122 |
| Santa Cruz | 80,703 | 41,727 | 38,976 | 94,013 | 47,510 | 11,181 | 10,276 | 15,110 | 7,083 | 2,853 |

Source: Instituto Nacional de Estadística. INE (2012)

highlighted a discrepancy between her own understanding of healing practices and modern medicine. So, she goes to a private doctor and also uses traditional remedies and herbs. It is common for different worldviews and beliefs to clash when it comes to attending to ailing bodies (Tapias, 2015). What might make sense from a Western medical worldview, such as fasting before an operation, is in tension with traditional understandings of looking after an ailing body, such as making sure it is fed properly with nutritious food.

Many interviewees considered the medical care provided by the state to be inadequate. Ernestina, for example, was living in a peri-urban area of Santa Cruz, in Plan 3000. She was caring for her mother, who is over 100 years old and bedridden. She complained about the cost of accessing medical care:

> I no longer go to Santa Cruz because they do not attend to us because if one is going to buy a ticket, I have to get hold of a ticket and then be there all day and in at the end, all the doctor does is they give a prescription, no more, he does not give us anything. (SC13)

So, they went to private health services, to the hospital of Jorochito, which is located on the old road to Cochabamba, in an area far from Santa Cruz. During the interview she commented that they used to have a free hospital for older citizens, but the government suspended it in 2011 (three years before the interview). She also complained that there was very little control over the type of drugs pharmacies sell and that some pharmacies sell fake medicines.

Access to adequate medical care in rural areas is even more difficult.[4] Health services in rural areas only provide very basic care in health posts and health centres. Health posts are attended by auxiliary personnel or nursing technicians. Health centres only provide primary and urgent care for subsequent referral to second-level establishments. Older adults living in these areas have to seek health services in larger towns or in cities, which, in many cases, entails not only significant additional costs but also difficulties in accessing adequate transport. In Tarija, interviewees spoke of having to walk long distances, because buses are often full. So even if they live on a bus route, on market days the busses do not stop to pick up because they are already full by the time they arrive at intermediate bus stops.

This situation is very common in rural areas throughout Bolivia. For example, Elmer, 79, fell ill in the Guaraní territory where he usually lives. He had a very common condition called pre-embolism and in the local health centre they only gave him an aspirin, telling him that there was no cure. So, his son took him to the city of Santa Cruz for better care. During the interview Elmer stated that he generally feels quite depressed and that he misses his *chaco*, the plot of land where he used to grow his own food. When things are okay, he walks to the market and buys a special health drink for hypertension, based on natural, traditional and herbal medicine (SC17). As will be seen later, natural medicine is considered to be an alternative for many older adults.

The situation is not much better in towns. Margarita, for example, 78 years old at the time of the interview, lived in Guarayo, a small town some five hours' drive from the city of Santa Cruz. Three years before the interview, she began to lose sight in one of her eyes. She had to travel five hours by bus to Santa Cruz to see an ophthalmologist. The local hospital used to be good, when it was run by a group of nuns, but now it has no specialised medicine. Her daughter was in Spain and sent remittances, but because there was no medical infrastructure or specialists close by, she had to travel to Santa Cruz (SC19).

## Migrants paying for parents' health needs

As mentioned at the beginning of this chapter, although older adults, due to different health problems and physical and mental deterioration, require support and care, of the total number of people interviewed in the different regions, only a small number of people require daily care and attention. The vast majority are relatively self-sufficient in terms of care. In fact, 73 per cent of the people interviewed were still working at the time of the interview. This percentage was highest in rural areas, where 86 per cent of those interviewed continued to work, followed by peri-urban areas, where 70 per cent of those interviewed continued to work, and lowest in urban areas, where 59 per cent continued to work at the time of the interview. Work in the formal sector was limited to those living in urban and peri-urban areas, and only covered 8 per cent of those who continued to be economically active.

However, there were a small number of interviewees who did require hands-on care, and we wanted to explore whether their adult children abroad played a role in either organising, paying or providing these hands-on-care needs.

The most striking example of people who did require hands-on care was Julia, who we interviewed in the city of La Paz. Julia was 88 years old at the time of the interview. She lived alone and had limited mobility: 'I don't want to go out because I can't stand alone, I can't sit alone, so if I went out. ... I'm always accompanied, though ... I can't get up alone or with my chair at all' (LP3). In the 1970s, for approximately five years, Julia lived in Houston, United States, together with her children and husband. However, due to language difficulties, her husband decided to return to Bolivia, taking the family with him. After finishing high school, their two children returned to the United States. This was some 35 years ago, in a move to better their professional lives. Both studied at US universities and became engineers.

They regularly sent remittances to their mother. Julia said that she was receiving at least Bs15,000 a month (approximately US$2,150) and she used this money to pay for five nurses who were with her 24 hours a day.

Her children called her every day. She commented that she speaks with her grandchildren in English because they do not speak Spanish. Despite the time they have been away, Julia felt sad due to the migration of her children. She explained that they cannot take her to live with them because health insurance in the United States is too expensive. The last time she went to visit them was three years prior to the interview, when her great-granddaughter was born. She was feeling very sorry when she talked about them: 'I have supported them, but I personally do not. … Because I miss them very much, but they have a better future there than here. They have good positions [jobs] and they are very well … they have their houses; they have their cars' (LP3). In some cases, adult children abroad provide remittances for medicines and, exceptionally, also to pay for private health insurance or nurses, as we discuss in the following, but this is the exception rather than the rule.

Access to private health services is expensive, which is why, in some cases, the children who migrated help their mothers and fathers in Bolivia pay for this service. Celia, already mentioned in Chapter 5, had two sons who lived abroad, and they were paying for her private health insurance:

[M]y children pay for insurance, medical insurance. … I am well looked after. The truth, the only thing I take care of, I do my annual check-ups, to see that everything is okay … thank God the only thing I have is the sugar that I have to keep under control, and I have to control that with food. (SC21)

This regular, organised support that was characteristic of older adults with higher socio-economic backgrounds was in marked contrast to more reactive responses to emergencies, which was more common among interviewees from lower socio-economic groups.

Parents with lower incomes resorted to asking their children abroad to send them money for medicines because they had no other source of income. Florencia, who is 75 years old, who we already introduced in the previous chapter, had lost everything to debt and relied on the *Renta Dignidad* and what her daughter could send her to cover all her needs. She had no health insurance, and her daughter was sending her money when she needed to see a doctor:

When I get sick, I don't have insurance, I don't have anything, I have to ask my daughter, tell her what I need and thank God my daughter solves all my needs, and my illnesses. I suffer from depression which has been really difficult to overcome and as a result of that I am diabetic. And I have moles everywhere that are caused by nerves, so I have also started a small treatment. And all of this is paid for by my daughter. (CBB19)

Martina, a woman in her 70s, interviewed in La Paz, also received money for emergency surgery from her son who was in the United States:

[M]y son just asks me: 'How are you mummy?' ... For example, the year before last, I got sick, I was bad, I had gallstones. ... 'How much is the operation going to be?' 'It's going to cost 10,000' [bolivianos, approximately US$1,400]. But there's another one up there, Asunción hospital clinic was cheaper, I already took the ultrasound, all that ... that's another Bs500, I was ill. My son told me: 'I'm sending you Bs10,000', so from there I went straight to the operation, they did tests, urine etc. All those things, Bs150. ... From there, they did a first ultrasound, I had a consultation and from there with the hospital doctor ... 'Mummy, you have the money, you can use it'. (LP4)

Amalia, who was 84 years old, had an operation not long before she was interviewed. Her daughter was in Chile, but she was not sending remittances: 'She is not sending any, she must be saving.' Amalia was living with her other daughter and with the children of the daughter who was in Chile. She had to pay for her operations privately, with the money she had saved from her husband's pension, which she had been receiving since he died in 2000. She did not have any health insurance and received some money from her son-in-law on a monthly basis, so that his children could study (CBB17).

In other cases, the children living in Bolivia are the ones who guarantee the health coverage of the people we interviewed. Consuelo, 74 years old, from Santa Cruz, had a daughter who was working for the telecommunications company Tigo and had added her mother to her occupational health insurance. As a result, she could buy her medicines with a discount. Consuelo's other daughter had been in Peru for five years but did not keep in touch. Consuelo did not know her whereabouts nor her occupation. Her daughter did not send remittances, even though she left her adolescent children in her mother's care (SC4).

Marina, 65 years old, said she usually does not get sick, but she had a health problem:

The doctor told me I was very angry and if I continued like that, I was going to have a stroke. Yes. A lot of anger, so many thoughts. So, this part was swollen [her left side of the body, from the leg to the shoulder, the whole half of her body hurt]. That was the only time I was sick. (SC8)

Although Marina was in daily contact with her daughter in Argentina, her daughter never sent her remittances. She was sending money to her husband, who was living in Santa Cruz, but Marina said that he spent it all on alcohol. Marina's healthcare bills were covered by her daughter who lives in the area. If Marina needed anything, the costs fell on the children living in Bolivia (SC8).

For most of our interviewees, the fact that the children had migrated did not imply greater access to health or living in better conditions.

Although sometimes interviewees had nobody to go with them when they had to visit the doctor, it was rare for older adults to be completely on their own. Most had children close by or in another town or city in Bolivia or were able to draw on neighbours or other people for help (see also Chapter 10). Hernan had stopped cultivating the land due to his health problems. He was easily out of breath and needed monthly check-ups to monitor his heart. The doctor told him to find somebody to accompany him to visits or he threatened that he will not see him anymore:

Then he [the doctor] had me have an operation. I went on my own and asked for an appointment. They gave me one and I went after eight. They took me to the operating theatre at eight and I left at nine. They brought me food; I could not sit up. The nurse had to give me the food while I was lying down and then at four, five in the afternoon I could just move and I could sit down, but I alone. ['You alone, have you not gone with your wife?'] She couldn't, she was with the *wawa* [baby/child]. The boy has to go to school [the grandson who lives with them, whose mum lives in Argentina]. (TRJ15)

Most of the interviewees who indicated that they were receiving support and help from their children abroad to pay for healthcare were women, suggesting that men received less support from their children. There is some background that might be useful in disentangling this relationship. Culturally, men are less likely to go to the doctor when they are ill. Men are also more likely to have health insurance and pensions so children might not be sending them money because they know that they already have some income that they can draw on. However, it is also the case that many of our interviewees mentioned that children tend to be closer to their mothers. Many interviewees mentioned that when their children call, they tend to talk and call their mothers rather than their fathers (see Chapter 10). Therefore, as an extension of this, it also seems to be the case that they are more likely to be helping their mothers access health services, both because women are more likely to attend clinics but also because children tend to have a closer relationship with their mothers.

Some particularities worth highlighting are the case of the regions of La Paz and Tarija. In the case of La Paz, the Autonomous Municipal Government provides basic medical services to older persons in centres called communal houses. These are spaces that allow the meeting and organisation of older adults, through the enhancement of their capacities and knowledge of their rights, of which there are about 35 located throughout the municipality of La Paz. Santa Cruz also has similar programmes, but they are sponsored by non-governmental organisations and international cooperation organised through the Catholic Church.

In the case of Tarija, as mentioned earlier, the close relationship that the group of older adults interviewed has with Argentina also extends to access to healthcare. This is a peculiarity not found in other regions and means that some of our interviewees in Tarija travelled to Argentina to access better healthcare. Guillermo, for example, who was suffering from osteoporosis and arthritis, used to go to the local hospital in Tarija. But then he also travelled to Argentina for some tests. There they gave him vitamins and other supplements, which helped, but once they were finished he did not have money to buy more (TRJ14). Similarly, Juliana mentioned having some health problems: pain in her feet, hip and heart. She said she usually goes to the health centre of San Andrés, but they only give her paracetamol and some analgesics, so she travelled to La Plata in Argentina, to see the doctor, taking advantage of the fact that her daughter was there (TRJ16).

## Traditional medicine

In line with the official data already cited, a large number of the interviewees turn to traditional medicine, either preventively or in a palliative way to mitigate the consequences of their health problems, and regardless of whether they have health insurance. This is especially the case for those who live in rural and peri-urban areas.

Albina, who lives in a rural area in La Paz, was told that she needs surgery, but she refused to undergo that procedure due to previous negative experiences she suffered in public hospitals: 'I have been told, but I do not want to have surgery … operations do not work.' She resorted to traditional medicine, 'just like that, herbs. … Pure grass with naturism. That's what I take but sometimes I forget. … When it's wanting to hurt, in that little moment while I'm just handling those things [pain] seriously [laughs], just so I can take something' (LP14).

Ezequiel, 71 years old, said he takes a vitamin and amino acid supplement (serum and tonic) twice a year. He also visits the doctor for check-ups but has never had any health problems. He drinks coffee and herbal remedies (TRJ11).

The cost of accessing good health services was clearly a big worry for most of our interviewees. Miguel said he was worried because he had to apply for a loan from the bank to buy the car he drives, which is why he did not want to get sick:

> Oh, no, it is forbidden to get sick … [I take] home medicine sometimes, and sometimes … eh thank God so far I have not had to go to a hospital, I always cure myself with homemade medicines, from time to time I go to the pharmacy to buy some things. (LP6)

Juliana also used herbal remedies to cure her rheumatism. She talked about boiling herbs (*molle*) to help induce sweating and relieve pain (TRJ16).

Although traditional medicine was much more popular in rural and peri-urban areas (7 per cent of interviewees in each of these areas respectively used traditional medicine), it was also accessed by some in urban areas (3 per cent, 1 person). Alfredo, 75 years old, had medical insurance based on the work he did in mining, but he distrusts the health service.[5] At the time of the interview, he was bedridden because of a problem in his back and had turned to the famous doctors known as the *hueseros Escobar*.[6]

> I have gone, I do not know, those friends have holy hands, with just seeing, and with touching, nothing else, it's all done, they have fixed it. They have put some bandages there, the ones that they make, then they put this one on me [he showed his splint]. … God knows how I have suffered, tremendous! He has seen me, he has put all these things on me, 'in a month you are going to walk', so he told me. (OR3)

Dolores, who was 79 years old, and lived in a peri-urban area in Santa Cruz, had never been to a Western doctor. She cured herself with traditional medicine and herbs if needed (SC15).

Bernardo, 63 years old, was living in a rural area of Oruro, and also did not have insurance. When he gets sick, he tries to cure himself at home because he does not have the economic resources to go to the private hospital (OR12).

Gladys, 67 years old, also living in a peri-urban area, in Tarija, sometimes requires medical attention but did not have enough money to go to the doctor. For the past six years, she has been drinking Herbalife (a vitamin and mineral supplement), which she claims to have cured her of her foot problems (TRJ5).

Ignacia, 73 years old, living in a rural area, also talked about having pain often, since she was pregnant with her first child, as well as pain in her feet and arm. She has used a veterinary cream[7] for pain relief and has accessed

Western and traditional healers to improve her symptoms. These seem to be targeting pain relief rather than the source of her disease (TRJ8).

Felisa, for example, who did not know her exact age, lived in a peri-urban area and said that her whole body hurts. But she did not have health insurance so when she is in pain, she said she does not go anywhere, she waits for it to pass or goes to the healer (OR8).

## Relying on spirituality and churches for support

Others rely on their religious beliefs and the churches they attend to manage their health and wellbeing. Adela, for example, from a peri-urban area in La Paz, did not have medical insurance. When she has had complications with her heart, she goes to the health centre, but she feels that her prayer group is also a support for her wellbeing:

> I go to the private hospital, here is a health centre, here I just come, there is a health centre. Of course, it is expensive, but I am ill, I am sick on the heart, I have polycythaemia [*poliglobulia*] I … he [the doctor] says that the blood is very thick, does not circulate well, does not pump to the brain and had grown my big heart, had grown with blood he says. I was under the care of a doctor, with a cardiologist, I am still with treatment, sometimes, anything, a strong emotion, a strong pain, he wants me to cover my chest. The doctor told me to be very careful because it can give me an embolism, he tells me. … I am strong, that's why prayers just help me, prayer helps me a lot. (LP7)

Likewise, there are those who also rely on spirituality to heal their health problems. Angela's daughter said that after going to several doctors without an answer about the illness of her 63-year-old mother, they sent the test results to Santa Cruz: '[S]he went around the whole of Oruro, but in Santa Cruz, they have helped her. She travelled there three times, but it is only aimed at soothing the pain … but later I took her to Bombori.[8] Now she is calm, calm' (OR9).

Eloy, who is 70, said he never went to the doctor. He runs every day for an hour and then goes to an evangelical church and that keeps him healthy. He said he recently broke his leg, and the pastor healed him (SC20). Other researchers working in Bolivia have also found that evangelism and evangelical churches are a source of support for curing physical illness in a context of absent state healthcare facilities (Godfrey-Wood and Mamani-Vargas, 2019).

## Conclusion

It is clear that access to healthcare varies by residence and socio-economic background. There is no provision for specialist medicine in rural areas.

Higher socio-economic groups have better access to healthcare and their migrant children are more likely to be contributing to their parents' health costs if needed.

Most of the people interviewed were still working at the time we spoke to them, either formally or informally, paid or unpaid. This is probably related to the lower percentage of adults interviewed who are in the fourth stage of dependency, that is, who are aged 80 and above. In this sense, despite the presence of health problems, few people require practical care to carry out daily activities.

Some health problems were visible at the time of the interview, such as restricted mobility. Other problems that interviewees mentioned included generalised pain, osteoarthritis, arthritis, hearing and visual problems, diabetes, sequelae of embolism, depression, silicosis and heart problems. Silicosis is related to working in the mines, and heart problems, including *poliglobulia*, mainly affect people who live at high altitude, as is the case in the western regions of the country.

Those who cannot access good quality healthcare tend to avoid the *Caja* and public services. They either do not go to the doctor, they use traditional medicine and/or rely on various churches and spirituality to maintain their health and cure injuries and illnesses.

We also found some instances of transnational use of health services, such as travelling to Argentina to access better healthcare, particularly in Tarija, by those who practice transnational livelihoods, which they extend to health service access and use.

It was not uncommon for interviewees to resort to traditional medicine, even more so if one considers the precariousness of the public health system, mainly in rural areas where there is no infrastructure or access to specialised medicine.

With regard to traditional medicine, the people interviewed have mainly alluded to the use of medicinal herbs intended to cure different ailments and the use of healers.

As we have already seen with respect to other indicators, there are clear differences between areas of residence and socio-economic level. Those who live in urban areas and those who belong to middle- and upper-middle-class socio-economic strata have greater access to some type of health insurance, because they have had a formal paid job. In addition, they have greater economic resources which enables them to access specialised medicine privately. Rural areas only have health posts that sometimes do not even have medical personnel, but only auxiliary staff or nursing technicians. For this reason, older adults self-medicate, resort to traditional medicine and, in some cases, are forced to make long trips to cities or even to other regions of the country in order to access specialised medical care.

Widespread distrust and discontent with short-term health services and social security force some older adults to endure illness and pain, as well as seek other traditional alternatives.

Only in some cases have interviewees had access to remittances for the private purchase of medicines, insurance and healthcare, as well as surgeries or urgent health problems. When remittances are received and used for health purposes, it is striking that better-off interviewees tend to have a more regular and organised support from their children abroad (for example, they make regular payments to their parents' health insurance), while those who are worse off tend to seek out their children's help only as a last resort.

Just as traditional medicine is important for the older adults interviewed, we cannot ignore aspects related to spirituality and the support found in religious organisations. In some cases, the people interviewed have expressed the vital support of their religious communities and have also indicated that they make their health requests to patron saints.

8

# Care

## Introduction

In this chapter we discuss how care is organised in transnational families. We include the practice of family members providing care for older people as well as examples of reciprocal care. We finish by highlighting the many ways in which older people continue to provide care for others as this is an important area of their lives, both in terms of the responsibilities that they continue to hold but also, for some, a source of joy and satisfaction that they would not want to do without. By doing this, we highlight the fact that older people are not just recipients of care but show how they continue to be active contributors to their families and communities where they live, not only through their work, which we discussed in previous chapters, but also through their unpaid care-work. Our findings support existing research that shows how older adults, particularly women, are not only self-sufficient but make an active and positive contribution to their households (Vera-Sanso, 2012; Vera-Sanso et al, 2023). Recognising older people's contribution, both paid and unpaid, is important, given they are often framed as a population that requires care, or even worse, as a 'resource burden', while they are often active contributors (Bastia et al, 2022b; Vera-Sanso et al, 2023; Vullnetari, 2023). In this chapter we also discuss challenges to self-care, particularly for older women who have experienced violence in their lives and continue to suffer both physical and emotional consequences of that violence.

## Family members providing care

In most cases, when interviewees required hands-on care, they relied on the children who have remained in Bolivia. This was either because help from their children abroad was not forthcoming or because the interviewees refused to receive help from their children abroad. Edgar, who we interviewed in the city of Santa Cruz, was 75 years old and had mobility problems. He required a lot of support to function in his daily life. Even though the doctors told him to walk, Edgar found walking very difficult. To see the doctor, he used to go to Prosalud,[1] but then he started going to a private doctor because he felt that she gave him better advice. His daughter, who was living in the same house, was his main carer. He said that all his children contributed to his medical expenses, but he has refused to accept remittances from his daughter, who was living in the United States, because he felt that her life was already difficult enough (SC9).

Diana, 63 years old, at the time of the interview lived in the Captaincy of the Guaraní Indigenous Peoples. Four years prior to the interview she had an embolism that left her disabled and did not allow her to work:

> Four years ago, I already got sick and had the embolism with a stroke and they operated on my head and from that I no longer work, and I walk like this, I walk with crutches because in the street I cannot function well. I always get that dizziness, I only see half of the person, the other half I see it in the dark, I don't know, I don't see well anymore. (SC12)

One of her daughters looked after her and cared for her, while her son, who was in Argentina, has not been in contact for at least five months.

Alfredo, 75 years old, was bedridden at the time of the interview. Two of his eight children, a son and a daughter, were in Argentina and although he spoke with both of them regularly – with his son once a week and his daughter every other day – they did not contribute to his care. He was being cared for by his wife and children in Bolivia (OR3).

When children set up their own families, either by marrying or by starting a de facto marriage by cohabiting with somebody, it is customary for the youngest child to remain nearby to provide care for ageing parents when and if this is needed, particularly in rural areas. For example, Genoveva, who we interviewed in a town in the Cochabamba region, said that her youngest son, despite wanting to go to Argentina with his brothers and sisters, decided to stay in Cochabamba so that she would not be alone: 'He wants to go too, but how is he going to leave me, he says, he does not want to leave me. He is sad' (CBB3). As could be seen in Chapter 5, especially in the case of Oruro, some children stay to cultivate the land together with their parents.

As will be seen later, other cases show a reciprocal care relationship with the older adults interviewed, especially those who live with their partner and at least one of their children.

Sometimes grandchildren become a source of support for ageing grandparents whose adult children are abroad. Lucia, for example, turned to her granddaughters when she needed help, since her own daughters were not a source of support for her (CBB11), as did Alejandro (CBB16).

Others reached out to younger people from their extended family networks for help. Gloria (TRJ7) did not need direct care, but if she needed to go to the doctor, she would 'borrow' one of the nieces or nephews who lived nearby. She had many extended family members who lived nearby, and her own daughters often kept an eye on her (TRJ7).

In exceptional cases, interviewees were helped by neighbours and non-family members, which is the case with Sonia, who we mentioned earlier in the book (CBB12) (see also the section on 'Turning points' in this chapter).

## Continuing to care for others

Care as part of social reproduction takes many forms, from taking care of other people when they are ill to the everyday tasks that are required to fulfil personal needs. In this section we place greater emphasis on instances when older people talked about care as an exception to the normal everyday activities. However, we do so without forgetting the contribution that women make, in particular in the forms of unpaid care and domestic work, especially in rural areas. Women are the ones who take care of grandchildren, husbands and close relatives, while at the same time working on the land. While our interviews focused more on activities to support people who require care (ailing spouses, younger children), parts of the fieldwork and data collection also allowed for instances of observation of everyday lives and routines. When Claudia and Sahara stayed with one family in a village in Oruro, they observed that the wife of one of the interviewees began her workday at 2am to cook and prepare everything and be ready by 5am when she, her husband and their son went to work on the plots where they grew quinoa (OR14). Although we did ask interviewees to talk us through their typical day routine, they did not often highlight the differentiated waking time or the extra work that women contribute to making sure that everything is ready for everyone else. This type of information generally did not feature in the interviews, so we wanted to mention it here as a backdrop to the examples we include in the following.

Often women, but sometimes also men, had significant caring responsibilities, despite having to manage their own health challenges. Eulogia, a 64-year-old woman from a rural area who was taking care of her husband, said:

> My husband cannot make any decisions; he is like a baby now [*ahora ya como wawa nomás ya es*]. He is already becoming like a baby, he had an accident, then now it hurts, 'it hurts me,' he says. ... This side hurts me, this side, everything is then, the car overturned. (LP9)

Maria also takes care of her husband who has health problems (OR1).

Angela, despite being in poor health, at the time of the interview was taking care of her husband who had fractures as a result of having fallen while building a wall (OR9). Braulio was taking care of his son, a university student, who had a concussion years ago as a result of a beating (OR13).

Of the total number of people interviewed, 20 per cent cared for their grandchildren whose parents were abroad and 6 per cent cared for grandchildren whose parents were in Bolivia. Seventeen of these are women and nine are men, highlighting the gendered nature of care.

The level of involvement in the care differs, as do the contributions they receive from the grandchildren's parents.

Consuelo, 72 years old, used to take care of her grandchildren since before her daughter left for Peru (SC4). Humberto continuously travelled from Challapata to Cochabamba to take care of his grandchildren, because his ex-son-in-law did not take care for them financially or in their everyday needs, so he was planning to take his grandchildren to live with him (OR2).

In some cases, the grandchildren were already adults and studied at the university when the grandparents took on responsibility (SC2). Beatriz, for example, lived with her son-in-law and her grandson who was at university and assisted in their care (OR10). Some only did pick-ups (SC12) or took care of the grandchildren with whom they lived, together with the father (SC14). None of these grandparents received money from their children, even in cases where they had full-time responsibility for the grandchildren (SC2, SC5, SC8, SC15). In these cases, the grandparents needed to work to support themselves as well as the grandchildren who were under their care.

Graciela, for example, had raised her daughter's son since he was one year old, when her daughter left for Argentina. Graciela's daughter never sent money for him, so she and her husband had to pay for education and materials as well as everyday subsistence with their own income. Her grandson was 20 years old at the time of the interview and had finished high school (*bachillerato*) (TRJ9).

Hernan, who lived in a rural area in Tarija, together with his wife took care of their eight-year-old grandson, whom they have cared for since he was a baby. His mother travelled to Argentina seasonally and was 24 years old at the time of the interview, so she was very young when she had him (TRJ15). Juliana, also from Tarija, lived with grandchildren she had raised since childhood, including one granddaughter she raised from when she was a week old (TRJ16).

Some of these grandchildren are in practice adopted and raised by their grandparents and sometimes also take on their grandparents' surname. For example, Néstor, who was a university professor, had two of his five children living abroad. He continued to work despite already having retired from his medical practice, because he had taken responsibility for his granddaughter:

My granddaughter still has to be taken care of, because. ... Well, she was born, and I don't know who her father is, so I gave my granddaughter my last name. So, I have to support her too. That's why I work at the university too, I have reached retirement age, but I continue to work at the university. (LP2)

The granddaughter's mother is in Bolivia, but they all live together in the same house.

Over time, this relationship is reversed. Dolores raised her grandson since he was eight months old. His father had separated from his mother when he was a baby and left him with Dolores. She raised him 'as her own son' and lives with him in a family compound. He was 18 years old at the time of the interview and went to work, and also contributed towards his expenses and those of his grandmother (SC15).

Although some men are involved in caring for grandchildren, the majority of those who have this responsibility are women (65 per cent).

Some people interviewed felt that grandchildren were a great responsibility, which they would like to avoid, particularly because they require additional expenses. Grandchildren involve additional costs, which are difficult to meet for resource-poor households:

> What if at some point they say that I should look after one of the grandchildren and it's dangerous having grandchildren, isn't it. … They are expensive, and I don't want to have that responsibility and they also don't want to stay with me … they have their father and their mother who are still young, let them work to support their children. (TRJ17)

However, others drew great emotional benefit from having grandchildren close by, particularly when they miss their own children, who have left, which we discuss in Chapter 10.

## Reciprocal care

Other cases reported examples of reciprocal care. For example, Amanda, 76 years old, lived alone. Her daughter, who was a widow, took care of her and always visited her. Despite her health condition – her hands and feet hurt, and she had no teeth which made it difficult for her to eat well – Amanda commented that she was happy when she was with her grandchildren. She would go to her daughter's house and take care of them: 'My hands hurt well, that's just how I am. … That's just how I am, down there for the *wawitas* [children] I cook too because … I cook there, here not so often, because I do not feel like eating alone.' Her daughter lost her husband when she was very young and Amanda always helped her: 'That's why I also help, if anything is missing, sometimes she buys, sometimes I do' (OR5). Similarly, Josefina, a woman of more than 60 years, lived with her eldest son who worked in the mine. He kept an eye on her. However, despite her health problems – knee and hip pain – during the interview, she was washing her son's clothes (OR7).

Gladys, 67 years old, had a good relationship with the grandchildren she was living with, so they helped her if she needed help. She was directly responsible for only one of the four grandchildren, she cooked for him, and they ate together. The other three ate separately. Their parents visited them every two weeks. They lived with her so they could access the school right next to the house, but she said it was also to keep her company (TRJ5).

Mercedes, 60 years old, divided her time between her two daughters, because she had no place to live or to seek help. She took care of the daughter who lived in Camargo, who was a trader and travelled for work. When Mercedes stayed with her, she could travel and work because there was somebody who could look after her children. Without Mercedes' help, she would not have been able to travel and work or she would have had to pay somebody to look after her children (TRJ4).

In exceptional cases, interviewees engaged in the type of transnational care that is more expected of higher income families and those who are better able to travel across borders.

Carmen, for example, a 61-year-old woman, had a university degree. She was working as a financial auditor and had a daughter in the United States. Her two other children were living in Bolivia. When her daughter was pregnant, Carmen travelled to the United States to help her:

> I have a visa for 10 years, the first time she was pregnant I went for six months, my daughter was pregnant, so for that reason I went, I asked for leave here without pay and I left for six months, that's the maximum amount of time I could take. They do not give more than six months to people who come from here, how much I would have liked to stay longer, but I could not. (LP19)

Only when she travelled to visit her could she verify that her daughter was fine: 'At first, I was very worried, how are you? Well, I thought maybe she is not telling me how things are, she's telling me not to worry, until I went and super, all was well' (LP19).

## Turning points

Care needs and practices were far from static. Finding balance between caring for others while at the same time fulfilling one's own care needs was sometimes challenging, as one's own needs as well as those of others evolve over time. For a small number of interviewees, the relationship between caring for grandchildren and receiving care from them was quite delicately balanced. In one case, we were able to capture the transition from when grandparents were caring for others to when they started needing care themselves. Sonia, already introduced earlier, was 83 years old at the time of the interview and originally from Potosí. When her husband passed away, one of her sons brought her to Cochabamba. This son had been her main carer but he also passed away a few months before the interview. When we spoke to her, she was living with two adolescent granddaughters, who were around 11 and 13 years old, whose mother was working in Spain. They were renting a small flat, consisting of two rooms and a kitchen. Another daughter and son were in Argentina. The death of her son had hit her hard. With no other family members around, she relied on the goodwill of her neighbour to cope with her daily needs, which included buying food and picking up remittances sent by Sonia's daughter in Spain.

Sonia was not working at the time of the interview because she was struggling to even walk from one room to another. 'I don't walk anymore, I used to go out. The feet no longer walk well. I would take the *wawas* [granddaughters] to school and pick them up.'

Since her daughter's migration to Spain, they had been able to buy a sofa, a table, a fridge, a table with chairs. According to one of her granddaughters, before her mother's migration they had nothing, but at the time of the interview, they were receiving between Bs2,000 to Bs2,500 (US$290–360) per month from their mother in Spain and had expenses of around Bs700 (US $100) for rent, spending the remainder on food. The neighbour, a tenant next door, helped them collect remittances and buy food. He would also lend them money if they needed that (CBB12).

During the visit, we noticed that her hair was matted, her clothes stained and she was eating spoiled food. She could not move easily. Despite feeling financially comfortable with remittances received from Spain, Sonia was in a very vulnerable situation, although she was reluctant to admit it in the interview. In this case, her vulnerability related to her physical wellbeing, poor health, additional responsibilities of caring for grandchildren, and lack of social networks. This story is in line with other research, which shows that migrants are not always able or willing to care from afar and that some older adults find it difficult to meet their daily needs (Schröder-Butterfill and Schonheinz, 2019).

While Sonia was the only adult responsible for her two grandchildren, she struggled to carry out everyday tasks, or to control the two adolescent girls. After the interview, she asked us to 'have a word' with them so that they understand that they need to do their homework. One of the girls was also wanting to go to a basketball match that was taking place somewhere on the other side of the city of Cochabamba and it seemed Sonia had little authority to deny permission to her granddaughter. The interview took place during the delicate turning point, when grandparent is in the process of no longer being able to take care of her granddaughters and starting to have to rely on them for everyday tasks such as shopping, cooking and cleaning. Given the age of the granddaughters, this was a worrying transition period and we do not know what the outcome of it was, given our interview only captured this moment.

## Violence against women

For some women, ageing entailed a continued sense of having to deal with the consequences of the violence that they endured during their lifetime at the hands of their partners. So, before concluding, we wanted to discuss how, for women, the violence that some experienced when they were younger continued to pose a challenge to their self-care.

Some women continue to feel pain and the consequences of having experienced violence on the part of their partners and husbands when they were younger. Even if they were no longer in those relationships, the physical consequences of the violence suffered were still with them.

Irene, 80 years old from a peri-urban area of Tarija, for example, had been hospitalised several times when she was younger and living with her husband, as a result of the violence she suffered at his hands. She started the interview recounting all her sadness and suffering, before talking about more mundane things like remittances or where her children live. In the interview, she described how she was given away by her mother to a man when she was 14 or 15 years old. He took her to Bermejo and had her living in a very basic house. A number of her babies died. One died in her womb when she was eight months pregnant as a result of a beating. Another baby was born dead, a baby boy, but his twin sister survived. She framed her whole interview with the suffering and the violence she experienced – almost a haunting presence of her ex-husband (she left him eventually) who she saw later on in the street with only one eye, the other one having fallen out, 'like a ball'. Maybe a punishment.

Irene's suffering goes further than just her husband. Her father died when she was eight years old, and her mother gave her to her grandmother to raise 'because she was tired of me crying'. She said they had a *'patrón'* (landowner). He came one day to tell her mother to give over her children so he could put them to work. This part of the interview is unclear, but it seems that she was raped, as she said that she 'was made to pay on the mattress'.

Irene underwent different surgeries. During the interview she said that she did not need help but is tired all the time and no longer feels like working. She complained of a knee problem but, given her age and history of violence, this is a minor ailment (TRJ10).

Similarly, Laura was married for a long time. She had six children, but her husband was violent. He beat her, including with a stone, and she describes how one day he tried to kill her. She used urine to treat a head injury and did not go to the hospital. She went to Argentina so she could be far from him and effectively end the relationship. She stayed with her eldest daughter, who was living there with her children, having also separated from her husband. Laura left her own children in Bolivia with her other eldest daughter. She seemed traumatised by so much violence, describing how her husband was jealous even of the priest and how he begged her to come back to him and would not leave her alone, trying to convince her to return to him (TRJ18).

Arminda, who was from a rural area in Cochabamba, also mentioned violence and aggression in her relationship with her husband. She had to stop working when she moved from Argentina to Bolivia, because her husband was jealous. She used to get on well with her mother-in-law, who only spoke Quechua. But moving to Bolivia meant that she lost the support of her own parents, who helped look after her children so she could work without her husband noticing. Her daughter has since migrated to Argentina and this seems to have triggered her husband's aggression again, because their son, who stayed with them, is often out so there is nobody else at home to provide a buffer against her husband's jealousy and aggression (CBB7).

Arminda's story is the only one that links violence directly to the migration of her children. But we included the other stories because we felt it was an important acknowledgement of the consequences of violence that women continue to suffer in older age. However, the other two testimonies are also linked to migration, albeit the interviewees'. Irene's experience of violence might not have been as extreme had she stayed closer to home. Although violence against women is endemic in Bolivia, there are also mechanisms that aim to mitigate against it (Harris, 1994). Laura, on the other hand, used migration to escape abuse from a violent partner, which is also not an unusual strategy for women who are in a violent relationship (Bastia, 2011).

## Conclusion

The organisation of care in transnational families is a core dimension of the research. Investigating how and who cares for older adults has meant finding examples of reciprocal care. We found that older adults continue to care for members of their family, since there is also an affective dimension that crosses this responsibility. In this sense, the majority of the people interviewed have shown concern and a sense of responsibility to care for their children and grandchildren, including the economic dimension through reverse remittances and the obligation they feel regarding leaving inheritance to all their children.

Older adults not only care for family members, but also contribute to their immediate communities, through paid but also unpaid work that also involves leadership roles and representation in different associations, which we discuss in Chapter 10.

Except for one case already mentioned which required everyday practical care, most of the people interviewed are cared for by their children in Bolivia, especially in rural areas. The average number of children in this area is higher than in other areas and some children stay with their parents to dedicate themselves to agricultural activity. As noted in Chapter 6, some children abroad have helped their parents when they needed healthcare, but older adults generally refuse to receive help from their children or ask for their children to visit them in Bolivia when they need care.

Likewise, in the organisation of care, in some families it is the grandchildren in Bolivia who support their older relatives, mainly in daily care. Other sources of support include extended family members and, to a lesser extent, neighbours and people in the immediate community.

We have found cases in which grandparents have assumed the care of their grandchildren, even without receiving any financial support. This is the reason why many of our interviewees have to work to ensure family support. Undoubtedly, this type of situation becomes more complex when older adults have health problems or other ailments related to the ageing process.

From a gender perspective, our study highlights the invisible work of women, who are the ones who dedicate the most time to caring for others. Women tend to care for grandchildren, husbands and other family members. Some women have travelled to help with their daughters' pregnancies. The cases found portray a latent reality in Bolivia. Despite not having official data that quantifies the unpaid domestic and care work carried out by women, it is estimated that they spend more than twice as much time on care and domestic work compared to men (OXFAM, 2019).

Overall, we found more instances of interviewees looking after others than the other way around. Women bear most of these responsibilities. As we will see in the chapter that follows, they also draw emotional satisfaction form these relationships and obligations. However, the fact remains that women bear higher responsibilities for care than men, even when they start to find the bearing of these responsibilities difficult.

Only women of higher socio-economic status are able to draw benefits of their children paying for care. Those belonging to the middle higher socio-economic groups and those who practice transnational livelihoods in Tarija are also able to participate in reciprocal care practices – for example, travelling abroad to help with childbirth and the post-partum period. However, these experiences are not available to most of the other interviewees who belong to the middle and lower socio-economic groups and whose mobility is constrained because of visa restrictions or lack of financial resources.

In exceptional cases, the care needs of older people are not being met. Sonia's testimony provides evidence that sometimes the delicate balance of making sure that one's needs are being met tips over and older people then find themselves in situations of extreme vulnerability. This happens when family support systems are not also complemented by wider social networks and there is no governmental (regional or municipal) institution that takes over the care that the ageing parent requires. In Sonia's case, this situation was further compounded by the fact that she herself continued to have care responsibilities for her adolescent granddaughters, despite the fact that neither she nor her granddaughters could meet her daily needs.

# 9

# Emotional responses to (adult) children's migration

## Introduction

Emotional care represents the third pillar of our transnational care framework. In this section, we expand on our definition of emotional care and then go on to analyse our interviewees' responses to their adult children's migration. As part of our interviews we asked how parents experienced and reacted to their adult children's migration. This question was for us a way of opening up discussion about emotions. We were also hoping to use answers to this question as the basis to then further unpack how migrant children supported (or not) their ageing parents' wellbeing (which we discuss in Chapter 10).

At the beginning of this research, we had expected that the departure of their adult children would represent a significant event in the interviewees' lives. The literature that was available at the time (2013) painted a rather bleak picture of the consequences that the migration of adult children had for their parents who remained in their countries of origin. For example, Vullnetari and King's papers on the mass exodus of people from Albania depicted migrants' parents as being in a desperate situation, effectively abandoned by their adult children to a sad life of hardship and loneliness (Vullnetari and King, 2008). They used language such as 'adult orphans' to describe the dire situation they were in. More recent literature from Eastern Europe continues to use this kind of language and argues that older people are abandoned and find it difficult to cope when their children leave (Iossifova, 2020). Reading about these findings, we had assumed a similar situation would be true in Bolivia, given that it is a relatively poor country in terms of its economic development and material resources available to most of the population. If this were the case, then, we had also assumed that the departure of the migrant adult children would have been felt as a significant turning point in the lives of our interviewees. However, while this was indeed a common experience, we were also surprised that in many cases the departure of one's children was not only expected, but sometimes it had been actively encouraged. Moreover, in some cases, the actual departure was hardly remembered. We argue in this chapter that the older people's experiences and how older people experience their children's migration were influenced by the region's migration history and practices, temporality and, to some extent, gender.

## The day sons and daughters left

In our interviews we were particularly interested in finding out how our interviewees felt when their children left to go to another country. In some cases, that first separation was marred by sadness, particularly for women. This was the case also when, overall, interviewees might have had a positive evaluation of their children's migrations. When we asked Patricia, a 63-year-old woman living in an urban area, about her son's first migration, she became sad and tearful. She said: 'I didn't know where he was going, what his life would be like over there. At the beginning he suffered a lot, he wasn't finding work. … He was calling us; we were calling him' (OR11). We need to remember that, at the time, it was expensive to call and people did not have access to mobile phones and WhatsApp like today.

Being far away from one's children raised anxiety about how they would cope if something happened. Monica, a 61-year-old woman living in an urban area, whose daughter was in Spain, talked about being more sentimental about potential changes in her life: 'more in emotional terms, isn't it. She was far … anything that might happen, you cannot do anything straight away, so I always said "Oh my God! What will we do if something happens, who will we reach out to?"' (OR16). Monica relates changes as being emotional, rather than economic.

Although these experiences of sadness were more common among women and those in urban areas, they were not confined to this group of interviewees. Gerónimo, a 70-year-old man, living in a rural area in Tarija, had a similar response:

> I felt sad, they left, as we were saying, because there was no water. They bought land but they didn't have water. … This has changed since there is no work … there is no one to help, they had sheep, goats, donkeys, cows. They looked after them. They sold everything. They only have a few cows now. … It is a loss when children leave [*Pérdida es cuando los hijos migran*]. (TRJ1)

Mercedes, also from Tarija, recalls how she could not stop crying when her eldest left for Argentina. She was very sad:

> Oh, it was sad, I was crying, nooo, my son is going away, I was crying like that. Will he come back or not? I was crying a lot because of my son, it was bad, and because of that, he came back. He was away for two years. … For me, it was all just crying, I was talking about him, waiting for him, he is going to come back any time, he is going to come in [to the house], I would make food for him in vain, and then I would feed the children, 'Mami don't cry, he is going to come back

any time'. And he did come back but he was no longer attached to me, not anymore, not anymore. (TRJ4)

Although her son did eventually return, she felt that she had lost that connection with him, they had lost the closeness that they used to have before he left (TRJ4).

Although it was more common for women to talk about their children's departure in emotional terms and for men to highlight a loss of work help and companionship, some men did also talk about their children's migration in emotional terms (see also section on 'Gender' in this chapter). Néstor, for example, was also very sad when his children left: '[A]h … very sad [his eyes teared up], I never separated from them, since they were small, the day they left I was very hurt. I still suffer' (LP2).

While for some there was a sense of inevitability that their children will leave, because of the constraints they would face in making a living (see Chapter 5), some also expressed that the sadness they felt when their children migrated was also inevitable. In the words of Lucia, who lived in a peri-urban area in Cochabamba: 'How will I not be sad, they are my children' (CBB11).

## Marriage and army service

However, while our focus was on migration, when asked about separation and how our interviewees responded to them, they sometimes brought up examples from other life cycle events that led to children moving out of their parents' homes and becoming independent of their parents: marriage and entering the compulsory army service.

In fact, in some of the interviews, interviewees started talking about migration but then shifted to marriage, conflating both events, given that both experiences involve separation and children setting up their own lives that are, to varying degrees, separate from their parents. Maria, from a rural area in Oruro, said:

> [S]he left, she called me from there … what am I going to tell her, she left with her husband, right? … Here she used to work, she used to sell things, she used to buy things and sell them off, she was in Santa Cruz, she lived there. They left from there. (OR1)

In this case, an internal migration had preceded her daughter's international migration but, in addition, she had also left with her husband. In this sense, she had already been 'apart'. To note here is also the fact that internal migration from the western parts of the country, like Oruro, towards Santa Cruz and Cochabamba is also expected and there seems to be little difference between internal and international migration. The western regions of La

Paz, Potosí and Oruro present a tendency to expel people, with migrants usually being in the economically active age range (INE, 2019).

For example, in her recollection of the day her children left, Eusebia, a 68-year-old woman from a rural town in Cochabamba, merged the separation from her daughter as a result of migration with her marriage. When asked about the day her children left, she said:

> I felt bad, at least when they got married [cries], each one, but I said, no, you want to get married, but why? Why don't you study? No, so I told them to study but unfortunately their partners didn't let them study any longer. ... [The day they left] I felt destroyed [*deshecha*] because we had always lived together, we had never been separated, but as they got married, they would distance themselves, they would have their own homes, so our lives would be like this. (CBB2)

Marisa made a similar slippage from our question asking about her son's migration. In her answer, she referred to her son going to do the military service. When asked whether she was sad when her first child left, she said: 'I was sad, but my son said, "You're not going to cry." When he came back from the military service, I prepared a barbecue for him' (CBB10).

For some, then, the inevitability is not necessarily linked to international migration but more related to life-course events and their children having reached the point in their lives when they become independent and start building their own lives. Growing up and becoming independent will, for some, involve moving or looking for work abroad. However, for some parents, moving abroad was not necessarily very different to their children making similar choices but more locally.

It is important to bear in mind that migration is only one of the reasons why adult children move away from their parents' home. Attitudes and experiences of separation due to migration need to be understood within this broader framework of life-course transitions.

## Depression and mental health

In some cases, the sadness that might be considered an expected response to a long separation to a distant destination became more persistent and developed into depression. Again, as already discussed, quite severe sadness and depression were talked about in these terms, particularly by women in urban areas. Depression was mentioned explicitly by a small number of women, particularly in Cochabamba (three) and Santa Cruz (one). Their 'sadness' was clearly linked to their isolation and feeling lonely. But this does not mean that only these four interviewees experienced depression. This number is more an indication of the background and context of the women who described their feelings in this ways and were also able to access medical support for their emotional state.

Juana, 68 years old, from Cochabamba, had three children in the United States. They had been away for 15 years, and she missed them a lot. She felt sad about them being so far away. She said she was depressed and had the feeling of having to solve all problems by herself, which she found difficult (CBB4).

Marta, a 63-year-old woman living in an urban area, whose daughter has an orthodontist practice in São Paulo, was financially well-off but mentioned that she had been depressed and felt lonely because her daughter was so far away. She talked about feeling disheartened and not wanting to get up or get dressed. 'The solitude, sometimes I feel lazy [*me da pereza*], I don't feel like getting changed, tidy myself up, I feel really down that I feel agitated [*me intranquiliza*], and I say I would like to die' (CBB18). She was sad when her daughter left, but she thought that she was going to return after she finished her studies in Brazil. However, her daughter stayed there and opened up an orthodontist practice. Marta was managing her finances and sometimes visited her.

Florencia, a 75-year-old woman living in an urban area, whose daughter had to leave for the United States 13 years ago because of Florencia's debts, used to sit in parks and cry. Then she started going to a Catholic church and started being active in its activities, organising events such as Easter. She served the church for ten years, which provided her with relief from the suffering she was experiencing as a result of her daughter not being there. Her daughter's departure had been particularly traumatic because it was linked to a business failure and accumulation of debt that they were not able to repay. Florencia still owed money to the bank at the time of the interview (CBB19).

Dona Celia (SC21), mentioned in more detail later in this chapter, described how she had sold her large house to move closer to her second son's young family and built a small house adjacent to his. However, her son then found a great job and moved abroad the year after. She fell into depression, did not want to leave the house and felt herself closing in. The house was lonely and silent. She was fine during the day because she kept busy with work, but evenings were difficult. She started getting better when she decided to seek professional help and then made an active plan to visit her friends regularly. She had private health insurance and her own job. She was able to access psychiatric support and eventually got better when she tapped into her wide social networks and set up regular weekly meetings to play cards with her friends. At some point, she had two groups going, with different friends.

Mixed feelings were also common. Alba, 70 years old, said that she felt both happiness and sadness:

[S]ometimes we are very selfish, we want to have them by our side, but they need to follow their own path, and I think sometimes, that's like a river, no? That the children are like the water that flows, and one cannot stop it, you have to allow it to flow its course. (OR17)

She was happy because her daughter had a professional job in France and was working as a commercial engineer. She was responsible for sales in an international pharmaceutical company. However, she was sometimes sad because she thinks that her daughter will not return to Bolivia. She has French nationality and has formed her own family there:

It was always my dream that she would go abroad and then come back after two or three years, but in her case it was different. She got married there, has French nationality not because she got married but because of her university degree, because of her studies. So, she also always dreamt of having a different life to the one that she had here, so she is also very happy. (OR17)

These experiences and ways of expressing emotional states such as sadness and depression were more common among parents in the higher socio-economic groups. Three of the four interviewees mentioned in this section had higher levels of education, good incomes and private insurance. They also had some support networks and were able to articulate their state of mind in this way. They were all in a much better position than Sonia, for example, discussed in the previous chapter, who, despite her difficult situation, said that 'everything was OK'.

## The inevitability of migration

These emotional responses to migration also need to be understood within a context where migration is seen as inevitable. In some regions, some interviewees expressed very little emotional reactions related to their children's migration. In Oruro, some interviewees talked about their children's migration as inevitable given migration has been taking place for a long time and the fact that the interviewees themselves had previously migrated internally. Victor, a 75-year-old man living in a peri-urban area of La Paz, commented:

[O]f course, that moment I felt, right? But then I thought … let him go … let him know what life is like, so that he can form himself, so that he can be a bit more responsible and so he went. I told his mother that he is going to leave, and she started crying, as any mother would, no? But afterwards … let him go! So he went, he went, it's been … 30 years, he has been there for so many years. (LP1)

While for those interviewees with higher levels of education and higher incomes, the migration of their children always took place when they were already adults – whether for studies, work or personal reasons – for those with limited or no formal education and lower income levels, their children sometimes had to start migrating when they were still children. As already discussed, child migration is common practice in Tarija, but it is not confined to this area. Felisa, a woman living in a peri-urban area of Oruro, said in Quechua, about her son: '[A]t the age of 12 he went to La Paz, from La Paz to Cochabamba, from Cochabamba to Mendoza and from Mendoza to Chile. He has also been in Santa Cruz' (OR8). 'When asked if he was sad when his children left, Guillermo replied: "Yes, always but what am I going to do, they grow up and they leave' (TRJ14). The same exact words were repeated by Hilda, who said that she was sad about her children being away but at the same time, there was little that they can do given there are no jobs locally: 'Of course, I feel sad but what am I going to do?' (TRJ17).

Often this sense of inevitability is linked to local work conditions, such as lack of water for farming, or a sense that further career prospects are not possible, unless one is politically well connected. For example, Angela said that her children migrated to Chile because there was no work locally: 'They went to work and they got lost there, they stayed there' (OR9). Florencia, whose daughter left for the United States 13 years prior to the interview, talked about how her daughter would never have been able to practise law, which she studied at university, had she stayed in Bolivia because, she said, 'it's all down to politics', meaning that to get a job one needs political connections (CBB18).

There is some sadness associated with them being abroad, but at the same time acceptance that this is the only option for them.

## Migration histories and practices

In some regions, migration is a well-established livelihood strategy that people have practised for decades. Tarija is a case in point. Many of the people we interviewed had engaged in seasonal migration since they were themselves young adults, sometimes even children. In many communities where water and access to local labour markets is scarce, it was customary for families to spend six months in Argentina and six months in Bolivia. When asked about their children's first migration, our interviewees indicated that they had started migrating when they were children, and they had themselves 'taught' their children how to migrate. This was the only region where it was customary for our interviewees' children to start to migrate *as children*, rather than when they were young adults. They did so with their families or with others who took them to Argentina to work. This was sometimes a relative or the landowner, who in some ways had a claim on the children's labour. This 'teaching' of migration to their children points to the fact that there was no clear beginning to a migration event, but that migration was not just embedded within local livelihood strategies but also part of the Bolivian migration *habitus* (Bourdieu and Nice, 1977; Hinojosa, 2010).

Emiliana, who was a 65-year-old woman from a rural area, for example, engaged in a migration practice that was typical in the region of Tarija, where families spent six months in Bolivia and six months in Argentina. Emiliana first went to Argentina when she was about ten years old, travelling with an aunt but after a year found her own job looking after children. She met her husband when she was 21 years old. He was also from the same village. After they became a couple, they started migrating together and continued to do so after they had their children (TRJ3).

There were many other examples. Isabel said that both her daughters left when they were 15 and 16 respectively (TRJ13). One left with her partner. The other was taken by a local man to work as a domestic worker. She then returned when she was older, with her own family.

Eva, 87 years old, also recalled that her children started migrating when they were still very young: her son first left when he was 12 years old to work as a *peón* or labourer. Her daughters left when they were 14 or 15, to work in people's homes, as domestic workers. Her son was in his 60s at the time of the interview but she still remembered being sad when he first went. She had to cross the border with him because they did not allow minors to travel by themselves. One of her daughters was 'taken away by a man, who didn't bring her back'. She had five children with him. Then he died and she came back (TRJ2).

Similarly, Guillermo had a very strong connection with Argentina. He started working in Argentina when he was 12 years old. He was taken by the *patrón*, who treated him badly, only paid him occasionally, until he was old enough to work on his own (17–18 years old). He then stayed in Mendoza for five years to work in agriculture. He had no communication with his parents during this time and he missed them. After a while, he returned. He had a wife and two daughters, but his wife left taking one of their daughters with her, leaving the other one who was still small with him. He said that she died at the age of three 'because she missed [her mum]'. He then remarried and had five children. To save them the suffering he had gone through, he took them to Argentina himself (his wife did not want to travel) until they were old enough (16–17) and they decided to stay there: 'And when they decided to stay there, what did you think? They were already grown up, they were young adults, *jóvenes*, and they took the decision themselves' (TRJ14).

These examples and others we introduced in earlier chapters (for example, Irene in Chapter 8) clearly point to a situation where migration is a structural element of the local economy, which has been practised for decades, if not centuries. Being passed down from parents to children, it does not point to something that is exceptional or out of the ordinary. Structural conditions, particularly in rural areas, are such that they do not allow young people to find sustainable livelihoods locally, either in agriculture or in the local paid economy. They therefore look to Argentina as the source of work and livelihoods.

The examples also show the very unequal social structure that exists in Tarija, as it does elsewhere in Bolivia. Young people are sometimes 'taken away' or 'given away' to better-off individuals, who might be related through the fictive relations system – *parentesco* – which ties poorer and better-off families in an unequal but mutual and reciprocal system of cooperation (see, for example, Miranda, 2017). The same system that allows children to work in the fields for local landowners or young rural girls to be given to better-off 'family members' in towns and cities to work as domestic workers, is also used trans-locally and transnationally. These children ended up becoming migrants, because the better-off relatives either lived or had economic interests in Argentina. The fact that there was no actual beginning of migration as a strategy that people could identify, meant that migration did not assume the significant 'turning point' in the older person's life that we had imagined.

In Bolivia, unlike other countries in the region, due to the prevalence of these cultural practices, Law No. 263, Comprehensive Law against Human Trafficking and Smuggling of 2012, recognises customary servitude as a type of human trafficking. This is defined as the action by which one person is subjected or exploited by another under ties associated with customary and traditional practices of the place, such as patronage, any other spiritual bond or relationship of power. It is punishable by deprivation of liberty for a term of 10–15 years. However, implementation is difficult given the widespread nature of these practices.

In other regions, where migration started or at least intensified more recently, our interviewees had a more marked experience of their children's migration. In Cochabamba and Santa Cruz, for example, it was much more common to find that interviewees at least remembered when their adult children migrated. In some cases, this was a significant experience for them, as shown at the beginning of this chapter. However, even here, we came across examples where our interviewees talked quite off-hand about their children's migration, as indicated earlier, where interviewees explained that their children 'just left' and this was seen as inevitable rather than surprising.

## Temporality

Temporality also influenced how our interviewees felt about their children's migration. In the case of Tarija, our interviewees were brought up in a context of frequent migration to Argentina and their children had started migrating when they were teenagers. At the time of the interview sometimes 40 years had passed since their children's first migration. Parents had assimilated their children's migrations and normalised their absence, so they did not feel there was anything unusual about them living in another country for at least part of the year. To the extent that these transnational living arrangements were practised by many other households within their communities, they represented what is normal within that context.

Strong emotional feelings of abandonment or solitude were more common in cases where the interviewees' children had migrated more recently or where their migration had not been envisaged. For example, Celia, mentioned earlier, was in her late 60s at the time of the interview. She continued to work and also had an active circle of friends. She had three sons, two of whom lived abroad. She was quite close to her two sons who took jobs abroad. In fact, she had built a house right next to one of them, just before he travelled to Peru. She was very sad when her sons left, especially the youngest one, and had to seek specialised support for depression (SC21).

> Well, I was very sad when my son left. I had never been away from them. They had their house here, right? He was already married, he had his two daughters and on the one hand I was happy, I mean, they were mixed feelings [*sentimientos encontrados*], right? I was happy that he had those achievements, because they sent him to Peru for a competition and he won and I was very proud to know that my son had achieved that [*mi hijo está realizado*], that he lives well, he works well. But on the other hand, so much sadness to be separated from him and from my granddaughters, right? Having granddaughters is incredible, for me, it was wonderful because I had only had sons, men, I was crazy about the girls … with my eldest granddaughters we used to play, right? We made houses, played dolls, everything that I hadn't played with my sons. We were so close with my granddaughters and the separation was really sad. So, as I said, they were mixed feelings. On the one hand, happy to see my son achieved what he had aimed to achieve [*realizado*], it is true, they are very well, happy. (SC21)

Temporality was so important that even in cases where the interviewees' children had passed away (for example, TRJ3) or they had lost contact with them, if significant time had passed, the interviewees had found ways of dealing with their loss. For Gladys, who was 67 years old at the time of the interview, a lot of time has passed. Two of her children travelled to Argentina, one when he was 15 years old and the other one when he was 20. However, she never regained contact with one of her sons. The one who migrated when he was 15 years old still lived in Buenos Aires and worked in agriculture. The other one she never heard back from since he left.

She did not know whether he was dead or alive and speculated he might be with his father in Santa Cruz. She used to worry about him, but 40 years had passed so she did not worry about him anymore (TRJ5).

In Eva's case, a woman who was 87 at the time of the interview, the migration of her children took place about 50 years ago, so a lot of time has passed since then, and their lives have moved on (TRJ2).

However, for some, when contact had been lost more recently, the emotional worry was sometimes compounded by physical ailments, as was the case for Diana. Her son left seven years prior to the interview but he had been 'lost' for five months. She continued to worry about him. He went silent after being in touch monthly for the first two years after he went to Argentina. She tried not to worry because the doctor told her that worrying is bad for her blood pressure (SC12).

## Gender

As is already clear from some of the examples included in the previous sections, gender was also a significant factor in explaining both how interviewees experienced their children's migration but also how they talked about it. The distinction between the experience and the way this is related is obviously difficult to untangle. Women and men often talk about their memories in quite different ways. In previous research, it was found that women use more speech and dialogue than men when they talk about their memories (Ely and McCabe, 2009; Leydesdorff et al, 2009). We also found that women were more likely to talk about their experiences in emotional terms. This could be because women were more affected by their children's absence, although it could also be that they just talked about this in different ways to men. Celia is a clear example of somebody who not only related to her children's migration in terms of loss, but she also talked about this in emotional terms (SC21). Other examples include Florencia, from Cochabamba, who talked about wandering the parks of the city, sitting on benches, on her own, and crying after her daughter left, until she was befriended by a member of a local church, who offered friendship and an open door to the church (CBB19).

Men also talked about their children's migration in terms of loss. However, they related the experience of their loss more in relation to something that was lost in conjunction with their children's departure, for example, loss of companionship or help in the fields. They rarely talked about just missing their children based on the close relationship they had, which was often how women framed their experience, particularly when the ones to leave were daughters. Men tended to add a more practical dimension to their 'missing the children'. For example, Luciano, 75 years old, from a rural area in Cochabamba, said that he was sad about his children being away, mostly because the children could not help with agricultural work and given he and his wife were getting older, it was more difficult for them to do physical work. His wife, on the other hand, said that she cried when they left and, again, when they went back to Argentina after visiting recently (CBB14). Similarly, Francisco said that he was initially very sad that they left, but after some time, he got used to the idea and was also happy that they had found their own way of making a living. He missed his son – not just the help that he provided in the fields, but also the companionship: 'His absence was difficult, I missed them a lot, every day I felt their absence in the house, at work, I missed them talking to me, their companionship, also at work and now I don't have anyone to help me' (CBB15).

Men, particularly those in rural areas, also expressed sadness when they saw their children's possibilities for education being truncated by their migration projects. In many Latin American countries, education is seen as the only way to escape poverty and manage to be 'somebody' in life (Crivello, 2011). In our interviews, leaving school and not going to university as a result of migration was associated with missed opportunities, which had both emotional and material connotations, as explained by Juvenal, a 72-year-old father from rural Cochabamba, whose four children all migrated to the United States and Spain. 'I never wanted him to go, I was demoralised, my eldest son, I wanted him to be a doctor, we would have had money as well, but it didn't happen' (CBB5). This was also the case for Humberto, who despite having been to Argentina himself, said to his children that they should prioritise their studies: 'I told them to study but ... no, he didn't want to, he left with his friends, and he hasn't come back.' He had been in Buenos Aires for more than 17 years at the time of the interview (OR2).

However, for some men the separation was emotionally difficult as well. Javier, 79 years old, from an urban area, was very sorry when his daughter left for Argentina. She went to visit her siblings and travelled with her mum, but then she just stayed there, some 30 or 40 years back. He said he cried for a long time and then was so cross that he sold his house and moved to Tarija (TRJ6). Similarly, Alvaro also talked about being sad when his daughters left: 'as any father, I was bitter sad ... maybe they were not going to find luck here in Bolivia so we let them go' (OR4).

Sometimes women described their partner's reaction, such as Elsa, who talked about her husband's reaction when their daughter left for Spain:

> Oh no [shouts], we cried, my husband and I, my husband cried and shouted at the airport, he said 'Lord, I feel like my heart is going to break'. We cried when the plane left, we walked all over Santa Cruz, without knowing where to go, it was so bad, we suffered a lot for my daughter, his daughter, he adored her [*era su adoración, su adoración*]. (SC2)

Overall, while both men and women missed their children, the way they expressed the consequences of their children's migrations in emotional terms differed. Women were more likely to be more expansive with their explanations of how they experienced the separation from their children emotionally. Women were also more likely to talk about mental health difficulties, including depression. Men also missed their children, but they tended to add a more 'practical' dimension to their emotional responses, such as missing their children's help in the fields. Those men who openly expressed sadness, for example, by crying or saying that they had cried when their son or daughter left, were exceptions.

## Conclusion

The emotional responses to the migration of adult children need to be understood in the context within which these events happened. Besides place and gender, the socio-economic background of the interviewees influenced how they spoke about their experiences and possibly also what they felt at the time their adult children left.

Regarding perceptions around the migration of children, although we had initially thought that migration would be a significant turning point in the lives of older adults, we found that migration is in a way something that is expected and encouraged, as it is synonymous with a better future or ideals of progress. As shown, it is likely that this is a result of the historical nature of migration, even more so in some regions, where there is a generational logic linked to smaller parcels of land as a result of inheritance practices in rural areas while urban areas suffer from structural issues linked to a lack of job opportunities.

In some contexts, seeking work abroad through migration is seen as inevitable. Where there is not enough land for everyone to practice subsistence agriculture or there is no irrigation to grow crops, young adults need to seek a living elsewhere. Similar needs arise also in middle-class families, whose children might have studied, but they lack the necessary connections to find a job to match their training. So for some interviewees, there is some acceptance of this inevitability.

Some interviewees did not feel comfortable talking about their emotions. But among those who did, gender, their socio-economic background as well as the history of migration in their locality strongly influenced how they spoke about their emotional responses to their children's migrations. Women tended to be more expansive, but this was generally true of women who have a medium or higher socio-economic background. This does not mean that men and women of lower socio-economic background did not have emotional responses to their children's migration. Their silence in this area shows a reticence to share their emotional responses in an interview setting or the need to express their emotions in different ways.

In regions where migration is customary, where younger people are expected to migrate and seek work elsewhere, there is less of a rupture of familial relations, given migration is inscribed within life-course expectations. Similarly, when a long time has passed since their children's migration, the feelings were less raw, even in cases where children abroad had passed away or communication had been lost, as we also discuss in the next chapter.

Undoubtedly, temporality, that is, the time that has passed since the children migrated, is an important factor. The feeling of isolation and abandonment was mentioned by older adults whose children had migrated more recently. But for those where significant time has passed, sometimes decades, compounded by a local history of migration, there was more of a sense of acceptance.

As we noted, women and men talked about their children's absence in different ways. Women were more likely to talk about depression, especially in urban areas. Children were often a source of companionship but this was not stressed in places like Tarija, where migration has historically been part of their livelihood strategies and usually some children stayed behind.

In general, mothers and fathers that we interviewed have been quite ambivalent about their children's migration. On the one hand, there is sadness and sorrow for the departure of the children, but on the other, they were expected to migrate for the sake of their own wellbeing and that of their families. Especially for mothers in urban areas, migration has led to problems of depression as a result of their sense of loneliness. This is even more so the case when they presume that the migration of their children has no return, as in cases of professional migration, when they have already acquired the nationality of the country of destination or when they have already consolidated their families abroad.

# 10

# Emotional care and wellbeing

Building on the previous chapter, in this chapter we explore emotional care within the transnational social spaces parents inhabit when their adult children leave. Overall, in this chapter we are interested in understanding how emotional care and wellbeing changes through the migration process. Does the migration of their (usually adult) children have an impact on the migrants' parents' emotional wellbeing? Do adult children abroad support their parents' emotional wellbeing? If so, in what ways? And how else do ageing parents ensure their emotional care and wellbeing?

We begin answering these questions by focusing on interviewees' closest relations – how they keep in touch and visit their children abroad – and then expand to assess their broader networks, including their communities and association lives. We play close attention to communication, including whether and how frequently ageing parents communicate with their children abroad, and the nature of their conversations, paying some attention also to instances when communication breaks down. Some parents stopped having contact with their migrant children, while others also experienced bereavement through their child's death abroad. We discuss these experiences in this chapter, before moving on to visiting practices – both of migrant children visiting their ageing parents and vice versa. We found that social networks, churches and associational life play an important role in how our interviewees related to their lives, so we discuss these in a section, before concluding with a discussion of how grandparents also draw support and satisfaction from exercising their role of grandparents.

## Communication

> Ah my son calls … twice a week, sometimes he says, be careful mami, take care mami, he always calls, sometimes he sings to me. (LP4)

Communication clearly plays an important role in enabling parents to feel connected with their children abroad. Among our interviewees, regular and open communication promoted closeness and a sense that the actual distance can be bridged. Those who were in contact regularly with their children abroad felt that they were to some extent participating in their daily activities. It also allowed children abroad to keep in close contact with the changing needs of their parents and provide emotional as well as practical support where needed.

Access to communication improved quite significantly during the duration of this project. While during the pilot study (2013) quite a few interviewees lacked direct access to phones or internet, this was quite rare during the last wave of data collection (2019–2020). Almost everyone (93 per cent) had a way of communicating with their children abroad and it was quite rare for parents not to be in contact with their children abroad. In fact, only 7 per cent were not in touch with their children abroad. The reasons for this were varied, but usually included losing contact with their children once they moved abroad, either because they stopped calling or because there was an argument, and their communication broke down.

Of those who were in communication with their children, over half (54 per cent) used the telephone, 41 per cent used WhatsApp, while the remainder used radio, messages passed on through other children or letters. There were significant differences between urban, peri-urban and rural areas, with the latter being the most disadvantaged in terms of access to mobile phones and signal coverage. In rural areas, everyone was in communication with their children abroad, while 10 per cent of respondents in both urban and peri-urban areas were not in touch with their children abroad, which was quite surprising given poorer access to signal and internet in rural areas, particularly during our pilot phase. However, the mode of communication differed between these areas. In rural areas, it was much more common to communicate via the telephone (69 per cent) as opposed to WhatsApp (26 per cent), while in peri-urban areas the modalities were 31 per cent and 48 per cent respectively and in urban areas 41 per cent and 45 per cent respectively.

If we look at this across socio-economic groups, the lack of access to smartphones with internet to be able to access WhatsApp and cheap, instantaneous messaging becomes most evident. While over two-thirds of those with higher socio-economic backgrounds had access to WhatsApp, this was the case for only half of those of medium socio-economic backgrounds and just over a fifth (22 per cent) of those with lower socio-economic backgrounds. Access to smartphones and internet then also translated into more frequent communication. While weekly communication was the most common frequency across all socio-economic groups, almost a third of those with higher socio-economic backgrounds reported having daily communication, while the next most common frequency for those of lower and medium socio-economic backgrounds was once a month (see Table 10.1).

During the pilot study in Cochabamba, which we carried out in 2013, Luciano mentioned that communication had improved, because they had mobile phones so their children could call often (CBB14). Interviewees who engaged in subsistence farming talked to their children once a week when they went to the *feria* – the weekly market – where there was mobile coverage (CBB21). However, even in urban areas, where some interviewees

**Table 10.1:** Communication mode and frequency by socio-economic group (%)

| | Socio-economic group | | | |
| --- | --- | --- | --- | --- |
| | Low (N=54) | Medium (N=30) | Higher (N=16) | Total |
| **Communication mode** | | | | |
| Internet café | 4 | 0 | 0 | 2 |
| Telephone | 65 | 37 | 25 | 50 |
| WhatsApp | 22 | 50 | 69 | 38 |
| Radio | 2 | 0 | 0 | 1 |
| Messages passed via others | 2 | 0 | 0 | 1 |
| Without information | 0 | 0 | 6 | 1 |
| Does not apply | 6 | 13 | 0 | 7 |
| *Total* | *100* | *100* | *100* | *100* |
| **Frequency** | | | | |
| Daily | 4 | 3 | 31 | 8 |
| Weekly | 44 | 40 | 50 | 44 |
| Every two weeks | 2 | 0 | 6 | 2 |
| Monthly | 37 | 37 | 6 | 32 |
| Only in emergencies | 2 | 0 | 0 | 1 |
| None | 2 | 0 | 0 | 1 |
| No information | 2 | 7 | 6 | 4 |
| Does not apply | 7 | 13 | 0 | 8 |
| *Total* | *100* | *100* | *100* | *100* |

had access to the internet, they used the internet for their own leisure, but not for talking to their children (CBB16). During the pilot, virtually nobody used the internet as a form of communication, save for Juvenal, who used it only when his youngest son, who was 18 years old, was online and he was able to connect too (CBB5), and Florencia, who has used it to talk to and 'see' (that is, video-call) her daughter, but not on a regular basis (CBB19).

By the time of the data collection in the last region, Oruro, everybody was using WhatsApp to communicate with their children – this was true across place of residence and socio-economic status (17/18 interviewees, with 1/18 interviewees for whom this question did not apply).

Interviewees also observed how much easier and cheaper it was to talk nowadays:

[B]efore we used to talk on the phone, now via WhatsApp. Before a call was 50 … a couple of words and it was already 50 bolivianos [just over US$7] but now it's free [he laughs]. (LP17)

> Thank god we have this WhatsApp, it's easier to talk, connect. Before with the phone, it was expensive … via WhatsApp we talk: 'How are you, my love?' 'I'm good, what are you doing?' 'I'm doing this thing, or the other, how is Dad?' 'Have you had your tea? Are you cooking?'. (LP10)

The technology is allowing families to stay together, despite the distance: 'I miss her, it is like our family has fragmented but now, luckily, with the technology, we are always in touch with video calls and this is really good … we call every week, including with the little one because I know a little bit of English' (LP19).

The most common frequency for communicating with their children abroad was weekly (44 per cent), then monthly (32 per cent), with 8 per cent communicating daily. Daily communication was most common for interviewees from higher socio-economic groups, as can be seen from Table 10.1. This is well illustrated by this quote from Inés, who was 61 years old and interviewed in La Paz:

> I have a very strong relationship with my daughter, every day, I am not exaggerating, I talk to her, thank God, I am grateful for the technology, these days I can talk to her every day. Before, imagine, without this technology, I think I would have died of sadness, impotence, desperation of not being able to talk to her, ask her how she is doing, if she needs anything. … I talk every day with my daughter, at least she says hello, she says 'Hi mum, I love you and I'm happy'. (LP5)

Often the children themselves bought the phones for their parents and taught them how to use them. Mercedes, for example, had a mobile phone and she knew how to answer it but not how to make phone calls. Others had a mobile phone but did not use it because they did not have credit (TRJ9). A couple of people relied on fixed telephones (for example, those in the home), while some received messages left with relatives who lived close by.

Radio was also used for communicating with children abroad. This was quite exceptional, and we came across this only in Santa Cruz. Efrain, for example, who used to go to the drop-in centre Hombres Nuevos in Plan 3000, said his son had not been in touch since he left seven years prior to the interview. He tried to call him via radio, leaving a message so he would get in touch, but he had not called. He said his son speaks to his sister though (SC10).

The modes and frequency of communication are useful indicators regarding whether parents and children are communicating but they do not tell us information about the quality of that communication. Transnational communication is complex and parents as well as children abroad often silence sensitive information about their wellbeing or their experiences (Sampaio, 2020). Our interviewees were well aware that children did not always 'tell it as it is'. For example, Consuelo, a 72-year-old woman interviewed in Santa Cruz, had a daughter who lived in Peru and had married a Peruvian man. Although her daughter only once mentioned that she would separate, she never talked to her mother about her relationship with her husband, but Consuelo found out through a friend that he was abusive towards her daughter. They had two children together and she also had another three children from previous relationships, who lived with Consuelo. Consuelo was worried both for her daughter being in a violent relationship and also what would happen to her grandchildren if their mother was to separate from her husband. But Consuelo did not feel that she could talk about this openly with her daughter (SC4).

Based on her research with Brazilian transnational families, Sampaio (2020) argues that what is not being said in transnational communication should also be understood as a form of caring, given migrants omit experiences and information from conversations as a form of protecting their parents from worrying and suffering (Sampaio, 2020).

Undocumentedness was also a source of worry and anxiety. Several interviewees mentioned continually being worried and anxious about their children abroad, because they lacked relevant documentation and this sometimes had an impact on their communications. Alejandro, for example, whose daughter was in Spain, mentioned that he did not know where she lived. He explained that she had not given him her contact details because she was undocumented and this would put her at risk (CBB16). Similarly, Eusebia's daughter in the United States was undocumented but, luckily, Eusebia was able to visit regularly and spend time with her grandchildren (CBB2).

## Deaths and disappearances

Sometimes communications did break down and this was clearly a source of worry and anxiety for ageing migrants' parents. Diana, interviewed in Santa Cruz, described how she had not heard from her son in Argentina for four or five months, when previously they would talk at least monthly. When asked 'What does your son do in Argentina?', she replied:

Well, I had information, people told me that he was working as a builder [*ayudante de albañil*] over there, but I don't know if that was true. Then somebody else said that he was working in a garment workshop. [Don't you talk?] Well, first he sent me messages, first he used to talk to me but lately he doesn't talk to me. He doesn't even send messages. I don't know what is happening with him, if he is dead or alive, I don't know, it's been four or five months since we talked. (SC12)

We came across a similar case in Oruro. Felisa, who we already introduced in Chapter 5, was over 60 years old, and had problems collecting her *Renta Dignidad* because of irregularities with some of her documents. She sold vegetables in the market to make ends meet. During the interview she was distressed because she lost communication with her son who migrated to Arica (Chile). In Quechua, she said that her son bought her a mobile phone that cost Bs1,000 (around US$144). She used to call him periodically, but about a year before the interview, she lost all contact with him. While crying she said that she even travelled to Arica to look for him, without success. She was also worried about the health of one of her daughters who was losing her sight. Sometimes her grandchildren get sick as well (OR8).

In a small number of cases, the children passed away or all communication stopped for no apparent reason and the parents did not have any information on the whereabouts of their children. This was the case for three interviewees in Tarija (TRJ3, TRJ5 and TRJ8), where they had children who died in Argentina. Similar to Diana, Gladys, who we mentioned earlier on, had not heard back from one of her sons since he left (TRJ5).

But contrary to Diana, who did not have information about her son, some of these parents knew that their children had died abroad. Emiliana had one child, a son, whom she raised on her own. He migrated to Argentina when he was about 25 years old. She went to see him a few times. Then he was killed a few years later (6–8) in a kidnapping or fight. He was stabbed multiple times. She had to go and get his body to bring him back to Tarija. She was sad when he left and did not want him to go. He used to help around the house and with the agricultural production (TRJ3).

Ignacia's eldest son went to Argentina when he was 20 but died a couple of years later, from an illness that they could not get a cure for. They tried both traditional and Western medicine, but he got ill in January and died in July (TRJ8).

Although anecdotal evidence suggests that deaths of Bolivians in regional migration centres, such as Buenos Aires, are not unusual, due to the racism and xenophobia that they experience (Bastia and vom Hau, 2014; Magliano and Ferreccio, 2017; Bastia, 2019), it is difficult to find reliable data on the actual number of deaths of Bolivians abroad, because this information is not being collected.

## Visiting

Besides more frequent and more accessible communication, the other aspect that helped people overcome the separation that is inherent in migration trajectories were visits – parents visiting children in their destinations or migrant children visiting their parents.

There seem to be two groups of people who are fairly mobile across borders and can therefore visit each other with relative ease: those of higher socio-economic backgrounds, who have the financial means to cover international visits; and those for whom transnational practice is a way of life. The former group includes older adults with higher levels of education and their adult children, who have been able to study to university level and sometimes beyond and find professional jobs abroad or those with better financial means. The latter group includes people with relatively low levels of education or no education at all, but who practice seasonal migration, which also includes regular periods of either agricultural or other work abroad, typically in Argentina. Some people have been able to develop this transnational way of living between Bolivia and the United States, despite having relatively low levels of education and working in agriculture (for example, those from Arbieto), but these were exceptions.

Visiting is an important part of transnational life (Baldassar, 2001; Miah et al, 2023). When migrants and/or their non-migrant relatives visit each other, they reassert their family bonds (Miah, 2022). In our interviews we found that those who can, engage in two-way visiting: parents visit children abroad and children visit their parents in the country of origin. However, restrictive migration regimes as well as sometimes exorbitant costs preclude these practices. Although just over a third (34 per cent) of our interviewees visited their adult children abroad, the ability to visit children abroad was concentrated among those with the financial means to do so or those whose livelihoods were embedded in transnational economic and social practices.

Travelling abroad for visits was directly correlated with socio-economic status. While 69 per cent of those with higher-middle socio-economic backgrounds visited their adult children abroad, only 24 per cent of those with lower socio-economic backgrounds did so. For those with middle socio-economic backgrounds the rate was 33 per cent. This information is quite illuminating. One would have expected that those with lower socio-economic backgrounds might also practice transnational visiting given their adult children are more likely to engage in regional migration movements, where borders are more porous, and travelling is economically more accessible. However, this is not the case. The much lower participation in transnational visiting can be explained by these parents' needs to keep working to make a living but also the fact that they are more likely to have large families. Some of their children would therefore most likely be still living close by, thereby reducing their need to visit those children who live abroad. For those of lower socio-economic backgrounds, whose children migrated to higher income countries, such as Europe or the United States, visa regimes and the cost of the trip makes visiting inaccessible.

Some interviewees decided not to visit their children abroad, despite being encouraged to do so by their children. This was sometimes because they did not know what to expect, for example, whether their daughters-in-law would treat them well. Mercedes, mentioned in the previous chapter, who cried when her son left, said that both her sons invited her to go to Argentina, but she did not want to go, in case her daughters-in-law are 'mean' and will not treat her well (TRJ4). At other times, their reluctance was related to responsibilities they had at home. Eva, who was 87 years old, introduced in the previous chapter, said there was nobody to help her look after her plants and animals. She also could not leave for long periods of time because she needed to attend weekly *Prosol* meetings and also regular community meetings, if she wanted to avoid a fine. She had visited her children in Argentina, and they wanted her to move there, but one of the places, Corrientes, was too cold, and the other one had lots of insects, and she said she could not get used to the changes (TRJ2).

Regional differences were also significant. While in La Paz, almost half (9/20) of all interviewees were able to visit their children abroad, in Santa Cruz this was possible for only two out of the 21 interviewees. The significant differences here are not only related to possible differences in sampling but largely to the fact that in Santa Cruz, international migration is a relatively recent phenomenon and migration largely focused on Spain. Visiting is therefore difficult given the existing migration regime in Spain and the fact that many of the newer migrants there will not have a settled migration status. For example, Marta's daughters have been away for ten years and said they will visit next year. They have not been back since they left (SC18). Undocumentedness also limits visiting and deters travelling across borders.

Interviewees told us that their children also make choices about where they live on the basis of their parents' perceived needs and to facilitate visiting, both in terms of accessing their parents in case something happened but also to make shorter and more frequent visits easier. Ezequiel, for example, had two children and both were in Argentina. They worked for themselves, renting land and growing vegetables. Their aim was to save money and go back to Tarija, but they have been away for 15–20 years. Over time, they have moved closer to where their father was living. They used to be in Santa Fe, but they felt it was too far, in case something happened. Ezequiel explained that his children were worried, that they used to say: 'if something happened to you daddy, we won't be able to come in time to see you, so they moved to near Jujuy, which is 2.5–3 hours from Tarija. They visit often, sometimes over weekends. He also travels there to see them. In fact, he was planning to go the day after the interviews (TRJ11).

Different children also visit more or less often, depending on where they live, their work and caring responsibilities, and how close they are to their parents.

Isabel was in regular contact with one of her daughters in Argentina, but she and her husband had a difficult relationship with another daughter, who set fire to plots and a house. They were not on talking terms. Isabel threw her out of her house, and they had no contact. There was a son as well, who was brought to her as a baby. Somebody left him at the hospital and she raised him. He visited from Argentina. She said she felt the absence of one of her daughters, but not of the other. They spoke on the mobile phone regularly. However, her daughter would spend more extended periods of time with Isabel, but she said she could not leave her family in Argentina for a very long time because she only has sons: 'Both of them are boys … they are both boys so she cannot leave them', referring to the gendered expectations that women and girls will be able to look after themselves but not men and boys, because they 'don't know' how to cook or wash clothes. She comes for a few days, three days or so, and then goes back (TRJ13).

Having animals also implies responsibilities that are not easily covered by other people and so preclude some interviewees from visiting their children abroad. Eva felt lonely and somehow tied to the house and the animals she had (dogs and chickens) as there was nobody to look after them when she was away. She said that if she did not have to look after her animals, she would go and visit her daughter in the city of Tarija and stay with her for a few days at a time. Of her three children abroad, one visited annually or twice a year, one visited three times a year, and one visited four to five times a year (TRJ2).

Those who visited less often usually made sure that they were there for the local saint's day. Ignacia said her children visit once a year, at the end of the year or in August. The year we carried out the interview, her daughter had visited in February so then she did not come in August. But when she visits in August, she makes sure the dates coincide with the Virgen de Chahuaya, a Virgin Mary they celebrate locally with *fiestas* (TRJ8).

In Oruro, the majority of the people interviewed (11/18) had travelled to visit their children abroad, especially to Argentina. Josefina commented that she had plans to go to Argentina to celebrate the end-of-year festivities with her three children (OR7). Beatriz said that her children will come to Oruro for the end of the year and that then she will travel to Chile with one of her daughters (OR10).

In La Paz almost half (nine out of 20) of our interviewees had visited their children abroad. Children's visits, in return, tended to coincide with the celebration of Santiago de Callapa, which is celebrated in the region of La Paz every 25 July to commemorate the anniversary of the Municipality and in honour of Saint Santiago. Every year migrants return to the village to celebrate the Municipality and the saint's day, usually to dance the *morenada*[1]: 'They arrive on the 25th of July … there will be *fiestas* … lots of *fiestas* … we have all sorts, *morenada*. … First, my eldest daughter arrived, this was last year. They danced. Then they left [laughs].' Like other older people from the community, Eulogia also danced:

> [Y]es, I think about dancing, but I think less about drinking [which often goes hand in hand] … I only dance now [she doesn't drink], this year I will dance on the 25th, every year I dance. One year I didn't dance, I can tell you Mam [laughs], one year I didn't dance, what will I be dancing for, wasting all that money [because the dresses are expensive] I said, but that year, Tata Santiago [the local saint] punished me. I was given lots of fake money, 200 … 800 bolivianos [laughs] [she is highlighting the high denomination of the bank notes], imagine, can you believe? (LP9)

Other people from La Paz had similar experiences:

> In July we will dance … they will be here any time, all of them will arrive. I don't know how they will be practising [over there], I've never been [laughs] … I dance … yes, I dance, last year I danced as well. (LP14)

> On the 25th we have a fiesta already, and they will come, last year they all came, with my grandchildren as well. We were all there, but they leave quickly. Once they left their garment workshops, for two days. Like, they come one day and the day after, or the day after that, they leave. They have contracts [that they cannot miss]. (LP11)

In our interviews, therefore, we found that socio-economic background as well as migration regimes influence visiting practices. Those of higher socio-economic backgrounds tend to practice visiting both ways, with parents visiting their children abroad and vice versa. Those of lower socio-economic backgrounds only tend to receive visits from their children abroad, and only if they have migrated regionally. When their children migrated further away, such as to the United States or to Europe, their lack of documentation and low-wage jobs tend to raise insurmountable barriers to visiting, leading to prolonged periods of parents and children not seeing each other.

## Belonging: churches and associational life

Family and communication with their children abroad were not the only things that mattered for interviewees from an emotional wellbeing point of view. They also cared about feeling connected with people outside of their family networks, such as their wider community, their neighbourhood and/ or their jobs. Although we did not quantify the breadth and depth of their social networks, the in-depth interviews gave us a sense of how important it was for interviewees to feel that they belong to a wider community, however they wished to define this. For some, this wider community was represented by their professional associations. For others, it was their church. Some were active in grassroots organisations or civic organisations representing older people. Some just took pleasure in having somebody to talk to. Virtually everybody talked about 'companionship' of one form or another. For example, both Ricardo (CBB1) and Marcos (CBB8) missed having a woman or partner (respectively) in their lives.

Churches played an important role in providing a wider community for many interviewees, as well as their main source of support for those who did not have close family nearby. Eusebia, for example, worked teaching Catholicism (*catequista*) and has done so since she arrived from the mining town where she lived, through the 'relocalisation' programme (Nash, 1993; Bastia, 2019). She said it was difficult for her to get used to living in rural areas and to live off agriculture. When she arrived some 15–20 years ago, she suffered a lot. She found solace in teaching the Catholic doctrine, running classes for young people, preparing couples for marriage and generally supporting her church and its programme of activities (CBB2).

Florencia turned to the church after her only child, her daughter, migrated to the United States. She found herself wandering around the city, sitting in 'plazas' on her own, crying. She was befriended by somebody from a church some ten years prior to the interview, and she has been helping out at the church ever since. She said she now spends most of her time at the church: '*me he entregado al señor*' (CBB19).

The neighbourhood in urban areas, including peri-urban areas, as well as the community in rural areas are important sources of support. Martin described reciprocal care and gifts from neighbours, traditional ways of giving and receiving within the community, for key celebrations, such as men returning from military service, weddings, birthdays, when the community comes together (CBB22). Others meet up with friends in local cafes in the city to talk about politics (CBB20), highlighting differences in socio-economic status in terms of where they choose to meet with peers.

Having family close by seemed to be more important for women than for men, given that the latter gave greater importance to continuing working. But both women and men were active in civil society and associational life.

For example, Walter's wellbeing centres around continuing to work. He enjoys working and keeping busy so he has kept his business going: 'I am used to it, it's my *costumbre*, my hobby, I cannot be without work, *sin trabajo no puedo estar.*' He did not express any sadness as a result of the fact that none of his children lived close to him (SC7).

Eloy, for example, said everyone loves him because of his work. He was in touch with his children abroad. The daughters in Spain took turns to visit him every year, staying for a month. He was keeping busy with the radio and had a close network with his church: 'Everybody loves me here because I have saved lives with this radio. I have served "half the world" [*he servido a medio mundo*].' He takes pride in his job and has a positive attitude towards his life and those who surround him (SC20).

Juvenal was president of the local peach association as well as the local transport route (CBB5), while Julián was active in the local pensioners' association. He used to have roles in the Christian workers' movement (Movimiento Obrero Cristiano) and a charity (the Sociedad de beneficiencia). These activities kept him active and also gave him additional income. He was living with his wife, who was poorly, and four children and did not mention being lonely. He also tried to keep active and mentioned walking to the place where he grew up (Orobo) and swimming across the river. At the time of the interview, he had liver problems so was less able to keep active. He worried about his migrant daughter's health problems and the fact that she needed to travel to Chile for some paperwork (SC6).

Some women were also active in civil society organisations. Ernestina mentioned attending weekly meetings of an older people's association (SC13). Juana was also very active in the local branch of the women's organisation Bartolina Sisa and was a leader of the local senior citizens' association. She said she missed her children and talked about going out to talk to friends, because she did not know what do to at home. She seemed to have a good and healthy local social network that filled her days and helped her deal with the absence of her children and grandchildren. She said nobody helped her when she had a problem, but then mentioned a cousin who she spoke to regularly on the phone. She also used to meet up in the plaza with other older women: '[W]e go there to talk now, *vamos a estar comadreando* [we are going to be gossiping], other people come, they tell us other stories, *otras gentes vienen, otros cuentitos nos cuentan*' (CBB4).

Arminda was also involved as treasurer of an organisation that works to bring drinking water and sewage (*alcantarillado*) to the town where she lives. She also held posts at the Municipality of where she lives on two occasions (CBB7).

Overall, we found that while both women and men were active in local associations, men were more likely to participate in work-related associations than women, given they were also more likely to have held professional jobs in their working years. However, both men and women participated as members but often also as representatives and leaders of organisations representing the interests of senior citizens, as well as neighbourhood-based associations. In fact, during the course of this research we observed the development at the national level of a senior citizen's identity, which was linked to grassroots as well as national associations that lobbied the government for the improvement of services and benefits for senior citizens.

## Grandchildren as a source of companionship: *Mejor me encuentro porque me he quedado con mis nietos*

Although in previous chapters we looked at grandchildren from the point of view of grandparents caring for them when the grandchildren's parents are unable to do so (whether as a result of migration or because they start new relationships or work elsewhere in Bolivia), in this section we address how grandparents relate emotionally to caring for grandchildren.

In this sense, grandchildren were a source of both companionship as well as worry. Some found companionship in the grandchildren who were left in their care when their children left (CBB11, CBB13). Lucia was living with eight grandchildren and despite some of them – in her words – giving her headaches, most provided companionship as well as practical help when needed (CBB11).

Paulina, who was living in the same neighbourhood, said: 'I feel better because my grandchildren stayed with me [*Mejor me encuentro porque me he quedado con mis nietos*]' (CBB13). Paulina enjoyed looking after her grandchildren. She had been looking after one of them since he was six months old. At the time of the interview he was already a teenager (15 or 16 years old). She was living with two of her own grandchildren (her daughter's children) and also a stepson. Her stepson had finished studying medicine in Cuba and, when he came back, he asked if he could live with her instead of his father (who was living somewhere else). She said she was happy when he is home because he controls and disciplines her grandchildren: '[W]hen he is here, they don't go out, they do their chores, he teaches them, they clean the house, do the dishes, he tells them off but he makes them understand, he doesn't beat them.' In this community, as elsewhere in Bolivia, men generally take on the role of disciplining children and this is something that women struggle with when their partners are away, or they are on their own (Bastia, 2019).

Similarly, Dolores, from Santa Cruz, who had not seen her daughter since she left for Spain 11 years prior to the interview, talked about missing her daughter. The interpreter who helped us translate from Guaraní, said: 'She has been feeling nostalgia for her daughter [has been missing her] since she left. Her only hope is to see her while she is still alive.' However, this sadness was alleviated by the fact that she was surrounded by her other children and grandchildren. When asked about what makes her sad, she responded: 'Only my housing situation. Then I am happy with my daughters. I am fine. My daughters are around me, my grandchildren' (SC15).

Similarly, Basilia, who lives in a rural town in Santa Cruz, said she was happy because her children lived close by. Her daughters have been away for ten years and have not been back since, but they said they will visit next year.

She says that she is *tranquila,* [calm, peaceful] because her children are around her and they take care of her, so she does not feel lonely. It's good that her daughter left. … All her children are close to her, so she is fine. One of her sons lives here, her sister lives on the other side. (SC18, via a translator)

Not living alone and having family members around ensured that ageing parents felt accompanied, engaged and embedded within their families.

In some instances, grandchildren can cause some attrition, for example, when they are older teenagers or in their 20s, and they start having their own independent lives, forming relationships or drinking (CBB10).

Grandmothers who had grandchildren in their care often worried whether they would be able to see them 'on a good path' before they died. Consuelo, for example, worried a lot about the youngest grandchild, who was 15 years old at the time of the interview and was difficult to control. She said that she would like to see him 'on a good path' before she dies (SC4).

This hope to see their grandchildren 'on a good path' was also a common thread, shared by others. Cristina worried about the grandchildren she was looking after, both in terms of some of them lacking their mum's love but also in terms of schooling, drugs, violence and 'bad influences' in the neighbourhood. She did not seem to have the strength to control them. She only hoped to be able to live long enough to see them on a good path (SC5).

As we saw in Chapter 8, Sonia from Cochabamba, who struggled with mobility, also found it difficult to control her adolescent granddaughters, which caused her to worry (CBB12). However, in Cochabamba and Santa Cruz, having responsibility for grandchildren was usually not a problem per se and interviewees did not complain about them.

This was different in Tarija, where grandchildren were usually seen as a 'cost' and, therefore, a problem, as we discussed in Chapter 8, and some interviewees resisted having grandchildren in their care. In Tarija, 26 per cent of interviewees had caring responsibilities, though these were not always towards the grandchildren whose parents were abroad (four were abroad, one in Bolivia). Grandparents sometimes cared for their grandchildren from birth (or thereabouts). Often, they did not receive any financial contribution from the grandchildren's parents towards the upkeep of the grandchildren.

Juliana did not receive any remittances from her two children abroad. They brought something when they visited – once a year – but at the time of the interview they were not on talking terms with one of their daughters abroad. Juliana sold petrol from a small shop she had set up at home, and her husband brought the petrol to sell. That was their only income, besides some vegetables they grew mostly for their own consumption. She said she had to pay to support the grandchildren and to send them to school. She was planning to send them to Argentina to their mother so they could go to school there (TRJ16).

However, at other times, grandchildren provided the companionship that the ageing grandparents sought. Hernan, 71 years old, and his wife had been looking after their eight-year-old grandson since he was very little. His mother was 24 years old and travelled to Argentina seasonally. When talking about him they said:

> [H]e keeps us company, he says 'Mami, now you are my mum, my mother had me, but she didn't raise me … she had me, but you are my mother. I am not going to go to my mother. I have to look after you.' He is no longer little, and it looks like he's come out well '*ha salido bien parece*'. (TRJ15)

Other interviewees who have grandchildren close by similarly tended to thrive in their company. Most people we spoke to drew on their extended family for support, especially if they lived close by. In fact, those who did not have grandchildren close by explicitly said that this is something that they would very much like. For example, Laura, who was living in a home, said that she would like to live in peace and close to her children and grandchildren and with enough food for everyone to eat (TRJ18).

## Conclusion

The pillar of emotional care cannot be separated from the history and practices of migration in the region, the temporality of the migratory event, and the motivations for the migration of children that are related to factors at the macro level. The perspective offered by Vullnetari and King (2008) on the mass exodus of people from Albania, coining the term 'adult orphans', as well as what was proposed for the case of Bulgaria by Iossifova (2020), in the Bolivian case is limited to some areas of the Altiplano located in the region of La Paz, where the only ones who have remained are older people. All the young adults migrated to Brazil and only visit once a year for two days for the day of the community's saint that is celebrated in July. In fact, although we did not focus on this aspect, it seemed to us that children's migration is also leading to significant changes in the traditional roles and responsibilities in some rural indigenous communities. Despite the expectation that community members take up traditional roles and responsibilities – *cargos* – such as the sponsoring of the annual saint's celebration, social and productive roles are not assumed by the younger migrants, but only by older adults, raising questions about their sustainability.

Communication and visiting are important and much improved but inequality persists in both areas: communications as well as transnational visiting. As we have shown, transnational visiting is accessible to interviewees of higher socio-economic backgrounds as well as those who practice transnational livelihoods but not to those between these extremes. This finding has important implications for the reproduction of inequalities across the migration process.

11

# Conclusion

## Introduction

As we get to the end of this book, we realise that many of the stories included in this book also reflect our own life experiences. Having left home at the age of 16 to study abroad with a scholarship, Tanja's ageing parents were the last thing on her mind then. Ageing as a process and older age as a stage in one's life were so far removed from her understanding of life, that she did not spare a single thought as to the long-term consequences of her decision to take up a scholarship abroad. She suspects that neither did her mother, with whom she was living at the time and who was the one supporting her in making that decision. More than three decades have passed, and she could have been interviewing her own parents for this research. Both are in their 70s. Both have a daughter living abroad. Would they remember the day she left? Probably not. She remembers her first day at the new school in Oxford, but she does not remember leaving. But now, both her parents are ageing and developing health problems that give rise to worry given the distance and the difficulties she would have in travelling to see them given other caring commitments.

As for many of our interviewees, their everyday lives became separated because of better opportunities abroad: more interesting studies than the ones that were on offer locally, which later translated into job opportunities, while meeting a partner early on and having children contributed to consolidating a life abroad. The strong mother–daughter relationships also emerged in our interviews, with many of our women interviewees, particularly in urban areas, indicating that the separation from their daughters was particularly emotionally challenging. Many women suffered depression and continue to experience loneliness. Those who managed to overcome these feelings did so with the help of churches or friendships, friendly support groups with whom they meet regularly to socialise and enjoy their spare time.

## Material conditions

The wellbeing of older adults is contingent on material subsistence. So to understand the material component of transnational care, as fundamental elements that make up this dimension, we asked about housing, working conditions, how older adults manage their livelihoods, businesses, pensions, savings, access to land, as well as subsistence farming.

Housing tenure, beyond the quality of the materials of the house, is highly valued by the people interviewed. In fact, since many interviews were conducted in the homes of the people we spoke to, we were able to observe the living conditions, which varied considerably according to socio-economic background and place of residence. Migration did not have a strong impact on housing and the quality of the houses of the people interviewed. Housing was closely related to the socio-economic situation of older adults. We have been able to identify only one case where one of our interviewees was able to build her home thanks to the money from the remittances she received. In fact, most of our interviewees, despite the fact most of them have health problems, have not stopped working. In fact, the majority, 73 per cent of those we interviewed, had some paid work, either formal or informal. Although the likelihood of working decreased with age, we also came across older adults who continued to work even though they were already past 80 years old; not to mention that many also held unpaid positions and, in the case of women, performed unpaid domestic and care work.

For many, paid work is the only way in which they can guarantee their subsistence, while for others it is part of their daily life and identity because the idea persists in the imaginary that if they stop working they will get sick or grow old.

As with the issue of housing, with respect to the work activity of the older adults interviewed, there is no direct relationship with the migration of their children abroad. We did not find cases in which older adults have stopped working as a result of the improvement in their socio-economic conditions due to migration. With the exception of one case, older adults did not depend exclusively on remittances from their children to guarantee their subsistence.

From a gender perspective, there are large gaps between women and men interviewed. In terms of economic autonomy, women received the lowest percentage of pensions. As a result, they had fewer possibilities of access to healthcare. In some cases, they stopped doing paid work to take care of their children, or because in some cases their husbands forbade them to work. This had a significant impact on their socio-economic conditions in older age. Added to this situation was the burden of unpaid care-work that they continue to carry out caring for their grandchildren – children of their children in Bolivia and/or abroad – and their husbands; while in rural areas they were also responsible for work related to agricultural production and animal husbandry.

With regard to land tenure in rural areas, migration has meant that the plots dedicated to cultivation are not fragmented according to the number of children, which is what is usually done according to the regulations referring to inheritance. In the region of Oruro, cases of conflicts between older siblings have been detected regarding the boundaries between their quinoa farmland. For the children who remain in their communities of origin, the migration of their siblings has meant the possibility of larger tracts of land. Although some children abroad support their parents financially for agricultural production, they do not make any demands or make any important decisions in this area. However, as they age, older adults face their own inability to fully engage in agricultural production without the help of their children, have to buy in agricultural help or are forced to share the crops, which significantly reduces their income.

In the case of peri-urban areas, it was common to find more productive investments linked to the migration of their children. Peri-urban areas had more diversified migration streams, which included both South–South and South–North migrations. They also had some access to education and plots of land, which could be used to build houses, which could in turn produce an income, when and if they were let out. There was little investment into business activities but there certainly was some geared towards buying plots of land as a form of investment, especially to build rental housing.

## Communication

Access to communication improved considerably since this research project started over ten years ago. While, at the beginning, most rural areas were largely cut off from accessible communication, when we finished data collection in 2020 almost everyone had access to mobile phones and was communicating via WhatsApp. Access to communication is the backbone of transnational care and, as expected, we found a wide variation of practices related to communication. Some parents talked daily to their children abroad. Others communicated once a week, or every two weeks. Only a small minority communicated only in emergencies and even fewer had no communication at all with their children abroad.

Clearly, it is not the communication per se that builds relationships but, rather, it facilitates the maintenance of already existing relationships. If parents have had a feud with their children, then no matter how good their access to communication might be, they are not going to be communicating very often. The data we gathered therefore indicates that most of the parents have functioning relationships with their children abroad. Some might have very close and caring relationships. Others might not be as close but they still enjoy support and warmth between them even if their communication is not as frequent. Overall, it is not surprising that parents and children abroad are communicating, given today's wide accessibility of mobile phones and access to the internet. However, it is at the same time surprising to find that most interviewees have some kind of regular (frequent or less frequent) communication with their children abroad, considering the diversity of destinations, migration practices, differences in interviewees' socio-economic backgrounds and temporality. Some of our interviewees' children started migrating when they were still children, some in their early teenage years. In some cases, five decades have passed. Others have not seen their children for over a decade. But in most cases, save for a few exceptions, they continue to communicate with one another, which is the basis for transnational care.

Intergenerational transnational ties are strong and persist across differences and varying forms of inequalities of land, housing and jobs.

## Diversity among regions

Although we were aware of regional variations in migration patterns and histories of migration, we did not except to find such great diversity of experiences of migration and, as a result, also transnational care. Despite some commonalities in transnational care practices among interviewees of higher or lower socio-economic backgrounds, which we discuss further in the following, the regional differences in migration practices and histories of migration really do stand out against the broader generalisations. Engaging in transnational livelihoods across Bolivia and neighbouring Argentina, in the way in which rural interviewees did in Tarija, leads to very different transnational care practices to the type of migrations that rural people from the Santa Cruz region engage in – long-distance migrations to Europe, largely long-term without the option of shorter return trips, particularly for irregular migrants, leading to very long separations. This again is very different from the type of migration that people undertake from Cochabamba, Oruro or La Paz, where we find a greater variety of destinations and modes of migration: migration for professional work to regional destinations such as Brazil or further away in Europe and the United States or lower-income work in neighbouring countries such as Chile and Argentina, both of which generally provide opportunities for visiting, at least annually.

The fact that in some regions our interviewees also had a significant experience of migration, including abroad, meant that their children's decision to migrate was not alien to their experience, given they had themselves taken this decision earlier in their lives. This provided some basis for understanding their children's decision and therefore, also, support them, building the basis on which such support can then be reciprocated by their children at a later date.

## Temporality

As with the regional diversity, we also encountered a great variety of temporal dimensions to the migration experiences and, as a result, of transnational care. The time that had passed since their children's first migration varied significantly, from a few years to many decades. Although this diversity made it difficult for us to generalise across different interviewees, the same diversity also allowed us to explore how transnational care changes over time. Is it easier to maintain transnational care if not much time has passed since their children's migration? Or is this more likely to peak as specific care needs emerge, regardless of the time that has passed since the children's migration?

We were surprised that the moment of migration – the specific day, or at least period – was not remembered by many of our interviewees. Although some did talk about going to the airport with their children and seeing them off, shedding tears afterwards, for most, the departure was not an event. Sometimes a long time had passed since the children's departure, so interviewees did not remember the day their children left. But in most cases, it was not so much that the day itself was not remembered, but that interviewees did not see their children's departure as exceptional. In some cases, children continued their parents' migrations. They started migrating with their parents as children, and then continued – sometimes travelling with other family members when they were still young, as teenagers, and later on alone or with friends, when they were old enough to do so. In these cases, we could not identify a before and an after the migration 'event', because migration was interwoven in the interviewees' everyday experience and livelihoods. Their children's migration was remembered as an event in cases where it led to a significant change in the interviewees' lives, as with mothers whose only daughters migrated and who then went on to experience periods of depression, or parents who were particularly attached to the child who migrated.

The mode of migration also seemed to have played a part. Those who remembered the day their child left were more likely to have taken them to the airport for longer-distance travel to the United States or to Europe, rather than seeing them off locally when their children would then travel by bus to regional destinations, albeit distant ones.[1]

## Differentiated transnational care

While we initially thought that we would find the greatest differences in the ways in which transnational care is practices between rural, urban and peri-urban areas, as we developed this research we realised that there were significant differences within these areas. Switching to socio-economic group allowed us to have a better starting point to explore differences in how transnational care is practised. As expected, we did indeed find that higher-income and better educated interviewees have more opportunities to receive transnational care: they are less reliant on others for care and support in the first place, because they are more likely to have had jobs in the formal sectors, which come with access to healthcare and private pensions. Moreover, their children are more likely to have had a higher degree of education and either studied abroad or migrated for professional jobs. Legal migration routes and secure incomes mean that children are not only able to visit their parents in Bolivia, but they are also able to sponsor them to come visit them in the United States, Europe or Brazil. They are able to get them visas, and also pay for their trips. These parents, besides living more comfortable lives, also get to enjoy paid visits to their children and grandchildren abroad.

Interviewees from lower socio-economic backgrounds usually have children who migrate for lower-paid jobs regionally or to Europe through irregular migration routes. These parents are more likely to have worked in the informal sector. They have lower incomes, no access to private pensions and only have access to the basic national healthcare. Their need for financial support from their children abroad is greater, yet their children are in a worse position to be able to provide this support. These parents rarely visit their children abroad, either because they do not have financial means to do so and/or because their children are not able to sponsor their visits – financially or by sponsoring a visa.

Interviewees from the rural areas of Tarija have proven to be an exception to this pattern. They generally have low incomes and few years of schooling. Their children are also mainly engaged in agricultural work in Argentina. Yet the transnational livelihoods they practice places migration as a learned experience at its core and, as a result, transnational care is much more accessible. Families come and go every six months. Parents help their children maintain their plots but they also wait for their return to undertake key tasks in the agricultural cycle. The 'coming and going' (Hinojosa Gordonava, 2000) and transnational migration as a way of life extends to transnational care, with some interviewees travelling to Argentina to access healthcare, or to provide care for their daughters after they have given birth.

With this research, we have therefore been able to shine a light on the different ways in which socio-economic background leads to different transnational care practices, because of the very different contexts and opportunities that are mediated by socio-economic background. While this was expected, this is the first study of transnational care that actually shows how it differs across socio-economic backgrounds.

## Vulnerability and abandonment

Because our starting point was the country of origin, we were also able to identify instances where transnational care has failed and is not available at all. While the early studies on ageing and migration that emerged from Eastern Europe also focused on the country of origin (Vullnetari and King,

2008; Iossifova, 2020), the concept itself was developed on the basis of the experience of migrants in Australia. Starting with the migrants' experiences and then working their way back to their parents in a number of countries, Baldassar et al (2007) showed that transnational care is possible, despite large distances.

We found that transnational care is indeed possible but it is not available to everyone. Some parents might be receiving remittances, but their situation can be classed as one of vulnerability and abandonment because their everyday needs are not being met. Clearly, money is useful but it stops playing a role if basic needs of physical comfort are not being met. At the same time, this contrasts sharply with those who receive sufficient remittances to pay for round-the-clock care. The difference between the two situations is largely determined by the older person's socio-economic background, international migration regimes and the absence of state support for older people in Bolivia.

## Migration regimes

Where children migrate to, their mode of migration, how long they migrate for and the type of jobs that they are able to access at destination all play a significant role in their ability to practice transnational care in relation to their ageing parents in Bolivia. Safer modes of migration, which include the possibility of two-way visiting, coupled with better jobs that allow migrants to build the financial means for regular visits home, gives them the opportunity to nourish their relationship with their parents and also visit them during holidays or when emergencies happen.

Insecure jobs and irregular modes of migration mean that migrants are not able to afford regular visits home and also preclude them from sponsoring their parents' visits, either financially or by supporting a visa request. Despite these difficulties, parents and their children maintain their relationship through regular communication. In addition, many interviewees usually have other children locally or somewhere else in Bolivia who can provide everyday care when needed. However, the nature of their relationship is quite different if there is a financial as well as a legal basis for transnational visiting than when this is missing.

## The role of the state

What sets this study apart from countries like Australia, is the – at best – weak state provision of services and support for older people, which in some places, like the rural areas we visited, is almost non-existent. Despite the quite elaborate and developed legal framework in place for supporting older citizens, which we discussed in Chapter 4, as well as the only universal cash-transfer available for older citizens in the whole region, many of our interviewees expressed disillusionment or outright despair at the lack of health services in some areas in Bolivia.

While the *Renta Dignidad* was generally welcomed and in fact provided a very significant financial contribution for subsistence farmers, it was nowhere near enough to be able to cover a person's daily subsistence. This meant that most of our interviewees had to continue working, despite their sometimes advanced age and debilitating physical conditions. Only in a small number of cases were interviewees able to use remittances sent from their children abroad to cover daily subsistence.

Access to healthcare was singled out as the most pressing problem for most of our interviewees, who talked about the difficulties they had in accessing anything other than very basic services in rural areas. However, more than that, most interviewees, irrespective of socio-economic status, found health service provision inadequate, except for what is privately provided. Their aversion to state-provided healthcare was clear in the very common practice we observed of many interviewees resorting to private healthcare, despite having health insurance through their jobs.

We found that remittances played an important role in substituting for the absent provision of services by the state or provision that is deemed inadequate by our interviewees. Many interviewees received in-kind gifts when their children visited or financial remittances on birthdays and special occasions like Mother's or Father's Day. Those who already had their basic needs covered usually used remittances to buy themselves special treats – a meal out, a haircut or some biscuits. However, for those who had ongoing health problems but lacked a regular income, remittances often proved to be – literally – a lifesaver, given that they often save them up so that they could pay for health services, such as medicines or check-ups, when the need arises.

However, as the migration and development literature has already acknowledged, remittances are not the panacea that is able to resolve all problems. As we saw in Chapter 6, not everybody receives them and many of our interviewees received no financial support from their children abroad.

## Looking ahead

As the world's population continues to age, there is an increasing urgency to address the needs of older people. In lower- and middle-income countries, this need is much more acute given the intensification of ageing in lower- and middle-income countries, which is coupled with relatively weaker state infrastructures. Mobility, which is also intensifying, both across and within national borders, presents its own set of challenges but also opportunities for migrants and for the family members who remain in their places of origin.

However, as our research has shown, mobility tends to intensify existing inequalities and although some people do benefit from their migration projects, these tend to be people who were already better off – whether in terms of income, education or networks – before they started engaging in migration. Therefore, it is imperative that states provide support for those who are not able to benefit from these opportunities.

We have also shown that older parents, rather than being passive recipients of their children's migrations, are often actively involved in their children's migration projects. They lend them money to travel, they look after their children, and they receive, manage and invest remittances. Rather than waiting on the state or their children to provide them with what they need for their survival, they are generally engaged in economic activities, subsistence agriculture or community organisations, for as long as they are able. They are far from being the 'cost' that most policies frame them to be. They are actively contributing to their families, communities and their countries, even when they should have every right to rest and enjoy receiving some care and resources, since they have had a full lifetime of giving to others.

Finally, there is much more that needs to be done in relation to older age and gender. The gender dimension, which was present for us from the outset, has really emerged as a strong element of the analysis of older people's lives, not just in terms of the often invisible work that many older women undertake – both paid and unpaid – but especially in terms of the consequences that a lifetime of violence continues to have for these women's lives. Even when they are no longer in violent relationships, having left their partners or becoming widowed, women continue to suffer as a result of the violence that was inflicted on them when they were younger. For us, this was an unsettling finding and one that is not receiving adequate attention from researchers or policy makers.

# Appendix: Interviewee data

| Number | Region | Code | Gender | Age | Residence | Socio-economic | # children | # children abroad |
|---|---|---|---|---|---|---|---|---|
| 1 | Cochabamba | CBB1 | M | 83 | Rural | Medium | 3 | 2 |
| 2 | Cochabamba | CBB2 | F | 69 | Rural | Medium | 5 | 1 |
| 3 | Cochabamba | CBB3 | F | 62 | Rural | Lower | 6 | 5 |
| 4 | Cochabamba | CBB4 | F | 68 | Rural | Medium | 3 | 3 |
| 5 | Cochabamba | CBB5 | M | 72 | Rural | Medium | 5 | 4 |
| 6 | Cochabamba | CBB6 | M | 82 | Rural | Medium | 6 | 2 |
| 7 | Cochabamba | CBB7 | F | 60 | Rural | Higher | 2 | 1 |
| 8 | Cochabamba | CBB8 | M | 61 | Rural | Medium | 5 | 5 |
| 9 | Cochabamba | CBB9 | M | 76 | Rural | Lower | 2 | 1 |
| 10 | Cochabamba | CBB10 | F | 69 | Peri-urban | Lower | 3 | 3 |
| 11 | Cochabamba | CBB11 | F | 82 | Peri-urban | Lower | 7 | 2 |
| 12 | Cochabamba | CBB12 | F | 83 | Urban | Lower | 4 | 3 |
| 13 | Cochabamba | CBB13 | F | 60 | Peri-urban | Lower | 5 | 4 |
| 14 | Cochabamba | CBB14 | M | 75 | Rural | Lower | 7 | 3 |
| 15 | Cochabamba | CBB15 | M | 65 | Rural | Lower | 3 | 2 |
| 16 | Cochabamba | CBB16 | M | 67 | Urban | Medium | 4 | 2 |
| 17 | Cochabamba | CBB17 | F | 83 | Urban | Medium | 2 | 1 |
| 18 | Cochabamba | CBB18 | F | 63 | Urban | Higher | 1 | 1 |
| 19 | Cochabamba | CBB19 | F | 75 | Urban | Lower | 1 | 1 |
| 20 | Cochabamba | CBB20 | M | 70 | Urban | Higher | 5 | 2 |
| 21 | Cochabamba | CBB21 | M | 61 | Rural | Lower | 7 | 4 |
| 22 | Cochabamba | CBB22 | M | 67 | Rural | Lower | 6 | 3 |
| 23 | Santa Cruz | SC1 | M | 79 | Urban | Lower | 2 | 1 |
| 24 | Santa Cruz | SC2 | F | 65 | Urban | Medium | 3 | 1 |
| 25 | Santa Cruz | SC3 | M | 85 | Urban | Medium | 1 | 1 |
| 26 | Santa Cruz | SC4 | F | 72 | Urban | Medium | 8 | 1 |
| 27 | Santa Cruz | SC5 | F | 65 | Peri-urban | Lower | 2 | 1 |
| 28 | Santa Cruz | SC6 | M | 74 | Urban | Higher | 9 | 1 |
| 29 | Santa Cruz | SC7 | M | 72 | Urban | Higher | 3 | 1 |
| 30 | Santa Cruz | SC8 | F | 65 | Peri-urban | Lower | 4 | 1 |
| 31 | Santa Cruz | SC9 | M | 75 | Urban | Medium | 5 | 2 |
| 32 | Santa Cruz | SC10 | M | 93 | Peri-urban | Lower | 4 | 1 |

| Number | Region | Code | Gender | Age | Residence | Socio-economic | # children | # children abroad |
|---|---|---|---|---|---|---|---|---|
| 33 | Santa Cruz | SC11 | M | 68 | Peri-urban | Medium | 8 | 2 |
| 34 | Santa Cruz | SC12 | F | 63 | Peri-urban | Lower | 8 | 1 |
| 35 | Santa Cruz | SC13 | F | 76 | Peri-urban | Lower | 7 | 2 |
| 36 | Santa Cruz | SC14 | F | 61 | Peri-urban | Lower | 3 | 2 |
| 37 | Santa Cruz | SC15 | F | 79 | Peri-urban | Lower | 6 | 1 |
| 38 | Santa Cruz | SC16 | F | 75 | Peri-urban | Lower | 5 | 1 |
| 39 | Santa Cruz | SC17 | F | 79 | Peri-urban | Lower | 4 | 3 |
| 40 | Santa Cruz | SC18 | F | 77 | Rural | Lower | 6 | 2 |
| 41 | Santa Cruz | SC19 | F | 78 | Rural | Lower | 12 | 1 |
| 42 | Santa Cruz | SC20 | M | 70 | Rural | Medium | 9 | 5 |
| 43 | Santa Cruz | SC21 | F | 68 | Urban | Higher | 3 | 2 |
| 44 | Tarija | TRJ1 | M | 70 | Rural | Lower | 10 | 7 |
| 45 | Tarija | TRJ2 | F | 87 | Rural | Lower | 6 | 3 |
| 46 | Tarija | TRJ3 | F | 75 | Rural | Lower | 1 | 0 |
| 47 | Tarija | TRJ4 | F | 60 | Rural | Lower | 4 | 2 |
| 48 | Tarija | TRJ5 | F | 67 | Peri-urban | Lower | 4 | 2 |
| 49 | Tarija | TRJ6 | M | 79 | Urban | Lower | 7 | 4 |
| 50 | Tarija | TRJ7 | F | 65 | Rural | Lower | 5 | 4 |
| 51 | Tarija | TRJ8 | F | 73 | Rural | Lower | 3 | 1 |
| 52 | Tarija | TRJ9 | F | 63 | Rural | Lower | 8 | 2 |
| 53 | Tarija | TRJ10 | F | 80 | Peri-urban | Lower | 9 | 2 |
| 54 | Tarija | TRJ11 | M | 71 | Rural | Lower | 3 | 2 |
| 55 | Tarija | TRJ12 | F | 62 | Rural | Lower | 5 | 3 |
| 56 | Tarija | TRJ13 | F | 74 | Rural | Lower | 7 | 3 |
| 57 | Tarija | TRJ14 | M | 67 | Rural | Lower | 5 | 5 |
| 58 | Tarija | TRJ15 | M | 71 | Rural | Lower | 3 | 3 |
| 59 | Tarija | TRJ16 | F | 70 | Rural | Lower | 4 | 2 |
| 60 | Tarija | TRJ17 | F | 65 | Rural | Lower | 7 | 4 |
| 61 | Tarija | TRJ18 | F | 83 | Urban | Lower | 6 | 6 |
| 62 | Tarija | TRJ19 | M | 90 | Urban | Medium | 7 | 1 |
| 63 | La Paz | LP1 | M | 75 | Peri-urban | Higher | 4 | 3 |
| 64 | La Paz | LP2 | M | 64 | Urban | Higher | 5 | 2 |
| 65 | La Paz | LP3 | F | 88 | Urban | Higher | 2 | 2 |
| 66 | La Paz | LP4 | F | 70 | Urban | Medium | 6 | 1 |
| 67 | La Paz | LP5 | F | 61 | Urban | Higher | 1 | 1 |
| 68 | La Paz | LP6 | M | 61 | Peri-urban | Medium | 4 | 1 |

| Number | Region | Code | Gender | Age | Residence | Socio-economic | # children | # children abroad |
|---|---|---|---|---|---|---|---|---|
| 69 | La Paz | LP7 | F | 62 | Peri-urban | Lower | 4 | 1 |
| 70 | La Paz | LP8 | F | 74 | Peri-urban | Higher | 2 | 1 |
| 71 | La Paz | LP9 | F | 64 | Rural | Lower | 9 | 2 |
| 72 | La Paz | LP10 | M | 80 | Rural | Lower | 8 | 2 |
| 73 | La Paz | LP11 | M | 83 | Rural | Lower | 3 | 1 |
| 74 | La Paz | LP12 | M | 80 | Rural | Lower | 8 | 2 |
| 75 | La Paz | LP13 | F | 80 | Rural | Medium | 3 | 2 |
| 76 | La Paz | LP14 | F | 63 | Rural | Medium | 4 | 2 |
| 77 | La Paz | LP15 | M | 73 | Peri-urban | Medium | 7 | 3 |
| 78 | La Paz | LP16 | M | 61 | Peri-urban | Medium | 1 | 1 |
| 79 | La Paz | LP17 | F | 74 | Peri-urban | Medium | 6 | 1 |
| 80 | La Paz | LP18 | M | 68 | Peri-urban | Medium | 3 | 1 |
| 81 | La Paz | LP19 | F | 61 | Urban | Higher | 3 | 1 |
| 82 | La Paz | LP20 | M | 73 | Peri-urban | Higher | 3 | 3 |
| 83 | Oruro | OR1 | F | 64 | Rural | Lower | 8 | 1 |
| 84 | Oruro | OR2 | M | 72 | Rural | Medium | 2 | 1 |
| 85 | Oruro | OR3 | M | 75 | Urban | Medium | 8 | 2 |
| 86 | Oruro | OR4 | M | 64 | Urban | Medium | 8 | 2 |
| 87 | Oruro | OR5 | F | 76 | Peri-urban | Lower | 7 | 2 |
| 88 | Oruro | OR6 | M | 74 | Peri-urban | Medium | 5 | 2 |
| 89 | Oruro | OR7 | F | 60 | Peri-urban | Medium | 5 | 2 |
| 90 | Oruro | OR8 | F | 60 | Peri-urban | Lower | 5 | 1 |
| 91 | Oruro | OR9 | F | 63 | Peri-urban | Lower | 9 | 3 |
| 92 | Oruro | OR10 | F | 63 | Urban | Medium | 4 | 2 |
| 93 | Oruro | OR11 | F | 64 | Urban | Medium | 4 | 1 |
| 94 | Oruro | OR12 | M | 63 | Rural | Lower | 5 | 1 |
| 95 | Oruro | OR13 | M | 67 | Rural | Lower | 8 | 6 |
| 96 | Oruro | OR14 | M | 64 | Rural | Lower | 7 | 1 |
| 97 | Oruro | OR15 | M | 64 | Rural | Lower | 12 | 4 |
| 98 | Oruro | OR16 | F | 61 | Urban | Higher | 3 | 1 |
| 99 | Oruro | OR17 | F | 70 | Urban | Higher | 2 | 1 |
| 100 | Oruro | OR18 | M | 70 | Urban | Higher | 2 | 1 |

# **Notes**

## Chapter 2

[1] We use 'stayers' rather than 'left behind', following Haagsman and Mazzucato (2020), who have argued that stayers conveys more of a sense of agency to the migrants' parents, who often contribute to the migration decision-making process of their adult children. This is also supported by our research, as will be seen later.

[2] Personal communication from recent returnee to one of the authors.

## Chapter 4

[1] Unfortunately we do not have more recent data. For example, this document from 2017 refers back to the data from 2012: https://www.ine.gob.bo/index.php/argentina-es-el-pais-de-mayor-preferencia-de-emigrantes-bolivianos/, last accessed 12 March 2025.

[2] The '*aguinaldo*' is an extra monthly payment – a wage or pension payment in this case – given at Christmas.

[3] In the first case Bs4,550 (US$659) per year equates to 11 monthly payments of Bs350 (US$50) and one payment of Bs700 (US$100), which includes the '*aguinaldo*' so the payment is doubled. In the second case, Bs3,900 (US$565) a year, equals 11 monthly payments of Bs300 (US$43) and one payment of Bs600 (US$86), which includes the '*aguinaldo*'.

[4] Local authority. The term dates to the colonial period.

[5] Demographic dividend refers to the potential economic growth created by the changes in the demographic distribution according to age (Pinto, 2015). It is characterised by the growth of the economically active population, with a simultaneous decrease in those aged below 15 years and above 60 years old.

## Chapter 5

[1] *Anticrético* is a modality of accessing housing where the tenant pays a large deposit that is then returned in full by the owner at the end of the contract. This modality allows property owners to access capital that they can use to finalise or expand their property, invest elsewhere or just earn interest in the bank, while the tenants effectively live in the house 'rent free', save for the loss of interest they would have earned elsewhere on their lump sum. The practice is inscribed in Bolivian property law. The contract usually specifies that if the owner does not return the lump sum, the house will be sold so that the person renting can have their lump sum returned.

[2] The mixed modality includes *anticrético* and rent.

[3] Dried potatoes.

[4] Of these, 14 per cent were receiving a contributory pension at the time of the interview; 6 per cent were beneficiaries from their spouse's pension; 5 per cent were contributing towards one and will receive it at a later date; 75 per cent will not receive a contributory pension.

[5] Traditional alcoholic drink made of fermented sweetcorn.

[6] Physically punishing thieves is common in rural and many peri-urban areas (Goldstein, 2012).

[7] This custom is recognised in the Bolivian Civil Code as '*usufructo*'. It is quite common for parents to leave land and/or houses to their children but retaining their right to live in the house or use the land until their death to secure their own access to housing and land and guarantee succession rights to their children.

[8] Oruro is the most important producer of camelid livestock. It has the largest number of llamas in all of Bolivia.

⁹  This practice involves the farmer giving land for someone else to grow quinoa and then the harvest is split in two, one part is for the owner of the land.

## Chapter 6

¹  4,000 pesos was US$290 at the time of the interview.

²  The Communal Solidarity Programme (*Prosol*) is a programme of the Autonomous Departmental Government of Tarija that administers and transfers departmental resources from oil revenues, for the benefit of peasant and indigenous communities for the execution of communal productive initiatives.

³  This is a role that is taken on by couples for the annual religious fiestas and requires the *pasante* to sponsor the fiesta, including the renting of clothes, beverages and food, and paying for the folkloric bands.

⁴  Folkloric dance of the Bolivian highlands.

## Chapter 7

¹  A common disease in Bolivia among people who live in the highlands, which involves an increase of red blood cells, and which can have serious consequences.

²  Since 2019, with the signing of the Law No. 1152 Bolivia established a free and universal medical service for the benefit of all the people who are not covered by the short-term social security provision. Article 7 establishes, moreover, that public health services are obliged to provide preferential treatment in providing services and administrative procedures to those people who find themselves in a vulnerable situation, including, among others, older people, those with disabilities and people belonging to one of the indigenous groups (*Pueblos Indígena Originario Campesinos*), intercultural and Afrobolivian communities.

³  These are hard foods, implying that he has strong teeth.

⁴  According to the national standard for the characterisation of first-level health facilities developed in 2013 by the Ministry of Health and Sports, the levels of care of health facilities are defined by their technical and resolutive capacity, and are classified as: First Level, Second Level and Third Level. The first level establishments are the gateway to the health system, through the function of comprehensive intercultural healthcare that does not have specialised medical services. The second level establishments offer services of general medicine, dentistry and specialties of internal medicine, gynaecology and obstetrics, general surgery, paediatrics, anaesthesiology and other specialties according to the local epidemiological profile. The tertiary level establishments are made up of hospitals and institutes that offer outpatient and inpatient services in specialties, subspecialties, diagnostic support and treatment (Ministerio de Salud y Deportes, 2013).

⁵  Many miners are of indigenous origins and therefore share many of their beliefs.

⁶  Bonesetters. It is estimated that there are at least five generations of the Escobar family, recognised for being specialists in the treatment and care of bone diseases. Their office is located in Cliza, a municipality of Cochabamba.

⁷  Despite the fact that this is a veterinary cream, it is highly recommended by medical practitioners for use on people because of its anti-inflammatory and painkiller properties. In fact, it has been recently recommended to one of the authors.

⁸  The Tata Bombori is a plaster image of St James the Apostle. It is famously recognised for its power to cure diseases, even terminal ones.

## Chapter 8

¹  Bolivian private non-profit organisation, which develops its activities within the framework of the National Health Policy.

## Chapter 10

[1] Dancing is understood as an offering to the saint that is celebrated. Those who dance can expect good fortune to follow that year. Dancers go to great expense to participate in the celebration, both in terms of investing time for rehearsals but also spending money to rent or get clothes made. *Padrinos* and *madrinas* often sponsor dance troupes and buy refreshments or pay for musicians.

## Chapter 11

[1] It takes three days to travel by bus from Cochabamba to Buenos Aires, Argentina, a journey that Tanja did as part of her PhD fieldwork (Bastia, 2019), and it takes a similar amount of time to travel to São Paulo, Brazil.

# References


Acosta, D., Blouin, C. and Freier, L.F. (2019). *La emigración venezolana: respuestas latinoamericanas. Cuadernos de trabajo 19*. Madrid: Fundación Carolina.

ADB (Asian Development Bank) (2024). *Aging Well in Asia: Asian Development Policy Report*. Manila: Asian Development Bank.

Ahmed, A. and Hall, K. (2016). 'Negotiating the challenges of aging as a British migrant in Spain', *GeroPsych: The Journal of Gerontopsychology and Geriatric Psychiatry*, 2(2), 105–114. DOI: 10.1024/1662-9647/a000147

Åkesson, L. and Eriksson Baaz, M. (2015). *Africa's Return Migrants: The New Developers?* London: Zed Books.

Amassari, S. (2009). *Migration and Development: Factoring Return into the Equation*. Newcastle upon Tyne: Cambridge Scholars Publishing.

Amrith, M. (2011). '"They think we are just caregivers": The ambivalence of care in the lives of Filipino medical workers in Singapore', *The Asia Pacific Journal of Anthropology*, 11(3–4), 410–427. https://doi.org/10.1080/14442213.2010.511631

Amrith, M. and Coe, C. (2022). 'Disposable kin: Shifting registers of belonging in global care economies', *American Anthropologist*, 124(2), 307–318. DOI: 10.1111/aman.13688

Anthias, F. (1983). 'Sexual divisions and ethnic adaptation: The case of Greek-Cypriot women', in Phizacklea, A. (ed) *One Way Ticket: Migration and Female Labour*. London: Routledge and Kegan Paul, pp 73–94.

Anzaldúa, G. (2015). *Light in the Dark/Luz en lo oscuro: Rewriting Identity, Spirituality, Reality*. Edited by A. Keating. Durham, NC: Duke University Press.

APS (2024). *Información Estadística Pensiones*. Autoridad de Fiscalización y Control de Seguros y Pensiones. Available at: https://www.aps.gob.bo/pensiones/informacion-estadistica (accessed 9 December 2024).

Ariza, M. and Jiménez Chaves, L.F. (2022). 'Migración femenina e interseccionalidad: El trabajo reproductivo de las inmigrantes latinoamericanas en México', *Revista interdisciplinaria de estudios de género de El Colegio de México*, 8, 1–42. DOI: 10.24201/reg.v8i1.957

Baars, J., Dohmen, J., Grenier, A. and Phillipson, C. (2014). *Ageing, Meaning and Social Structure*. Bristol: Policy Press.

Baby-Collin, V. and Cortes, G. (2014). 'New trends of the Bolivian migration in a context of crisis', *Revista CIDOB d'Afers Internacionals*, 106–107, 61–83.

Bairros, L. (1995). 'Nossos Feminismos Revisitados', *Revista Estudos Feministas*, 3(2), 458–463. DOI: 10.1590/%x

Bakewell, O. (2009). *South-South Migration and Human Development: Reflections on African Experiences*. New York: United Nations Development Programme. Available at: https://hdr.undp.org/content/south-south-migration-and-human-development (accessed 12 March 2025).

Baldassar, L. (2001). *Visits Home: Migration Experiences between Italy and Australia*. Carlton South: Melbourne University Press.

Baldassar, L., Baldock, C.V. and Wilding, R. (2007). *Families Caring across Borders: Migration, Ageing, and Transnational Caregiving*. Basingstoke: Palgrave Macmillan.

Balslev Clausen, H. and Velazquez Garcia, M. (2011). 'En búsqueda del México auténtico. Las comunidades norteamericanas en ciudades turísticas de México', in Mazón Martínez, T., Huete, R. and Mantecón, A. (eds) *Construir una nueva vida. Los espacios del turismo y la migración residencial*. Santander: Milrazones, pp 61–80.

Barrientos, A. (2006). 'Poverty reduction: The missing piece of pension reform in Latin America', *Social Policy & Administration*, 40(4), 369–384. DOI: 10.1111/j.1467-9515.2006.00495.x

Barrientos, A. (2009). 'Social pensions in low-income countries', in Holzmann, R., Robalino, D.A. and Takayama, N. (eds) *Closing the Coverage Gap: The Role of Social Pensions and Other Retirement Income Transfers*. Washington, DC: World Bank, pp 73–83.

Barrientos, A. (2024). *Social Protection in Latin America: Causality, Stratification and Outcomes*. London: Palgrave Macmillan.

Barrientos, A. and Lloyd-Sherlock, P. (2002). 'Older and poorer? Ageing and poverty in the South', *Journal of International Development*, 14(8), 1129–1131. DOI: 10.1002/jid.954

Barrios de Chungara, D. and Viezzer, M. (1979). *Let Me Speak! Testimony of Domitila, a Woman of the Bolivian Mines*. London: Monthly Review Press.

Basch, L.G., Schiller, N.G. and Szanton Blanc, C. (1993). *Nations Unbound: Transnational Projects, Postcolonial Predicaments, and Deterritorialized Nation-states*. Basel: Gordon and Breach.

Bastia, T. (2007). 'From mining to garment workshops: Bolivian migrants in Buenos Aires', *Journal of Ethnic and Migration Studies*, 33(4), 655–669. DOI: 10.1080/13691830701265628

Bastia, T. (2009). 'Women's migration and the crisis of care: Grandmothers caring for grandchildren in urban Bolivia', *Gender & Development*, 17(3), 389–401. DOI: 10.1080/13552070903298378

Bastia, T. (2011). 'Migration as protest? Negotiating gender, class, and ethnicity in urban Bolivia', *Environment and Planning A*, 43(7), 1514–1529. DOI: 10.1068/a43365

Bastia, T. (2014). 'Intersectionality, migration and development', *Progress in Development Studies*, 14(3), 237–248. DOI: 10.1177/1464993414521

Bastia, T. (2015). '"Looking after granny": A transnational ethic of care and responsibility', *Geoforum*, 64, 121–129. DOI: 10.1016/j.geoforum.2015.06.014

Bastia, T. (2019). *Gender, Migration and Social Transformation: Intersectionality in Bolivian Itinerant Migration*. Abingdon: Routledge.

Bastia, T. (2023). 'Gender and intersectionality', in Clarke, M. and Zhao, X.A. (eds) *Elgar Encyclopedia of Development*. Cheltenham: Edward Elgar, pp 276–277.

Bastia, T. and Calsina Valenzuela, C. (2022). 'Desigualdades en el cuidado transnacional: una mirada desde las migraciones y los adultos mayores en cinco regiones bolivianas', *Périplos: Revista De Estudios Sobre Migraciones*, 6(2), 71–101.

Bastia, T. and Montero Bressán, J. (2018). 'Between a guest and an okupa: Migration and the making of insurgent citizenship in Buenos Aires' informal settlements', *Environment and Planning A: Economy and Space*, 50(1), 31–50. DOI: 10.1177/0308518x17736312

Bastia, T. and vom Hau, M. (2014). 'Migration, race and nationhood in Argentina', *Journal of Ethnic and Migration Studies*, 40(3), 475–492. DOI: 10.1080/1369183X.2013.782153

Bastia, T., Calsina Valenzuela, C. and Pozo, M.E. (2021a). 'The consequences of migration for the migrants' parents in Bolivia', *Global Networks*, 21(2), 393–412. DOI: 10.1111/glob.12276

Bastia, T., Calsina Valenzuela, C. and Pozo, M.E. (2021b). 'Entrepreneurial grannies: migration and "older left-behind" in Cochabamba, Bolivia', in Repetti, M., Calsanti, T. and Phillipson, C. (eds) *Ageing and Migration in a Global Context: Challenges for Welfare States*. London: Springer, pp 29–43.

Bastia, T., Datta, K., Hujo, K., Piper, N. and Walsham, M. (2022a). 'Navigating the challenges of fieldwork and childcare: Revisiting "muddy glee"', *Area*, 54(4), 569–573. DOI: 10.1111/area.12834

Bastia, T., Lulle, A. and King, R. (2022b). 'Migration and development: The overlooked roles of older people and ageing', *Progress in Human Geography*, 46(4), 1009–1027. DOI: 10.1177/03091325221090535

Bastia, T., Datta, K., Hujo, K., Piper, N. and Walsham, M. (2023). 'Reflections on intersectionality: A journey through the worlds of migration research, policy and advocacy', *Gender, Place & Culture*, 30(3), 460–483. DOI: 10.1080/0966369X.2022.2126826

Benencia, R. (1997). 'De peones a patrones quinteros: movilidad social de familias bolivianas en la periferia bonaerense', *Estudios migratorios latinoamericanos*, 12(35), 63–101.

Benencia, R. (2003). 'El fenómeno de la inmigración en la formación de la Argentina moderna', *Memoria, revista mensual de política y cultura*, 168, 27–34.

Benencia, R. and Gazzotti, A. (1995). 'Migración limítrofe y empleo: precisiones e interrogantes', *Estudios migratorios latinoamericanos*, 10(31), 573–611.

Benencia, R. and Karasik, G. (1994). 'Bolivianos en Buenos Aires: aspectos de su integración laboral y cultural', *Estudios migratorios latinoamericanos*, 9(27), 261–299.

Benencia, R. and Karasik, G. (1995). *Inmigración limítrofe: Los bolivianos en Buenos Aires*. Buenos Aires: Centro Editor de América Latina.

Berlinger, N. and Kaebnick, R. (2013). 'Whose hands? Global migration, elder care, and the mothers of others', *Virtual Mentor*, 15(9), 761–766. DOI: 10.1001/virtualmentor.2013.15.9.jdsc1-1309

Biao, X. (2007). 'How far are the left-behind left behind? A preliminary study in rural China', *Population, Space and Place*, 13(3), 179–191. DOI: https://doi.org/10.1002/psp.437

Blouin, C. (ed) (2019). *Después de la llegada: realidades de la migración Venezolana*. Lima: Themis.

Blouin, C. (2021). 'Complejidades y contradicciones de la política migratoria hacia la migración venezolana en el Perú', *Colombia Internacional*, 106, 141–164. DOI: 10.7440/colombiaint106.2021.06

Bolzman, C., Poncioni, R., Vial, M. and Fibbi, R. (2004). 'Older labour migrants' wellbeing in Europe: The case of Switzerland', *Ageing and Society*, 24(3), 411–429.

Botterill, K. (2017). 'Discordant lifestyle mobilities in East Asia: Privilege and precarity of British retirement in Thailand', *Population, Space and Place*, 23(5), e2011. DOI: 10.1002/psp.2011

Bourdieu, P. and Nice, R. (1977). *Outline of a Theory of Practice*. Cambridge: Cambridge University Press.

Brown, R.P.C. (1998). 'Do migrants' remittances decline over time? Evidence from Tongans and Western Samoans in Australia', *The Contemporary Pacific*, 10(1), 107–151. http://www.jstor.org/stable/23706841

Buffel, T. (2017). 'Ageing migrants and the creation of home: Mobility and the maintenance of transnational ties', *Population, Space and Place*, 23(5), e1994. DOI: 10.1002/psp.1994

Calderón, F. and Rivera, A. (1984). *La cancha: una gran feria campesina en la ciudad de Cochabamba*. Cochabamba: CERES, Centro de Estudios de la Realidad Económica y Social.

The Care Collective (2020). *The Care Manifesto: The Politics of Interdependence*. London: Verso Books.

Carling, J. (2002). 'Migration in the age of involuntary immobility: Theoretical reflections and Cape Verdean experiences', *Journal of Ethnic and Migration Studies*, 28(1), 5–42. DOI: 10.1080/13691830120103912

Carling, J. and Schewel, K. (2018). 'Revisiting aspiration and ability in international migration', *Journal of Ethnic and Migration Studies*, 44(6), 945–963. DOI: 10.1080/1369183X.2017.1384146

Carrillo Chambi, J.J. (2015). 'Estructuras y jerarquías en las autoridades de cabildo de Calamarca: Entre el poder local y la colonialidad', *Temas Sociales*, 36, 57–85.

Casado-Díaz, M.A., Kaiser, C. and Warnes, A.M. (2004). 'Northern European retired residents in nine southern European areas: Characteristics, motivations and adjustment', *Ageing and Society*, 24(3), 353–381. DOI: 10.1017/S0144686X04001898

Cela, T., Charles, K., Rigaud Dubuisson, P., Fortin, O., Estinvil, D. and Herns Marcelin, L. (2022a). 'Migration, memory and longing in Haitian songs', *Zanj: The Journal of Critical Global South Studies*, 5(1/2), 193–227. DOI: 10.13169/zanjglobsoutstud.5.1.0013

Cela, T., Fidalgo, M. and Marcelin, L.H. (2022b). 'The COVID-19 pandemic and Haiti's changing remittance landscape', *Revista Relaciones Internacionales*, 95, 128–158. DOI: 10.15359/ri.95/2.6

CEPAL (2024). *Violencia feminicida en cifras: América Latina y el Caribe*. Santiago: United Nations Economic Commission for Latin America and the Caribbean. Available at: https://www.cepal.org/es/publicaciones/81001-actuar-sentido-urgencia-prevenir-poner-fin-feminicidios (accessed 12 March 2025).

Cerase, F.P. (1974). 'Expectations and reality: A case study of return migration from the United States to southern Italy', *The International Migration Review*, 8(2), 245–262. DOI: 10.2307/3002783

Chomik, R., O'Keefe, P. and Piggott, J. (2024). *Pensions in Aging Asia and the Pacific: Policy Insights and Priorities*. Manila: Asian Development Bank.

Cintra, N., Owen, D. and Riggirozzi, P. (2023). *Displacement, Human Rights and Sexual and Reproductive Health: Conceptualizing Gender Protection Gaps in Latin America*. Bristol: Bristol University Press.

Ciobanu, R.O. and Hunter, A. (2017). 'Older migrants and (im)mobilities of ageing: An introduction', *Population, Space and Place*, 23(5), e2075. DOI: 10.1002/psp.2075

Ciobanu, R.O. and Ramos, A.C. (2015). 'Is there a way back? A state-of-the-art review of the literature on retirement return migration', in Karl, U. and Torres, S. (eds) *Ageing in Contexts of Migration*. London: Routledge.

Ciobanu, R.O., Fokkema, T. and Nedelcu, M. (2017). 'Ageing as a migrant: vulnerabilities, agency and policy implications', *Journal of Ethnic and Migration Studies*, 43(2), 164–181. DOI: 10.1080/1369183X.2016.1238903

Coe, C. (2016). 'Orchestrating care in time: Ghanaian migrant women, family, and reciprocity', *American Anthropologist*, 118(1), 37–48. DOI: 10.1111/aman.12446

Coe, C. (2017). 'Transnational migration and the commodification of eldercare in urban Ghana', *Identities*, 24(5), 542–556. DOI: 10.1080/1070289X.2017.1346510

Coe, C. (2022). *Changes in Care: Aging, Migration, and Social Class in West Africa*. New Brunswick: Rutgers University Press.

Colectivo Ioé (2012). *Impacto de la crisis sobre la población migrante*. Madrid: Colectivo Ioé. Available at: https://www.colectivoioe.org/uploads/0bae582aa3b0842a9eaf50cde16f4f97d9527bcb.pdf (accessed 12 March 2025).

Conkova, N., Vullnetari, J., King, R. and Fokkema, T. (2018). ' "Left like stones in the middle of the road": Narratives of aging alone and coping strategies in rural Albania and Bulgaria', *The Journals of Gerontology: Series B*, 74(8), 1492–1500. DOI: 10.1093/geronb/gby127

Cortés, G. (2004). *Partir para quedarse: supervivencia y cambio en las sociedades campesinas andinas*. La Paz: Plural.

Cox, R., Hope, J., Jenkins, K. and Ray, C. (2024). 'Care and the academy: Navigating fieldwork, funding and care responsibilities', *Area*, 56(1), e12909. DOI: 10.1111/area.12909

Crawley, H. and Teye, J. (2023). 'South-South migration and inequality: An introduction', in Crawley, H. and Teye, J. (eds) *The Palgrave Handbook of South-South Migration and Inequality*. Cham: Palgrave, pp 1–22.

Crenshaw, K. (1989). 'Demarginalizing the intersection of race and sex: A black feminist critique of antidiscrimination doctrine, feminist theory and antiracist politics', *University of Chicago Legal Forum*, 1, 139–167.

Crenshaw, K. (1991). 'Mapping the margins: Intersectionality, identity politics, and violence against women of color', *Stanford Law Review*, 43(6), 1241–1299.

Crivello, G. (2011). ' "Becoming somebody": Youth transitions through education and migration in Peru', *Journal of Youth Studies*, 14(4), 395–411. DOI: 10.1080/13676261.2010.538043

Curiel, O. (2007). 'Crítica poscolonial desde las prácticas políticas del feminismo antirracista', *Nómadas*, 28, 92–101.

Cylwik, H. (2002). 'Expectations of inter-generational reciprocity among older Greek Cypriot migrants in London', *Ageing and Society*, 22(5), 599–613. DOI: 10.1017/S0144686X02008863

De Haas, H., Castles, S. and Miller, M.J. (2020). *The Age of Migration: International Population Movements in the Modern World*. London: Macmillan International and Red Globe Press.

de la Torre Avila, L. (2006). *No llores, prenda, pronto volveré. Migración, movilidad social, herida familiar y desarrollo*. La Paz: PIEB.

de la Torre Avila, L. and Alfaro Aramayo, Y. (2007). *La cheqanchada: caminos y sendas de desarrollo en los municipios migrantes de Arbieto y Toco*. La Paz: PIEB.

Díaz Gómez, L. and Marroni, M.d.G. (2017). 'Abuelas en la migración. Migración circular, servicios de cuidados y reunificación familiar en una localidad del occidente michoacano', *Relaciones. Estudios de Historia y Sociedad*, 38(151), 263–295. DOI: 10.24901/rehs.v38i151.336

Dossa, P. and Coe, C. (2017). *Transnational Aging and Reconfigurations of Kin Work*. New Brunswick: Rutgers University Press.

DTUDA (Danish Trade Union Development Agency) (2021). *Labour Market Profile 2021 – Bolivia*. Copenhagen: Danish Trade Union Development Agency. Available at: https://www.ulandssekretariatet.dk/wp-content/uploads/2021/01/LMP-Bolivia-2021-Final.pdf (accessed 12 March 2025).

ECLAC (Economic Commission for Latin America and the Caribbean) (2022) *Ageing in Latin America and the Caribbean: Inclusion and Rights of Older Persons. Report of Latin America and the Caribbean for the Fourth Review and Appraisal of the Madrid International Plan of Action on Ageing.* Santiago. Available at: https://repositorio.cepal.org/server/api/core/bit streams/703b8179-ba9d-4838-8ec1-61405dbcbd18/content (accessed 12 March 2025).

Ely, R. and McCabe, A. (2009). 'Gender differences in memories for speech', in Leydesdorff, S., Passerini, L. and Thompson, P. (eds) *Gender and Memory*. New Brunswick: Transaction Publishers, pp 17–30.

England, K. and Henry, C. (2013). 'Care work, migration and citizenship: international nurses in the UK', *Social & Cultural Geography*, 14(5), 558–574. DOI: 10.1080/14649365.2013.786789

Erbol (2013). 'Exportación de quinua multiplicó por 26 en 10 años', *Erbol*. Available at: https://anteriorportal.erbol.com.bo/noticia/economia/21022 013/exportacion_de_quinua_multiplico_por_26_en_10_anos (accessed 12 March 2025).

Escóbar, S. (2014). *Trabajando de por vida, los adultos mayores en el mundo del trabajo rural, La Paz, Bolivia*. Available at: http://www.helpagela.org/public aciones/publicaciones-destacadas/ (accessed 9 December 2024).

Escóbar de Pabón, S. (2012). *Los adultos mayores en el mundo del trabajo urbano*. La Paz: HelpAge International and CEDLA.

Espinosa Miñoso, Y. (2007). *Escritos de una lesbiana oscura: reflexiones críticas sobre feminismo y política de identidad en América Latina*. Buenos Aires: en la frontera.

Espinosa Miñoso, Y., Gómez Correal, D. and Ochoa Muñoz, K. (eds) (2014). *Tejiendo de otro modo: Feminismo, epistemología y apuestas descoloniales en Abya Yala*. Popayán: Editorial Universidad de Calcuta.

Farah Henrich, I., Sánchez, M.d.C. and Castro Mantilla, M.D. (2012). *La participación política y el liderazgo de las mujeres adultas mayores*. La Paz: HelpAge International.

Finch, J. (1989). *Family Obligations and Social Change*. Cambridge: Polity Press.

Freier, L.F. and Vera Espinoza, M. (2021). 'COVID-19 and immigrants' increased exclusion: The politics of immigrant integration in Chile and Peru', *Frontiers in Human Dynamics*, 3. DOI: 10.3389/fhumd.2021.606871

Gamboa, R. (2006). 'Evaluación de la Sostenibilidad del Pago del Bonosol', *Revista de Análisis Económico*, 21, 62–82.

Gamburd, M.R. (2020). *Linked Lives: Elder Care, Migration, and Kinship in Sri Lanka*. New Brunswick: Rutgers University Press.

Gandini, L., Prieto Rosas, V. and Lozano-Ascencio, F. (2020). 'Nuevas movilidades en América Latina: la migración venezolana en contextos de crisis y las respuestas en la región', *Cuadernos Geográficos*, 59(3), 103–121. DOI: 10.30827/cuadgeo.v59i3.9294

Gao, Q., Prina, A.M., Ma, Y., Aceituno, D. and Mayston, R. (2022). 'Inequalities in older age and primary health care utilization in low-and middle-income countries: A systematic review', *International Journal of Health Services*, 52(1), 99–114. DOI: 10.1177/00207314211041234

Garcés-Estrada, C., Leiva-Gómez, S. and Comelin-Fornés, A. (2021). 'Interseccionalidades y trabajo de cuidado: migración circular boliviana en el norte Chile', *Apuntes. Revista De Ciencias Sociales*, 49(90), 119–145. DOI: 10.21678/apuntes.90.1409

Gardner, K. (1999). 'Narrating location: Space, age and gender among Bengali elders in East London', *Oral History*, 27(1), 65–74.

Gardner, K. (2002). *Age, Narrative and Migration: The Life Course and Life Histories of Bengali Elders in London*. Abingdon: Routledge.

Gavazzo, N., Gerbaudo Suárez, D., Espul, S. and Morales, Y. (2020). 'Intersecciones entre migración, clase, género y generación', *RevIISE – Revista De Ciencias Sociales y Humanas*, 16(6), 115–130.

Gissi, N., Aruj, R. and Polo, S. (2021). 'Políticas migratorias y cooperación regional en el Cono Sur: gestión institucional de la migración venezolana en Argentina, Chile y Bolivia', *Sociedade e Estado*, 36(3), 1015–1035. DOI: 10.1590/s0102-6992-202136030008

Godfrey-Wood, R. and Mamani-Vargas, G. (2017). 'The coercive side of collective capabilities: Evidence from the Bolivian Altiplano', *Journal of Human Development and Capabilities*, 18(1), 75–88. DOI: 10.1080/19452829.2016.1199169

Godfrey-Wood, R. and Mamani-Vargas, G. (2019). '"It really saves us" versus "it doesn't cover everything": The benefits and limitations of a non-contributory pension in the Bolivian Altiplano', *Ageing and Society*, 39(1), 17–44. DOI: 10.1017/S0144686X17000460

Goldstein, D.M. (2012). *Outlawed: Between Security and Rights in a Bolivian City*. Durham, NC: Duke University Press.

Gonzalez, L. (2020). *Por um Feminismo Afro-latino-americano: ensaios, intervenções e diálogos*. São Paulo: Zahar.

Green, M. and Lawson, V. (2011). 'Recentring care: Interrogating the commodification of care', *Social & Cultural Geography*, 12(6), 639–654. DOI: 10.1080/14649365.2011.601262

Green, P. (2013). 'Contested realities and economic circumstances: British later-life migrants in Malaysia', in Janoschka, M. and Haas, H. (eds) *Contested Spatialities, Lifestyle Migration and Residential Tourism*. Abingdon: Routledge, pp 145–157.

Green, P. (2015). 'Mobility, subjectivity and interpersonal relationships: Older, Western migrants and retirees in Malaysia and Indonesia', *Asian Anthropology*, 14(2), 150–165. DOI: 10.1080/1683478X.2015.1046033

Haagsman, K. and Mazzucato, V. (2020). 'The well-being of stay behind family members in migrant households', in Bastia, T. and Skeldon, R. (eds) *Routledge Handbook of Migration and Development*. Abingdon: Routledge, pp 181–190.

Harper, S. and Laws, G. (1995). 'Rethinking the geography of ageing', *Progress in Human Geography*, 19(2), 199–221. DOI: 10.1177/030913259501900

Harris, O. (1994). 'Condor and bull: The ambiguities of masculinity in Northern Potosí', in Harvey, P. and Gow, P. (eds) *Sex and Violence*. Abingdon: Routledge, pp 40–65.

Hayes, M. (2014). '"We gained a lot over what we would have had": The geographic arbitrage of North American lifestyle migrants to Cuenca, Ecuador', *Journal of Ethnic and Migration Studies*, 40(12), 1953–1971. DOI: 10.1080/1369183X.2014.880335

Hayes, M. (2015). 'Moving south: The economic motives and structural context of North America's emigrants in Cuenca, Ecuador', *Mobilities*, 10(2), 267–284. DOI: 10.1080/17450101.2013.858940

Hayes, M. (2018). 'The gringos of Cuenca: How retirement migrants perceive their impact on lower income communities', *Area*, 50(4), 467–475. DOI: 10.1111/area.12460

He, C. and Ye, J. (2014). 'Lonely sunsets: Impacts of rural–urban migration on the left-behind elderly in rural China', *Population, Space and Place*, 20(4), 352–369. DOI: 10.1002/psp.1829

HelpAge International and UNFPA (United Nations Population Fund) (2012). *Ageing in the Twenty-first Century: A Celebration and a Challenge*. New York and London: UNFPA and HelpAge International.

Herrera, G. (2013). *Lejos de tus pupilas: familias transnacionales, cuidados y desigualdad social en Ecuador*. Quito: Onu-Muejres, FLACSO.

Herrera, G. (2020). 'Care and migration', in Bastia, T. and Skeldon, R. (eds) *Routledge Handbook of Migration and Development*. Abingdon: Routledge, pp 232–241.

Heslop, A. and Gorman, M. (2002). *Chronic Poverty and Older People in the Developing World*, with HelpAge International, CPRC Working Paper No 10. Brighton: University of Sussex.

Higgs, P. and Gilleard, C. (2017). 'Ageing, dementia and the social mind: Past, present and future perspectives', *Sociology of Health and Illness*, 39(2), 175–181. DOI: 10.1111/1467-9566.12536

Hinojosa, A. (2010). *Buscando la vida: familias bolivianas transnacionales en España*. La Paz: CLACSO; Fundación PIEB.

Hinojosa Gordonava, A. (2000). *Idas y venidas: campesinos tarijeños en el norte argentino*. La Paz: Fundación PIEB.

Ho, E.S. and Chiang, L.-h.N. (2017). 'Long-distance filial piety: Chinese families in Australasia caring for elderly parents across borders (長距離的孝道：紐西蘭與澳洲華人家庭的跨國父母照顧)', *Translocal Chinese: East Asian Perspectives*, 11(2), 278–311. DOI: 10.1163/24522015-01102006

Hochschild, A.R. (2000). 'Global care chains and emotional surplus value', in Giddens, A. and Hutton, W. (eds) *On the Edge: Living with Global Capitalism*. London: Jonathan Cape, pp 130–146.

Hope, J., Lemanski, C., Bastia, T., Moeller, N., Meth, P. and Williams, G. (2020). 'Childcare and academia: An intervention', *International Development Planning Review*, 42(4), 391–405. DOI: 10.3828/idpr.2019.40

Huete, N.R., Mantecón Terán, A. and Mazón Martínez, T. (2008). 'De qué hablamos cuando hablamos de turismo residencial?', *Cuadernos del Turismo*, 22, 101–121.

Hunter, A. (2011). 'Theory and practice of return migration at retirement: The case of migrant worker hostel residents in France', *Population, Space and Place*, 17(2), 179–192. DOI: 10.1002/psp.610

Hunter, A. (2018a). 'Journey's end? Old age in France's migrant worker hostels', in *Retirement Home? Ageing Migrant Workers in France and the Question of Return*. Cham: Springer International Publishing, pp 1–28.

Hunter, A. (2018b). *Retirement Home? Ageing Migrant Workers in France and the Question of Return*. 1st edn. Cham: Springer.

IBCE (Instituto Boliviano de Comercio Exterior) (2021). *Exportaciones de quinua*. Instituto Boliviano de Comercio Exterior. Available at: https://ibce.org.bo/images/ibcecifras_documentos/Cifras-959-Exportaciones-quinua.pdf (accessed 12 March 2025).

INE (Instituto Nacional de Estadística) (2012). *Censo nacional de población y vivienda*. Available at: https://www.ine.gob.bo/index.php/estadisticas-sociales/vivienda-y-servicios-basicos/censos-vivienda/ (accessed 9 December 2024).

INE (2015). *Censo de población y vivienda 2012: características de la población*. La Paz: INE. Available at: https://www.ine.gob.bo/index.php/publicaciones/censo-de-poblacion-y-vivienda-2012-caracteristicas-de-la-poblacion/ (accessed 12 March 2025).

INE (2017a). *Argentina es el país de mayor preferencia de emigrantes bolivianos*. Available at: https://www.ine.gob.bo/index.php/argentina-es-el-pais-de-mayor-preferencia-de-emigrantes-bolivianos/#:~:text=El%20Censo%202012%20establece%20que,vive%20habitualmente%20en%20el%20pa%C3%ADs (accessed 12 March 2025).

INE (2017b). *Población adulta mayor boliviana tiende a incrementarse en los próximos años*. Available at: https://www.ine.gob.bo/index.php/poblacion-adulta-mayor-boliviana-tiende-a-incrementarse-en-los-proximos-anos/ (accessed 9 December 2024).

INE (2019). *Estudio post-censal del adulto mayor: estado de situación de los adultos mayores en Bolivia*. La Paz: INE.

INE (2020). *Encuesta de Hogares*. La Paz: INE. Available at: https://www.ine.gob.bo/index.php/estadisticas-economicas/encuestas-de-hogares-ingre sos/# (accessed 9 December 2024).

INE (2023). *Censos y proyecciones de población sociales*. La Paz. Available at: https://www.ine.gob.bo/index.php/censos-y-proyecciones-de-poblac ion-sociales/ (accessed 9 December 2024).

INE (various dates). Census and Household Survey data. La Paz: Instituto Nacional de Estadística. Available at: https://www.ine.gob.bo/ (accessed 12 March 2025).

IOM (International Organization for Migration) (2011). *Perfil Migratorio de Bolivia 2011*. Buenos Aires: IOM. Available at: https://publications.iom. int/es/books/perfil-migratorio-de-bolivia-2011 (accessed 12 March 2025).

Iossifova, D. (2020). *Translocal Ageing in the Global East: Bulgaria's Abandoned Elderly*. Cham: Palgrave Macmillan.

Isbell, B.J. (1979). *To Defend Ourselves: Ecology and Ritual in an Andean Village*. Austin: Institute of Latin American Studies, University of Texas at Austin.

Janoschka, M. (2011). 'Imaginario del turismo residencial en Costa Rica', in Mazón Martínez, T., Huete Nieves, R. and Mantecón, A. (eds) *Construir una nueva vida. Los espacios del turismo y la migración residencial*. Santander: Milrazones, pp 81–102.

Janoschka, M. and Haas, H. (2014). 'Contested spatialities of lifestyle migration: approaches and research questions', in Janoschka, M. and Haas, H. (eds) *Contested Spatialities, Lifestyle Migration and Residential Tourism*. Abingdon: Routledge, pp 1–12.

Jenkins, K. (2020). 'Academic motherhood and fieldwork: Juggling time, emotions, and competing demands', *Transactions of the Institute of British Geographers*, 45(3), 693–704. DOI: 10.1111/tran.12376

Jokela, M. (2009). 'Personality predicts migration within and between U.S. states', *Journal of Research in Personality*, 43(1), 79–83. DOI: 10.1016/ j.jrp.2008.09.005

Jones, R. (2016). *Violent Borders: Refugees and the Right to Move*. London: Verso.

Jones, R. and De La Torre, L. (2011). 'Diminished tradition of return? Transnational migration in Bolivia's Valle Alto', *Global Networks*, 11(2), 180–202. DOI: 10.1111/j.1471-0374.2011.00314.x

Jurdao Arrones, F. (1970). *España en venta: compra de suelos por extranjeros y colonización de campesinos en la Costa del Sol*. Madrid: Enclymon.

Karl, U. and Torres, S. (2016). *Ageing in Contexts of Migration*. Abindgdon: Routledge.

Kilkey, M. and Merla, L. (2014). 'Situating transnational families' care-giving arrangements: The role of institutional contexts', *Global Networks*, 14(2), 210–229. DOI: 10.1111/glob.12034

King, R. and Lulle, A. (2015). 'Rhythmic island: Latvian migrants in Guernsey and their enfolded patterns of space-time mobility', *Population, Space and Place*, 21(7), 599–611. DOI: 10.1002/psp.1915

King, R. and Vullnetari, J. (2006). 'Orphan pensioners and migrating grandparents: The impact of mass migration on older people in rural Albania', *Ageing and Society*, 26(5), 783–816. DOI: 10.1017/S0144686X 06005125

King, R., Warnes, A.M. and Williams, A.M. (2000). *Sunset Lives: British Retirement Migration to the Mediterranean*. Oxford: Berg.

King, R., Cela, E., Fokkema, T. and Vullnetari, J. (2014). 'The migration and well-being of the zero generation: Transgenerational care, grandparenting, and loneliness amongst Albanian older people', 20(8), 728–738. DOI: https://doi.org/10.1002/psp.1895

King, R., Lulle, A., Sampaio, D. and Vullnetari, J. (2017). 'Unpacking the ageing–migration nexus and challenging the vulnerability trope', *Journal of Ethnic and Migration Studies*, 43(2), 182–198. DOI: 10.1080/ 1369183X.2016.1238904

Klein, H.S. (1995). *Haciendas y ayllus en Bolivia: ss XVIII y XIX. Serie Estudios Históricos 18*. 1st edn. Lima: IEP.

Klein, H.S. (2003). *A Concise History of Bolivia*. Cambridge: Cambridge University Press.

Kleist, N. (2015). 'Pushing development: A case study of highly skilled male return migration to Ghana', in Åkesson, L. and Eriksson Baaz, M. (eds) *Africa's Return Migrants: The New Developers?* London: Zed Books, pp 64–86.

Koch-Schulte, J. (2011). 'La migración residencial en Udon, Thani, Thailandia', in Mazón Martínez, T., Huete Nieves, R. and Mantecón Terán, A. (eds) *Construir una nueva vida. Los espacios del turismo y la migración residencial*. Santander: Milrasones, pp 129–153.

Kofman, E. and Raghuram, P. (2015). *Gendered Migrations and Global Social Reproduction*. London: Palgrave.

Kowal, P., Kahn, K., Ng, N., Naidoo, N., Abdullah, S., Bawah, A. et al (2010). 'Ageing and adult health status in eight lower-income countries: The INDEPTH WHO-SAGE collaboration', *Global Health Action*, 3(1), 5302.

Kreager, P. (2006). 'Migration, social structure and old-age support networks: A comparison of three Indonesian communities', *Ageing and Society*, 26(1), 37–60. DOI: 10.1017/S0144686X05004411

Kreager, P. and Schröder-Butterfill, E. (2007). 'Gaps in the family networks of older people in three Indonesian communities', *Journal of Cross-Cultural Gerontology*, 22(1), 1–25. DOI: 10.1007/s10823-006-9013-3

Laliberte Rudman, D. (2006). 'Shaping the active, autonomous and responsible modern retiree: An analysis of discursive technologies and their links with neo-liberal political rationality', *Ageing and Society*, 26(2), 181–201. DOI: 10.1017/S0144686X05004253

Lamb, S.E. (2009). *Aging and the Indian Diaspora: Cosmopolitan Families in India and Abroad*. Bloomington: Indiana University Press.

Laslett, P. (1987). 'The emergence of the third age', *Ageing and Society*, 7(2), 133–160. DOI: 10.1017/S0144686X00012538

Leydesdorff, S., Passerini, L. and Thompson, P. (2009). *Gender and Memory*. New Brunswick: Transaction Publishers.

Lloyd-Sherlock, P. (1996). *The Growth of and Socio-economic Conditions in Shanty Towns within Greater Buenos Aires*. Glasgow: University of Glasgow, Institute of Latin American Studies.

Lloyd-Sherlock, P. (2004). *Living Longer: Ageing, Development and Social Protection*. London: Zed Books.

Lloyd-Sherlock, P. (2010). *Population Ageing and International Development: From Generalisation to Evidence*. Bristol: Policy Press.

Lloyd-Sherlock, P., Barrientos, A., Moller, V. and Saboia, J. (2012). 'Pensions, poverty and wellbeing in later life: Comparative research from South Africa and Brazil', *Journal of Aging Studies*, 26(3), 243–252. DOI: 10.1016/j.jaging.2012.02.003

Lozano, A.G. (1975). 'Syntactic borrowing in Spanish from Quechua: The noun phrase', in Avales de Matos, R. and Ravines, R. (eds) *Lingüística e indigenismo moderno de América: Trabajos presentados al XXXIX Congreso Internacional de Americanistas*. Lima: Instituto de Estudios Peruanos, pp 297–305.

Lugones, M. (2008). 'Colonialidad y Género', *Tábula Rasa*, 9, 73–101.

Lulle, A. (2024). *Midlife Geographies: Changing Lifecourses across Generations, Spaces and Time*. Bristol: Policy Press.

Lulle, A. and King, R. (2016). *Ageing, Gender, and Labour Migration*. New York: Palgrave Macmillan.

Magliano, M.J. (2015). 'Interseccionalidad y migraciones: potencialidades y desafíos', *Revista Estudos Feministas*, 23, 691–712. DOI: 10.1590/0104-026X2015v23n3p691

Magliano, M.J. and Ferreccio, N.V.G. (2017). 'Interseccionalidades que condenan: gestos coloniales del sistema jurídico en Argentina', *Crítica Penal y Poder*, 13, 112–127.

Marcelin, L.H. and Cela, T. (2023). 'The making of migration trails in the Americas: Ethnographic network tracing of Haitians on the move', in Crawley, H. and Teye, J. (eds) *The Palgrave Handbook of South–South Migration and Inequality*. Cham: Springer International Publishing, pp 271–294.

Martínez Espínola, M.V. and Delmonte Allasia, A. (2022). 'Feminismos, interseccionalidad y cuidados. Reflexiones a partir de experiencias de mujeres venezolanas en la Argentina actual', *Pacha. Revista de Estudios Contemporáneos del Sur Global*, 3(9), e210153. DOI: 10.46652/pacha.v3i9.153

Mata-Codesal, D. (2015). 'Ways of staying put in Ecuador: Social and embodied experiences of mobility–immobility interactions', *Journal of Ethnic and Migration Studies*, 41(14), 2274–2290. DOI: 10.1080/1369183X.2015.1053850

Mazzucato, V. (2011). 'Reverse remittances in the migration–development nexus: Two-way flows between Ghana and the Netherlands', *Population, Space and Place*, 17, 454–468. https://doi.org/10.1002/psp.646

McKay, D. (2016). *An Archipelago of Care: Filipino Migrants and Global Networks*. Bloomington: Indiana University Press.

Mehta, K. and Singh, A. (2008). *Indian Diaspora: Voices of the Diasporic Elders in Five Countries*. Leiden: Brill.

Membrado Tena, J.C. (2015). 'Migración residencial y urbanismo expansivo en el Mediterráneo español', *Cuadernos de Turismo*, 35, 259–286. DOI: 10.6018/turismo.35.221611

Miah, M.F. (2022). 'Return visits and other return mobilities', in King, R. and Kuschminder, K. (eds) *Handbook of Return Migration*. Cheltenham: Edward Elgar, pp 96–106.

Miah, M.F., King, R. and Lulle, A. (2023). 'Visiting migrants: An introduction', *Global Networks*, 23(1), 150–159. DOI: 10.1111/glob.12426

Ministerio de Salud y Deportes (2013). *Norma nacional de caracterización de establecimientos de salud de primer nivel*. La Paz: Ministerio de Salud y Deportes, Estado plurinacional de Bolivia. Available at: https://www.minsalud.gob.bo/images/Libros/DGSS/ursc/redes/dgss_redes_Inivelseguro.pdf (accessed 12 March 2025).

Miranda, B. (2017). '"Uno ya sabe a lo que viene": la movilidad laboral de migrantes andino-bolivianos entre talleres de costura de São Paulo explicada a la luz de la producción del consentimiento', *REMHU – Revista Interdisciplinar da Mobilidade Humana*, 25(49), 197–213. DOI: 10.1590/1980-85852503880004911

Miranda, B. (2019). 'La migración de retorno vista a través de la circularidad. Desplazamientos entre Bolivia y Brasil', *Andamios*, 16, 257–282. DOI: 10.29092/uacm.v16i41.725

Miyawaki, C.E. and Hooyman, N.R. (2023). 'A systematic review of the literature on transnational caregiving: Immigrant adult children to ageing parents in home country', *Journal of Family Studies*, 29(1), 453–470. DOI: 10.1080/13229400.2021.1908908

Montero Bressán, J. and Arcos, A. (2016). 'How do migrants respond to labour abuses in local sweatshops?', *Antipode*, 49, 437–454. DOI: 10.1111/anti.12250

Montes de Oca, V., Molina, A. and Avalos, R. (2008). *Migración, redes transnacionales y envejecimiento: estudio de las redes familiares transnacionales de la vejez en Guanajuato*. México, DF: México Universidad Nacional Autónoma de México.

Moonga, F. (2024). 'Poverty among rural older people in Zambia', *The Routledge Handbook of Poverty in the Global South*. Abingdon: Routledge, pp 182–199.

Müller, K. (2009). 'Contested universalism: From Bonosol to Renta Dignidad in Bolivia', 18(2), 163–172. DOI: 10.1111/j.1468-2397.2008.00579.x

Murra, J. (1972). 'El "control vertical" de un máximo de pisos ecológicos en la economía de las sociedades andinas', in Murra, J. (ed) *Visita de la Provincia de Leon de Huanuco en 1562*. Huanuco: Universidad Nacional Hermilio Valdizan, pp 427–476.

Muysken, P.C. (1984). 'The Spanish that Quechua speakers learn: L2 learning as norm-governed behaviour', in Andersen, R. (ed) *Second Languages: A Cross-linguistic Perspective*. Rowley: Newbury House, pp 101–124.

Näre, L. (2017). 'Identity and ambivalence in everyday transnationalism: Older-aged Gujaratis in London', *Identities*, 24(5), 625–640. DOI: 10.1080/1070289X.2017.1345550

Nash, J. (1993). *We Eat the Mines and the Mines Eat Us: Dependency and Exploitation in Bolivian Tin Mines*. New York: Columbia University Press.

Nazareno, J., Parreñas, R.S. and Fan, Y.-K. (2014). *Can I ever retire? The plight of migrant Filipino elderly caregivers in Los Angeles*. Los Angeles: Institute for Research on Labor and Employment.

Nedelcu, M., Tomás, L., Ravazzini, L. and Azevedo, L. (2023). 'A retirement mobilities approach to transnational ageing', *Mobilities*, 19(2), 208–226. DOI: 10.1080/17450101.2023.2213402

Neira Orjuela, F. (2022). 'Migraciones sur-sur: Los flujos andinos en Argentina, Brasil y Chile', in Paniagua Vásquez, A., Maza Ávila, F.J., Borunda Escobedo, J.E. and Camargo González, I. (eds) *La migración en Latinoamérica: estado actual, oportunidades y retos*. Ciudad Juárez: El Colegio de Chihuahua, pp 169–212.

Nobbs-Thiessen, B. (2020). *Landscape of Migration: Mobility and Environmental Change on Bolivia's Tropical Frontier, 1952 to the Present*. Chapel Hill: The University of North Carolina Press.

O'Reilly, K. (2012). *Structuration, Practice Theory, Ethnography and Migration: Bringing It All Together*. Working Paper. Oxford: International Migration Institute. Available at: https://www.migrationinstitute.org/publi cations/wp-61-12 (accessed 12 March 2025).

Ono, M. (2017). 'Fleeing from constraints: Japanese retirement migrants in Malaysia', in Guarné, B. and Hansen, P. (eds) *Escaping Japan: Reflections on Estrangement and Exile in the Twenty-First Century*. Abingdon: Routledge, pp 199–218.

OSUMI (2019). *Resumen perfil del país*. La Paz: Observatorio Sudamericano sobre migraciones. Available at: https://csmigraciones.org/sites/default/files/2021-01/estadisticas_sobre_migracion_en_bolivia.pdf (accessed 12 March 2025).

OXFAM (2019). *Tiempo para cuidar. Compartir el cuidado para la sostenibilidad de la vida*. La Paz: Oxfam. Available at: https://actions.oxfam.org/media/assets/file/Tiempo_para_cuidar.pdf (accessed 12 March 2025).

Oxford University (2024). *Global & Regional Population Pyramids*. Oxford: Oxford Institute of Population Ageing. Available at: https://www.ageing.ox.ac.uk/population-horizons/data/gpt (accessed 9 December 2024).

Parella, S. (2005). 'La maternidad a distancia de las empleadas domésticas latinoamericanas en España. La vulneración del derecho a la vida familiar en el contexto de la internacionalización de la reproducción', in Giró, J. (ed) *El género quebrantado. Sobre la violencia, la libertad y los derechos de la mujer en el nuevo milenio*. Madrid: Asociación Los Libros de la Catarata, pp 238–273.

Parella, S. (2011). 'Familia transnacional y redefinición de los roles de género: El caso de la migración boliviana en España', *Papers: revista de sociologia*, 97(3), 661–684. DOI: 10.5565/rev/papers/v97n3.454

Parella, S., Petroff, A. and Serradell Pumareda, O. (2014). 'Programas de retorno voluntario en Bolivia y España en contextos de crisis', *Revista CIDOB d'Afers Internacionals*, 106/107, 171–192.

Parreñas, R.S. (2001). *Servants of Globalization: Women, Migration and Domestic Work*. Stanford: Stanford University Press.

Parreñas, R.S. (2012). 'The reproductive labour of migrant workers', *Global Networks*, 12(2), 269–275. DOI: 10.1111/j.1471-0374.2012.00351.x

Parreñas, R.S., Silvey, R., Hwang, M.C. and Choi, C.A. (2019). 'Serial labor migration: Precarity and itinerancy among Filipino and Indonesian domestic workers', *International Migration Review*, 53(4), 1230–1258. DOI: 10.1177/0197918318804769

Pérez Orozco, A. (2021). 'Amenaza tormenta: la crisis de los cuidados y la reorganización del sistema económico', *Revista de Economía Crítica*, 1(5), 8–37.

Phillips, D.R. and Feng, Z. (2018). 'Global ageing', in Skinner, M.W., Andrews, G.J. and Cutchin, M.P. (eds) *Geographical Gerontology: Perspectives, Concepts, Approaches*. Abingdon: Routledge, pp 93–109.

Phizacklea, A.E. (1983). *One Way Ticket: Migration and Female Labour*. London: R.K.P.

Pinto, G. (2015). 'El bono demográfico en América Latina: El efecto económico de los cambios en la estructura por edad de una población', *Población y Salud en Mesoamérica*, 13(2), 191–210. DOI: 10.15517/psm.v13i2.21863

Pinto Baleisan, C. and Cisternas Collao, N. (2021). 'Reflexiones sobre el uso de la interseccionalidad en los estudios migratorios en Chile', *Revista Punto Género*, 14, 49–70. DOI: 10.5354/2735-7473.2020.60866

Pratt, G. (2012). *Families Apart: Migrant Mothers and the Conflicts of Labor and Love*. Minneapolis: University of Minnesota Press.

Price, M. (2016). 'Many destinations, one place called home: Migration and livelihood for rural Bolivians', *Focus on Geography*, 59. DOI: 10.21690/foge/2016.59.1p

Quijano, A. (2000). 'Colonialidad del poder, eurocentrismo y América Latina', in Lander, E. (ed) *Colonialidad del saber, eurocentrismo y ciencias sociales.* Buenos Aires: CLACSO-UNESCO, pp 201–246.

Randel, J., German, T. and Ewing, D. (2017). *The Ageing and Development Report: Poverty, Independence and the World's Older People.* Abingdon: Routledge.

Ratha, D. and Shaw, W. (2007). *South-South Migration and Remittances.* Washington, DC: World Bank.

Regalsky, P. (2003). *Etnicidad y clase: el estado boliviano y las estrategias andinas de manejo de su espacio.* La Paz: Plural.

Repetti, M. and Calasanti, T. (2024). *Retirement Migration and Precarity in Later Life.* Bristol: Bristol University Press.

Reyes Muñoz, V.L. and Reyes Muñoz, Y.T. (2021). 'Transnacionalidad e interseccionalidad para abordar la localización/posición de migrantes etnoracializados', *ODISEA. Revista de Estudios Migratorios*, 8, 49–75.

Rishworth, A. and Elliot, S.J. (2018). 'Ageing in low- and middle-income countries', in Skinner, M.W., Andrews, G.J. and Cutchin, M.P. (eds) *Geographical Gerontology: Perspectives, Concepts, Approaches.* Abingdon: Routledge, pp 110–122.

Román, O. (2009). *Mientras no estamos: migración de mujeres-madres de Cochabamba a España.* Cochabamba: UMSS, CESU.

Romero, M. (2018). 'Reflections on globalized care chains and migrant women workers', *Critical Sociology*, 44(7–8), 1179–1189. DOI: 10.1177/0896920517748497

Ryburn, M. (2016). 'Living the Chilean dream? Bolivian migrants' incorporation in the space of economic citizenship', *Geoforum*, 76, 48–58. DOI: 10.1016/j.geoforum.2016.08.006

Ryburn, M. (2018). *Uncertain Citizenship: Everyday Practices of Bolivian Migrants in Chile.* Berkeley: University of California Press.

Saffioti, H. (1978). *Women in Class Society.* New York: Monthly Review Press.

Saffioti, H. (1992). 'Rearticulando gênero e classe social', in Costa, A.d.O. and Bruschini, C. (eds) *Uma questão de gênero.* São Paulo: Fundação Carlos Chagas, pp 183–215.

Sampaio, D. (2020). 'Caring by silence: How (un)documented Brazilian migrants enact silence as a care practice for aging parents', *Journal of Intergenerational Relationships*, 18(3), 281–300. DOI: 10.1080/15350770.2020.1787038

Sampaio, D. (2022). *Migration, Diversity and Inequality in Later Life: Ageing at a Crossroads.* Cham: Palgrave Macmillan.

Sampaio, D. and Walsh, K. (2023). 'Ageing in place', in Torres, S. and Hunter, A. (eds) *Handbook of Ageing and Migration.* Cheltenham: Edward Elgar Publishing, pp 98–106.

Sassone, S. (1989). 'Migraciones limítrofes en la Argentina: Áreas de asentamiento y efectos geográficos', *Signos Universitarios: ciencias sociales y geográficas (Revista de la Universidad del Salvador)*, 8(15), 149–196.

Savaş, E.B., Spaan, J., Henkens, K., Kalmjin, M. and van Dalen, H.P. (2023). 'Migrating to a new country in late life: A review of the literature on international retirement migration', *Demographic Research*, 48(9), 233–270. DOI: 10.4054/DemRes.2023.48.9

Schröder-Butterfill, E. (2004). 'Inter-generational family support provided by older people in Indonesia', *Ageing and Society*, 24(4), 497–530. DOI: 10.1017/S0144686X0400234X

Schröder-Butterfill, E. and Schonheinz, J. (2019). 'Transnational families and the circulation of care: A Romanian–German case study', *Ageing and Society*, 39(1), 45–73. DOI:10.1017/S0144686X1700099X

Scuzzarello, S. (2020). 'Practising privilege: How settling in Thailand enables older Western migrants to enact privilege over local people', *Journal of Ethnic and Migration Studies*, 46(8), 1606–1628. DOI: 10.1080/1369183X.2020.1711570

Shetty, P. (2012). 'Grey matter: Ageing in developing countries', *The Lancet*, 379(9823), 1285–1287. DOI: 10.1016/S0140-6736(12)60541-8

Silvey, R. and Parreñas, R. (2020). 'Precarity chains: Cycles of domestic worker migration from Southeast Asia to the Middle East', *Journal of Ethnic and Migration Studies*, 46(16), 3457–3471. DOI: 10.1080/1369183X.2019.1592398

Simon, G. (1995). *Géodynamique des migrations internationales dans le monde.* Paris: Presses Universitaires de France.

Sinatti, G. (2015). ' "Come back, invest, and advance the country": Policy myths and migrant realities of return and development in Senegal', in Åkesson, L. and Eriksson Baaz, M. (eds) *Africa's Return Migrants: The New Developers?* London: Zed Books, pp 87–108.

Skeldon, R. (2021). *Advanced Introduction to Migration Studies.* Cheltenham: Edward Elgar Publishing.

Skinner, M.W., Cloutier, D. and Andrews, G.J. (2015). 'Geographies of ageing: Progress and possibilities after two decades of change', *Progress in Human Geography*, 39(6), 776–799. DOI: 10.1177/0309132514558444

Skinner, M.W., Andrews, G.J. and Cutchin, M.P. (2018). *Geographical Gerontology: Perspectives, Concepts, Approaches.* Abingdon: Routledge.

Souchaud, S. and Baeninger, R. (2009). 'Étudier les liens entre les migrations intérieures et internationales en suivant les trajectoires migratoires des Boliviens au Brésil', *Revue européenne des migrations internationales*, 25(1), 195–213. DOI: 10.4000/remi.4892

Squires, J. (2008). 'Intersecting inequalities: Reflecting on the subjects and objects of equality', *The Political Quarterly*, 79(1), 53–61. DOI: 10.1111/j.1467-923X.2008.00902.x

Stark, O. and Bloom, D.E. (1985). 'The new economics of labor migration', *The American Economic Review*, 75(2), 173–178.

Stefoni, C., Ramírez, C., Carbajal, M., Cavagnoud, R. and López-Yucra, K. (2022). 'Cuidados transnacionales y vejez. Aproximaciones teóricas y debates pendientes', *Si Somos Americanos*, 22(2), 107–129. DOI: 10.4067/S0719-09482022000200107

Strunk, C. (2015). 'Practicing citizenship: Bolivian migrant identities and spaces of belonging in Washington DC', *Journal of Intercultural Studies*, 36(5), 620–639. DOI: 10.1080/07256868.2015.1072910

Sun, K.C.-Y. (2014). 'Transnational healthcare seeking: How ageing Taiwanese return migrants view homeland public benefits', *Global Networks*, 14(4), 533–550. DOI: 10.1111/glob.12050

Sun, K.C.-Y. (2016). 'Professional remittances: How ageing returnees seek to contribute to the homeland', *Journal of Ethnic and Migration Studies*, 42(14), 2413–2429. DOI: 10.1080/1369183X.2016.1179106

Sunil, T.S., Rojas, V. and Bradley, D.E. (2007). 'United States' international retirement migration: The reasons for retiring to the environs of Lake Chapala, Mexico', *Ageing and Society*, 27(4), 489–510. DOI: 10.1017/S0144686X07005934

Tan, M.P. (2022). 'Healthcare for older people in lower and middle income countries', *Age and Ageing*, 51(4), afac016. DOI: 10.1093/ageing/afac016

Tapias, M. (2015). *Embodied Protests: Emotions and Women's Health in Bolivia*. Chicago: University of Illinois Press.

Tarija (2024). *PROSOL*. Tarija: Regional Government of Tarija. Available at: https://www.tarija.gob.bo/gobierno/programas-departamentales/prosol (accessed 9 December 2024).

Torres, S. and Hunter, A. (eds) (2023). *Handbook of Ageing and Migration*. Cheltenham: Edward Elgar Publishing.

Torres, S. and Serrat, R. (2019). 'Older migrants' civic participation: A topic in need of attention', *Journal of Aging Studies*, 50, 100790. DOI: 10.1016/j.jaging.2019.100790

Toyota, M., Yeoh, B.S.A. and Nguyen, L. (2007). 'Bringing the "left behind" back into view in Asia: A framework for understanding the "migration–left behind nexus"', *Population, Space and Place*, 13(3), 157–161. DOI: 10.1002/psp.433

Tronto, J.C. (2013). *Caring Democracy: Markets, Equality, and Justice*. New York: New York University Press.

Tronto, J.C. (2015). *Who Cares? How to Reshape a Democratic Politics*. Ithaca: Cornell Selects, an imprint of Cornell University Press.

Tronto, J.C. and Fisher, B. (1990). 'Toward a feminist theory of caring', in Abel, E. and Nelson, M. (eds) *Circles of Care*. Albany: SUNY Press, pp 36–54.

Truly, D. (2002). 'International retirement migration and tourism along the Lake Chapala Riviera: Developing a matrix of retirement migration behaviour', *Tourism Geographies*, 4(3), 261–281. DOI: 10.1080/14616680210147427

UN (United Nations) (2018). 'Old age: Responding to a rapidly ageing population'. In *The Report on the World Social Situation 2018: Promoting Inclusion through Social Protection*. https://doi.org/10.18356/39d66529-en

UNDESA (United Nations Department of Economic and Social Affairs) (2013). *World Population Prospects: The 2012 Revision*. New York: United Nations Department of Economic and Social Affairs Population Division.

UNDESA (2015). *World Population Ageing 2015*. New York: United Nations Department of Economic and Social Affairs.

UNDESA (2017). *World Population Ageing*. New York: United Nations Department of Economic and Social Affairs.

UNDESA (2019). *International Migration 2019 Wallchart*. New York: United Nations Department of Economic and Social Affairs. Available at: https://www.un.org/development/desa/pd/sites/www.un.org.development.desa.pd/files/files/documents/2020/Feb/un_2019_internationalmigration_wallchart.pdf (accessed 12 March 2025).

UNDESA (2020). *World Population Ageing 2019*. New York: United Nations Department of Economic and Social Affairs Population Division. Available at: https://www.un.org/en/development/desa/population/publications/pdf/ageing/WorldPopulationAgeing2019-Report.pdf

Valentine, G. (2007). 'Theorizing and researching intersectionality: A challenge for feminist geography', *The Professional Geographer*, 59(1), 10–21. DOI: 10.1111/j.1467-9272.2007.00587.x

Van Buren, M. (1996). 'Rethinking the vertical archipelago: Ethnicity, exchange, and history in the South Central Andes', *American Anthropologist*, 98(2), 338–351.

Van Dalen, H.P. and Henkens, K. (2007). 'Longing for the good life: Understanding emigration from a high-income country', *Population and Development Review*, 33(1), 37–66. DOI: 10.1111/j.1728-4457.2007.00158.x

Vargas, J.P.M. and Garriga, S. (2015). 'Explaining inequality and poverty reduction in Bolivia'. Working Paper WP/15/265. Washington, DC: IMF. Available https://www.imf.org/external/pubs/ft/wp/2015/wp15265.pdf (accessed 12 March 2025).

Vargas, V. (1985). 'Movimiento feminista en el Perú: balance y perspectivas', *Debates en sociología*, 10, 121–146. DOI: 10.18800/debatesensociologia.198501.005

Vassas Toral, A. (2016). *Partir y cultivar*. Marseille: IRD Éditions, Plural editores.

Vera-Sanso, P. (2004). ' "They don't need it and I can't give it": Filial support in South India', in Kreager, P. and Schröder-Butterfill, E. (eds) *Ageing without Children*. New York: Berghahn, pp 77–105.

Vera-Sanso, P. (2006). 'Experiences in old age: A South Indian example of how functional age is socially structured', *Oxford Development Studies*, 34(4), 457–472. DOI: 10.1080/13600810601045817

Vera-Sanso, P. (2012). 'Gender, poverty and old-age livelihoods in urban South India in an era of globalisation', *Oxford Development Studies*, 40(3), 324–340. DOI: 10.1080/13600818.2012.710322

Vera-Sanso, P. (2018). 'Ageing, poverty and neoliberalism in urban South India', in Walker, A. (ed) *New Dynamics of Ageing*. Bristol: Bristol University Press, pp 325–345.

Vera-Sanso, P. (2023). 'Will the SDGs and the UN decade of healthy ageing leave older people behind?', *Progress in Development Studies*, 23(4), 391–407. DOI: 10.1177/14649934231193808

Vera-Sanso, P., Vullnetari, J. and Bastia, T. (2023). 'Ageing and later life: Unsettling development assumptions', *Progress in Development Studies*, 23(4), 379–390. DOI: 10.1177/14649934231197348

Viveros Vigoya, M. (2016). 'La interseccionalidad: una aproximación situada a la dominación', *Debate Feminista*, 52, 1–17. DOI: 10.1016/j.df.2016.09.005

Vullnetari, J. (2023). 'Older people's contribution to development through carework: The role of childcare by grandparents in migration and development', *Progress in Development Studies*, 23(4), 444–460. DOI: 10.1177/14649934231195511

Vullnetari, J. and King, R. (2008). ' "Does your granny eat grass?": On mass migration, care drain and the fate of older people in rural Albania', *Global Networks*, 8(2), 139–171. DOI: 10.1111/j.1471-0374.2008.00189.x

Walsh, K. and Näre, L. (2016). 'Introduction: Trasnational migration and home in older age', in Walsh, K. and Näre, L. (eds) *Trasnational Migration and Home in Older Age*. London: Routledge, pp 1–24.

Warnes, A.M. and Williams, A. (2006). 'Older migrants in Europe: A new focus for migration studies', *Journal of Ethnic and Migration Studies*, 32(8), 1257–1281. DOI: 10.1080/13691830600927617

Warnes, A.M., Friedrich, K., Kellaher, L. and Torres, S. (2004). 'The diversity and welfare of older migrants in Europe', *Ageing and Society*, 24(3), 307–326. DOI: 10.1017/S0144686X04002296

WB (World Bank) (2022). *Data: Bolivia Indicators*. Washington, DC: World Bank. Available at: https://data.worldbank.org/indicator/NY.GDP.PCAP.CD?locations=BO (accessed 9 December 2024).

WB (2023). *Indicators: Fertility Rates, Total Births*. Washington, DC: World Bank. Available at: https://data.worldbank.org/indicator/SP.DYN.TFRT.IN?locations=ZJ (accessed 9 December 2024).

WB (2024). *Hospital Beds per 1,000 People*. Washington, DC: World Bank. Available at: https://data.worldbank.org/indicator/SH.MED.BEDS.ZS (accessed 9 December 2024).

Wengraf, T. (2001). *Qualitative Research Interviewing: Biographic Narrative and Semi-Structured Methods*. London: SAGE.

WHO (World Health Organization) (2024). *Making Older Persons Visible in the Sustainable Development Goals' Monitoring Framework and Indicators*. Geneva: World Health Organization.

Williams, A.M., King, R. and Warnes, T. (1997). 'A place in the sun: International retirement migration from northern to southern Europe', *European Urban and Regional Studies*, 4(2), 115–134. DOI: 10.1177/0969776 49700400202

Williams, S.J., Higgs, P. and Katz, S. (2012). 'Neuroculture, active ageing and the "older brain": Problems, promises and prospects', *Sociology of Health & Illness*, 34(1), 64–78. DOI: 10.1111/j.1467-9566.2011.01364.x

Yarnall, K. and Price, M. (2010). 'Migration, development and a new rurality in the Valle Alto, Bolivia', *Journal of Latin American Geography*, 9(1), pp 107–124.

Yarris, K.E. (2017). *Care across Generations: Solidarity and Sacrifice in Transnational Families*. Stanford: Stanford University Press.

Yépez, I.d.C. and Herrera, G. (2007). *Nuevas migraciones latinoamericanas a Europa: Balances y desafíos*. Quito: FLACSO, Obreal, Grial, UB.

Yépez, I.d.C. and Marzadro, M. (2014). 'Entre crisis, agencia y retorno: vulnerabilidad de las migrantes bolivianas en Italia/Between crisis, agency and return: The vulnerability of Bolivian migrants in Italy', *Revista CIDOB d'Afers Internacionals*, 106/107, pp 129–149.

Yépez, I.d.C., Ledo, C. and Marzadro, M. (2011). '"If you want me to stay here, you have to take care of our children": Migration and transnational motherhood between Cochabamba (Bolivia) and Bergamo (Italy)', *Autrepart*, 57–58(1), 199–213.

Yuval-Davis, N. (2006). 'Intersectionality and feminist politics', *European Journal of Women's Studies*, 13(3), 193–209. DOI: 10.1177/1350506806065752

Zapata, G.P., Gandini, L., Vera Espinoza, M. and Prieto Rosas, V. (2023). 'Weakening practices amidst progressive laws: Refugee governance in Latin America during COVID-19', *Journal of Immigrant & Refugee Studies*, 21(4), 547–565. DOI: 10.1080/15562948.2022.2163521

# Index